Lucy's People

An Ethiopian Memoir

Saba & Lucy's People
Book 1

Mesfin Tadesse

ianet Bastyan

Yerada Lij
AUSTRALIA

Lucy's People: An Ethiopian Memoir

Second edition

ISBN 978-0-6488287-2-3

© 2020, 2021 Mesfin Tadesse & ianet Bastyan

Published by J.R Bastyan & M Tadesse, Wilson, WA

www.ianetbastyan.com | info@ianetbastyan.com

The moral rights of the authors have been asserted. All rights reserved. Reproduction, transmission and adaptation of any part is not permitted. Fair Dealing permitted. For enquiries, email the publisher.

This book is intended for mature readers only, 16+.

 A catalogue record for this work is available from the National Library of Australia

Editor: Sam Cooney. Designer: Tess McCabe using cover images from iStockphoto.com

Cover image represents Lake Tana with a boat and author as sailor. Above is a golden disk containing a female profile with braids: the sun, Ethiopia, and woman all in one.

For Tewode and Samual

But when they pried his fingers
open, this nobody,
they found a whole country.

— Hama Tuma "Just a
Nobody"

Contents

Introduction	ix
Preface	xi
Chapter 1 *Gouder to Addis Ababa*	1
Chapter 2 *Harer*	11
Chapter 3 *Big Men*	31
Chapter 4 *Patriot*	45
Chapter 5 *Mama Teliqwa*	57
Chapter 6 *Arat Kilo*	75
Chapter 7 *Revolution*	89
Chapter 8 *Advisor*	103
Chapter 9 *Red Terror*	115
Chapter 10 *Books*	127
Chapter 11 *The Bean*	143
Chapter 12 *Heritage*	157
Chapter 13 *Calculator*	173
Chapter 14 *Forgive Me*	189
Chapter 15 *Enough*	207
Chapter 16 *Khalid*	223
Chapter 17 *Western Influenced*	235

Chapter 18 *Second Home*	251
Chapter 19 *Hagere Mariyam*	265
Chapter 20 *Market Day*	275
Chapter 21 *Departure*	283
Postscript	289
Addendum	291
The Gold Chain	293
Glossary	297
Events	299
People	303
Acknowledgments	305
About the Authors	307
Bibliography	311

Introduction

People ask, 'Is this story true?' It is, so we use first names for privacy. Addressing Ethiopians by their first name is polite. We use full names for prominent people.

Lucy's People has some Ethiopian words, for flavour. Of 85 Ethiopian languages, Mesfin uses Amharic, Ge'ez and Hebrew. Amharic is the national language, Ge'ez is classical Ethiopian and some Jews speak Hebrew.

All our dates follow the Gregorian calendar of the West. Early 1991 was 1983 in Ethiopia.

In 2021, we returned from Addis Ababa where we first released our book. Some chapters are now re-arranged. More Derg jokes crept in while we inserted a bibliography.

Perth
August 2021

Preface

Today in Australia, an Indian immigrant waits at the airport taxi rank. An Aussie raps knuckles on his cab window. 'You Ethiopian?'

'No.'

The customer gets in. To a yes, he would have moved down the queue. The driver wonders why some customers avoid Ethiopians. What if they think he is one? Riled, they might do anything.

He visits the local library to read up on Ethiopia. Staff say, 'Nothing much is available in English.'

It is the same at the State Library. The driver resorts to the internet. He finds out about the Battle of Adwa 1896, led by Emperor Menelik II. Inspired by Ethiopia's triumph over Italian invaders, he phones his pregnant wife in India.

She says, 'Our child will be named Menelik, boy or girl.'

The driver displays Menelik's photo in the back window of his taxi. He sports a Menelik beard and hat. Aussies admire it. He

Preface

says, 'This style originally belonged to Emperor Menelik II of Ethiopia.'

One day he leans over the fence of his rental and says to his neighbour, 'The hens in your backyard remind me of home. I asked the landlord to install a wire mesh dividing fence – this one needs replacing. She refused.'

They introduce themselves. The neighbour's name is Mesfin. He also wears a Menelik-style hat and is Ethiopian.

Mesfin was born during the reign of Emperor Haile Selassie I. Among millions, he suffered under the communist Derg. A fine engineer, he gave all to family and motherland. 1991 brought fresh disaster. Should youth stay or flee?

Lucy's People is his memoir. It is for readers ready to accept a ride with one of the greatest cultures on earth.

Chapter 1
Gouder to Addis Ababa

Ten soldiers shouldered and levelled AK-47s and Kalashnikovs. Cadre frowned at the site plan. I inverted my drawing. 'Other way.' The party members nodded. 'Go ahead.' I escaped their praise of the communist president, all mumbo jumbo.

My boss chased me with my risk reduction report. Alemayehu had said, 'Let me handle this.' He removed my references to Chernobyl. The facts remained, all 27 pages. Reinforced concrete was magnetic. Radiation melted zinc alum. Basaltic stone sparked: it contained cast iron with carbon from coal. Construction had to be with reinforced concrete containing pure metal.

The civil engineer ruffled my hair. 'Order Portland cement with hydrated lime river sand.' We were still within gunsights. Two workers together had a time limit of three minutes. In the dining room, cadre separated us by 1.5 metres. If three spoke they were dead. I left to buy construction materials.

Water expanses were my love: weirs, dams and irrigation. Ethiopia's only employer was the Planning and Labour Commission. It stuck me at the Gouder Tank and Missile Factory. Party insiders kept me underground in one zone for two years.

I was building the yellowcake silo water system and the chemical waste and nuclear waste treatment plants. Silo walls had to resist concrete bunker missiles, floods, landslides and earthquakes. What would happen in a catastrophe? In one nuclear explosion, half of Addis Ababa would go.

The next morning, government forces rounded up 47 technicians and engineers. We were aged between 17 and 32. They said we were from Western influenced worksites. The squad detained us without charge. They took us 180 kilometres north, outside the city. We were ravenous and thirsty.

At 2.30 a.m. soldiers bound us severely with ropes. They threw us into a truck and drove for 25 minutes to the forest beyond Gulele outside Addis Ababa. Five men died of asphyxiation.

A jeep with rocket-propelled grenades stopped us. It was impossible to run. Guards had *chichi*, twice the size of Kalashnikovs, and AK-47s. One climbed into a waiting bulldozer and started the engine. 'Get on with it. Shower them.'

Prisoners cried, but a debate began among soldiers.

'This is wrong, Major. They have done nothing. Let our sons and brothers go.'

'Colonel, what about our careers? We will be at risk if word gets out that we have disobeyed orders.'

'Not if you keep quiet about it. Finish digging the trench. Make it look real.'

The major relented after 20 minutes. The colonel called the army nurse. 'Verify that those five are dead.' The recruit had never seen a dead goat, let alone a human corpse. 'I do not know how. It is too dark.' 'Hold your torch. Use a mirror. If there is mist on the glass, he is alive. Stop crying and be a man.' The nurse, major and colonel laid the five bodies in the trench dug for show.

They yelled to the remaining 42, 'Run for your lives!'

Lucy's People

'Here is ten *birr*.' 'Take my watch.' 'Go! Live.'

We fled until sunrise, lost. All reeked of the urine and excrement of the dying or terrified piled in the truck. An engineer from the country said, 'Keep out of the eucalyptus plantation. Guards will shoot.'

Oromo farmers found us. The mothers gave us under-wing shelter. They muddied us to hide city skin, dressed us in their clothes, took us out at night. Too poor to eat meat themselves, they slaughtered chickens and goats to feed the thin ones among us. Many Ethiopians born between 1950 and 1975 experienced how Oromo people treated fugitives as though they were their own.

Oromo and Amhara formed the two largest Ethiopian ethnic groups. The national language was Amharic. As they combed our hair, I worked out what they said in Oromigna: 'His mother must be good. He has no lice.'

After three months, the communists lost interest in their campaign against the educated. We returned home. In Arat Kilo, my girlfriend Hewan had slept on the floor. She lit church candles, for whom she would not say. Barely expecting to reach 30, we married.

I returned to Gouder. We were on Oromo land the size of a province. The president sacrificed all inhabitants: birds, mammals and traditional owners. Ethiopian President Mengistu Haile Mariam's nuclear force was part of his Red Star Action.

The site would have no launch station. Gouder would manufacture its own steel for T55 tanks with chain wheels. Those would dig their own bunkers. From anywhere, they could launch guided missiles: 27 metres long with nuclear-coated heads. Attack the factory all you like. Its missiles would be long gone, sped to the other side of the country.

Seven stonemasons had disappeared from the silo. To

another subdivision? Had they insisted on a pay rise? In prison, their fingernails and teeth would be pulled while cadre stood at attention, red star on cap.

Thousands of North Koreans remained. Ideal communist workers, they shunned alcohol, books, magazines and music. I invited them to share our leisure area; they dispersed. Uniformly dressed, they chain-smoked tailor- made cigarettes rationed by their government. None smiled, laughed, talked, whistled, made requests or showed anger and happiness. Did any dream of the future?

Our city boys called them the Brain Dead. Each wore a tag with a photo of the North Korean leader, and mouthed praise. 'Our leader is our god.' Nobody in Ethiopia said that about her communist dictator Mengistu.

One day the loudspeaker system crackled. Another mournful socialist song? I fumbled for ear plugs, but it was an announcement. 'All workers report to the muster area.' Mengistu was visiting.

We lined up according to profession, with engineers front and others behind: North Korean plasterers, masons, bar benders, welders, excavators, landscapers, concrete workers and builders, and Cuban masons. I wished I was in the back. Every two metres a machine gunner's barrel pointed straight at us.

After 30 minutes, cadre told us that Mengistu had arrived. 'All applaud.'

I clapped half-heartedly. 'Stop.' Relaxing, I put my hand in my pocket.

Was the president flying or driving? Workers joked about it. Some said that, on one trip, seven donkeys had blocked the road. Mengistu's driver tooted. The animals would not budge. It was a donkey conference.

Lucy's People

Cadre said, 'This is an imperialist plot – sabotage.'

One got out of the vehicle and whispered into an animal's ear. All donkeys walked off.

Mengistu asked, 'How did you do that? Do you speak donkey? What did you tell them?'

'I said they were welcome to join the Communist Party.'

When the president appeared that day, time was short, but his honorifics droned on. In Kenya, an event organiser had asked if they could abridge the titles that went with his name. She said, 'The tea will get cold.'

At Gouder, the usual Marxist-Leninist rant followed. Afterward, workers sprinted to the construction site. Television news crew caught footage of the leader with us.

Two weeks later, I received a five-page letter. For having my hand in my pocket, cadre was docking half a month's pay. I needed help.

'Gash Alemayehu, I will not be able to send any money to my mother.'

'Mesfine, this has happened to others too. One man lit a cigarette; two exchanged a word. Though I cannot reverse it, I can help you in another way.' He arranged two construction-design trips to Addis Ababa and paid travel expenses. Twelve young ones in our family ate.

Red Star Action had begun in the late 1970s; yet in May 1991, the factory was not finished. One day, the North Koreans vanished. Ethiopia's régime was failing.

Communism had already ended in Russia with Gorbachev's 1989 Perestroika. Nevertheless, Ethiopian cadre had forced workers to celebrate May Day 1991. For three days they marched in blue and black overalls.

Later that week, I was guiding a grader and caterpillar and

surveying a site. Cadre came with soldiers. 'Site Engineer Mesfin? Stop work now. Return equipment and plans. Report to Head Office tomorrow.' Hopeless faces denied all questions. Mengistu's nationalist dream had evaporated.

The US and UK would dismantle the Gouder Tank and Missile Factory. They gained access to European Eastern bloc secret nuclear military science. Ethiopia's new leaders sold our technology to North Korea. Israel and the US would build similar factories.

I got a lift to the city to chase my salary.

In Addis Ababa, the site driver adjusted my backpack. I had loaded it with candles, sugar cane, false-banana root porridge, and honey.

He said, 'Pregnant women eat that twice a day. Sometimes babies arrive while mothers are in the fields. Honey gives them energy.'

'My wife is expecting in September, after Ethiopian New Year.'

'It will keep her strong. My aunt used it during Mussolini's invasion. People coughed blood from poisonous gases. Son, bring her to stay with my family until things settle down.'

At the Ministry of Defence Construction, the head engineer shook hands. He asked, 'What are your plans, Mesfine? You are bright. You need to protect yourself. Anything might happen now. We could lose another million people.' I was beyond answers.

'I am giving you an advance of two months' pay, plus another as travel expense,' he said. 'Report here when it is safe. There will be a job waiting for you.'

Finance's token cadre said, 'I do not believe you are due three months' pay. Too young. See my boss.'

The head smiled. 'At the very last, my clerk wants to use her insider's power. You were supposed to have been born before these times.'

Tessema handed me curfew exemption and travel documents. 'Mesfine, let us exchange smiles. This may be the last. We are surrounded by fire. *Selam.*'

Planning and Labour Commission forced the university professor and dean to work in industry and military construction. He was still not free. For me, there would be no more death-dealing missile factory.

The transport queue that morning was short. However, I did not want to step off a bus to stare at a Derg gun barrel. I walked home to Arat Kilo. When it rained, a security guard sheltered me in his hut.

'The rebels are heading south,' he said. These were the forces of the Tigray People's Liberation Front (TPLF). It called itself Woyane, which meant committee in Tigrinya. The communist Derg was the Armed Forces Co-ordinating Committee. Derg was Ge'ez.

'Who is their leader?'

'Meles, liked by the West.'

TPLF forces were like foreign invaders, dirty and undisciplined. Rebels had no military qualifications. Breaking unwritten combat rules, they shot parachutists in mid-air. They lopped the tops off Coca Cola bottles with bayonets.

'Is there fighting?' I asked.

'No, but Mengistu could be armed with North Korean nuclear rockets. The world hopes for a bloodbath.'

I gave the guard two candles and paddled along the footpath. Two Mary's belts shone in the south-east – a double rainbow. Compounds had wild peach, mango, lemon and false banana. Jacaranda flowered purple, another species whispered, and junipers wore tutus.

Derg soldiers were displaced in the city. They held non-jamming machine guns at an inoffensive angle, barrel up. Some had stick bombs. Many of the guns also had poisoned bayonets. None looted. They begged for 10 cents or a cigarette.

Around our corner I met Mum. From a jerry can she filled soldiers' water containers. She applied Vaseline to their lips. They had walked for days. Mum said, 'They have not been paid for six months, even years. Some places are without water.'

Others shunned them. 'You did not fight for me.' The boys never retaliated. Many had been taken from village streets and farms. Dropped in the middle of war zones, they made up Ethiopia's regular forces. Branded as cadre, they were not insiders.

A teenager in an outsize sweater waited for our mother. She took her pulse and told her to eat this and drink that. 'Turn your bed to face the moon.' Mum could tell that she was carrying a girl. For every 25 girls in my brother's Year 10 class, there were only six or seven boys.

For 17 years the Derg had slaughtered boys and young men. Now it forced women to abort female foetuses. Mum would deliver the young woman's baby to spare her a late termination. Visiting home ten years later, I met girls around Arat Kilo and Kazanchis with Mum's name, Tewode.

Near our house, our youngest brother Samual fed strays.

He bent to hug me. '*Gashe*.' He called me 'my older brother'.

At our compound I whistled my signature tune, "Death to Derg". The steel gate swung open. Three birds flew onto Samual's head and shoulders. He fed them wheat straight from his mouth. A dog, cat, goat, sheep, peacock, rooster and hens jumped at me. Sisters and their children hugged us, sticky from honey buns.

Mum called, '*Maye*'. Her hen Tatuta followed her inside the house. 'No mess.' The hen talked back to her, sitting when she did. Another sang and danced, wings outspread, for Samual. Then she crouched in the grass to lay an egg.

A pigeon with burgundy feathers, white head and black beak had a key tied to her leg. When he was 11, Samual had asked me to install a lock on his door. His room was safe from all borrowers of eggs, sport shoes or premises for coffee parties; the pigeon only flew to him.

We sat with Mum by the sitting-room wall, warm from the built-in pizza oven. Our youngest sister wore a crochet dress; her older sister had made it with no pattern. In wooden cradles, spun-cotton spools awaited the loom; Mum spun cotton daily. She had also set up her lace-making machine.

Communists said handcrafts were the expression of exploiters. 'Do not show that you are better than others.' Mum lived by selling them. Nobody wanted to exist in a Derg condominium box that was identical to others.

At dinner Samual apportioned his meal for his birds. 'For the rooster, the peacock, the pigeon, the dancing hen... ' The 16-year-old left nothing for himself, so we contributed to his meal.

He strummed his guitar. Covering the sound box, he played a puppy's whimper. The neighbour's child came running. King of the Indoors—our yellow cat—sprang away from the startled peacock's tail. A brother collected the fallen feathers. He would paint their edges, then sell them for 10 cents: the price of two lead pencils.

Samual played a Konso waltz on his bamboo flute. Mum said, 'Too quiet.'

Where was the *ratatata* of gunfire? The chopping of low-flying helicopters? Silence followed shootings and heralded house-to-house searches with bayonets. Monasteries had once rung bells. Mengistu stopped them.

We shut away the hens. Finding a spent cartridge I asked Samual, 'When was the last time?'

'Friday.' 'Drum kit?' 'Intact.'

Derg forces would come to our home. They kicked everything.

Hens and peacock lost confidence and grew very quiet. Our dog Medfir crouched low, a warrior bracing for action. Then he dug over and over at the ground. Toddlers wet themselves. Departing with their loot, Security fired AK-47s into the air. The sound of popcorn followed. My family picked up spent cartridges.

Chapter 2
Harer

I was born in Harer Province in Ethiopia's east. This was in the early 1960s when Emperor Haile Selassie I reigned. My father was a graduate of Britain's Royal Military Academy at Sandhurst. He was Border Security Commanding Officer and taught at Harer Military Academy. Dad too was born in Harer where his father was governor. My mother was a nurse, midwife and herbal healer. Five sisters came before me; three brothers and a sister followed. We lived at Harer Military Camp.

My birth lasted only 30 minutes even though I weighed 5.1 kilograms. Most of it was muscle. It took effort to pry open my fists. I was delivered with an intact amniotic sac; this brings luck or protection. My placenta was buried in Harer; I am prepared to die for that land.

At 40 days old I was circumcised with ceremony and gained an illustrious eye father, equivalent to a god father: Lieutenant General Aman. Ethiopians take their mother's religion, so we were Orit Orthodox or *Falasha:* Ethiopian Jews from the tribe of Jesus Christ. My father's family had been Orthodox Christian for generations. Such marriages were common in Ethiopia. Some families included Christians and Muslims.

Quiet and wakeful, I crawled early. My sisters and Mum took turns watching me. In case they fell asleep, an army-issue mosquito net prevented my escape. At two, I buttoned my shirt, tied my shoelaces and weaned myself. My sisters tempted me by smearing honey around Mum's nipples, but I backed away and covered my mouth for big men ate food.

Obsessed with books, I piled up bricks. 'Look at my books!' The top collapsed on my hand and the household came running, unused to hearing me cry. Itete comforted me. She was my eldest sister.

Outdoors, workers hugged me when I made wire roosters, which we called *kukulu*. Indoors, I sketched Mum with her *Yehuda* (Ethiopian Jewish) tattoos at chin and throat. She taught me Hebrew and Ge'ez.

Our parents waltzed together. He was 191 centimetres tall, and dark with brown eyes and curly hair. She was 185 centimetres, and fair with green eyes and straight hair. From a generation without modern conveniences, Mum was chic. She even served pretty food.

My parents Tewode Alemayehu and Colonel Tadesse Shwasegid. Imperial Ethiopian Government. Ministry of Information, 1971?

My warrior eye father's name Aman meant peace walker. The French had tried to assassinate him, and the UK had recently bad-mouthed Ethiopia. Lieutenant General Aman visited the London office of the BBC. 'From this matchbox you disturb the world,' he said.

In the Ogaden desert he slept on a stretcher that folded into a backpack. His water canteen was his pillow. Captains ate off silver dishes while he cooked rations.

Dressed sharply at Harer, Lieutenant General Aman mucked in at the camp with paint and cement. He spoke nothings into horses' ears and they surrendered to him. Aman would wash them with buckets of water, splashing shoes, suit and face with soapsuds. Then he neigh-laughed. So did the horses before running off. Dogs loved him too.

When my eye father worked, I followed him all day with toy bucket and putty knife, copying his ways. During levelling the plumb line pulled down my hand; he encouraged me to remain firm.

I sandpapered an M1 gun and polished it with linseed varnish. M16 and Bren machine guns—refined in Ethiopia—were mounted on jeeps. My eye father told recruits, 'Leave them for Mesfine to do.'

I could not wait to return to him after lunch. If the sister fetching me stepped in manure on the way, I refused to sit at the same table.

When I was four, I took Dad's service pistol. It was probably loaded. I refused to hand it over, loving the feel of it in my hand. The household did not appreciate my assurances: 'I am not shooting anybody. Just holding it.' My sisters called Lieutenant General Aman to disarm me. Then Dad taught me weapons safety. Later, I would know firearms too well.

I enjoyed household chores: polishing buttons and shoes and

pressing my clothes with a charcoal-heated iron, heavy and hot. When Mum stopped me, Scout recruits taught me *dama* – like chess.

My eyebrows joined, forming a single one like the emperor's. Wary of those close to him, Mum removed the central hairs with roasted ground cow dung.

At kindergarten in Harer, children avoided sitting beside me. I was evil eye. My gaze could make them ill or kill them. The teacher had said, 'Do not look at me eye-to-eye.' I refused school. Dad arrested him and put him in the brigade gaol. He brought two chairs and sat us opposite each other.

'Look at him.'

The teacher met my gaze although he was unnerved by the blue ring around my brown irises.

He went back to work and I changed schools.

Rumours about *Falasha* began with the Portuguese, who invaded in the sixteenth century. Our warriors defeated them. They wielded buffalo-hide shields, spears and arrows that were developed by Orthodox. The Portuguese said, 'Jews have high sight. Their evil eye kills.'

Mesfin Tadesse & ianet Bastyan

Me at two, hands in pockets. My father, 1962?

Lucy's People

I loved lions, especially Ethiopia's black-headed lions, and had a toy Lion of Judah: *Mo Anbesa*.

Long before my birth, a real cat had stalked into our family. Lion-cub sized Wuro had yellow fur and yellow-black eyes. Many remember him that were associates of 4th Brigade Battalion.

It comprised two major generals, four brigadier generals, four colonels, four lieutenant colonels, eight majors, 60 captains, 62 lieutenants, 120 sergeant majors, 12,000 soldiers, 50 nurses, 20 radio operators, two black-headed lions and 20 carrier pigeons. It also had military clocks: roosters. Wuro was boss of the cats.

He drank milk and ate lung and liver. On Fridays he fasted with our family. No meat or milk until Sabbath ended on Saturday. If a recruit put liver or milk down, he would not touch it. Ants covered it.

The brigade ranked him corporal. At the border with Somalia and Djibouti, my father's colleague Major Sihale was murdered. Wuro shared in the camp's sorrow. He scratched at the floor, mourning. For honest military, border protection work was perilous.

Wuro was Flag Master. Each morning he stood at attention. The flag's bands of colour flapped in the breeze: green for growth, yellow for peace and hope and the return of the sun in the morning, red for blood spilt in defence of our country. When the soldiers did their about turn, he would miaow and dash off to Dad's office. They would say, 'The corporal has finished the ceremony.'

Wuro would leap onto the gun box that held our father's files and groom his face with both paws. When Dad went to a drawer, Wuro's tail twirled in anticipation of smoked chilli-beef jerky. Wars were won on it, but the corporal fell asleep. Paperwork complete, Dad saluted the cat. 'Hey Corporal, I am going to work.' Corporal Wuro crossed and re-crossed his paws in acknowledgment. 'Dismissed.' He only made this show of respect for Dad.

Us kids bored him with our salutes. Corporals and drivers tried it with no more success. Tea and coffee makers joked about it. 'Ah, do not try to trick him. He knows the real killers.' Dad was Corporal Wuro's special human.

Our yellow cat King of the Indoors: Corporal Wuro's lookalike. Mesfin Tadesse, 197–?

From the 1950s, the United Kingdom (UK), France and Somalia broke borders with Ethiopia. Their soldiers were thieves. They smuggled minerals and animal exotica, such as peacocks sought by British zookeepers. Dad would fine them; they would threaten him.

'Our government will be angry,' they would say.

'So be it. I have the evidence. You are not a peaceful soldier and commit crimes in uniform.'

Near Berbera in Northern Somalia, Dad apprehended five uniformed UK soldiers with contraband frankincense, tiger pelts and ivory. The UK ambassador travelled to the border to confront him, though this was illegal. He slouched outside Dad's office, hands in pockets.

'Man, what do you see before you?' My father kept quiet.

'The one standing in front of you represents the whole of England, the Crown.'

'I can see in front of my office one stupid, long-nosed man. Sit down.' Dad caught the eye of two soldiers who sat the boor down. 'I will put you in prison until you act like a human being. How did your government make a person with no manners ambassador?'

He had the five soldiers do ten days' labour at the military camp, then deported them. UK officials complained to the emperor about excessive use of force by his major.

The UK sought to malign him through the press, trying to provoke him in front of cameras. BBC news recorded Dad while he was eating lunch. The interviewer waited until he picked up a bone in his fingers. 'You serve as Border Security Commanding Officer, ensuring valuable things remain in Ethiopia. Now tell me, if you eat all the bones, what will be left for dogs in Ethiopia?'

'Why, in Ethiopia we give dogs fish-and-chips. Then for dessert we give them a big bowl of ice cream.'

Dad stopped the French and English from wearing military uniform inside Ethiopia unless they held a military attaché or diplomat licence. The UK and US pestered Emperor Haile Selassie I to get rid of him. He ignored them, but others returned recommendations for Dad's promotion. My father stayed a major for eight years.

My father in eastern Ethiopia with Border Security Force establishment soldiers. Colonel Tadesse is second from left. Imperial Ethiopian Government. Ministry of Defence, 1955.

Lucy's People

While at Harer we visited our home in Arat Kilo, Addis Ababa. It was in our father's family for 800 years – a fairy tale mansion with spires. Stonemasons were building a new section. Hammer on chisel and chisel on stone, they honed grey Ambo granite slabs. Some revealed ammonite fossils. To protect their lungs from dust, masons chewed a leaf or gum – a 700-year-old Lalibela recipe.

At the forty-hectare complex of Menelik II Palace, I fed pea snacks to the royal horses. I punched an older prince who would not share. With another prince I stole sugared carrots and vomited.

Emperor Haile Selassie I was fatherly. Toddlers got as close as possible to him. On formal days he wore a burgundy and purple velvet cape bordered with tinkling gold bells. We pulled and swung on it. He told his attendants to let us be.

One day in the Throne Room, he sneezed. The court bowed to the floor; I did not. 'When the emperor sneezes, I must kiss the floor?'

Haile Selassie laughed and called me to him. His thin hands smoothed my curls, each rolling up tightly. 'Didn't your mother tell you how to behave?'

'How? ... By kissing the ground?'

'Everyone be good to this boy. Give him a lolly and send him back to his mum.'

Later, we visited when the emperor received citizens. Mum needed to speak to him, but there was a queue. People from the country were asleep under palace trees. Officials made them wait so long that they begged on the streets.

Haile Selassie's dog Lulu was playing with me. She ignored an older boy, who kicked me. I headbutted him. The boy's minders made to grab me, but the emperor stopped them. 'Do not touch him. Bring that boy to me.'

Attendants waited with hands clasped behind backs. Haile Selassie said, 'You are a tough boy. Where is your father?'

'At the Somali border.' 'What is his name?'

I told him and he straightened. 'Is your mother here? Can I speak to her?'

Our father's bosses had exiled him. The feudal lords of Bale Province in the south adored the evergreen land's milk, butter and barley. They imposed heavy tithes and seized lands.

A farmer named Waqo protested. Educated neither by church, mosque nor madrassa, he led peasant resistance.[1] Belly-filler lords had allies at the palace. They told the emperor, 'This group is anti-government. He ordered the Ministry of Defence to investigate.

Instead of defusing tension, the military slaughtered peasants, who fought armed professionals with bare hands and sticks. Survivors dubbed Waqo 'General'.

Conflict continued, so the emperor sent trusted men to Bale: General Jegama, who spoke Oromigna, and my father. They negotiated Waqo's surrender and he accompanied them to the city. Belly-filler officials blocked him from Haile Selassie. Dad got him an audience and General Jegama interpreted. Speaking Oromigna, Haile Selassie comprehended the greed of the feudal lords and his ministers.

Restoring all seized farmland to the Bale Province peasants, he also opened a direct line of communication with the general and farmers. Waqo returned home with organic fertiliser and farming tools that Haile Selassie bought himself.

Superiors punished General Jegama and Dad. They kept the general in Addis Ababa to lead the royal guard for visits by heads of state. This paralysed his military and negotiating career. It would have disastrous consequences for Ethiopians.

The military sent Dad to the Somali–Kenyan border at Ogaden and Gode and forbade him from teaching recruits. Colleagues protested though Dad kept quiet. The Harer Military Academy suffered. Emperor Haile Selassie I had built it 1942–49 despite British opposition. Within twenty years, it had lost its leader.

The emperor had nothing to do with Dad's exile and recalled him to Harer.

On the way home that afternoon we passed rows of army trees in palace grounds. Gardeners painted their trunks part-way up. They were upright and steady like Dad.

My future wife's father served with him as a signaller. He referred to him as 'Sir'. 'He was like the sky for us. At the sound of his footsteps, we would rush to line up. "Colonel Tadesse is coming!" Shaving cream on faces, we would push out our chests. He never picked an individual fault. When he said, "Dismissed," we felt well-rewarded.'

The English asked Dad to take Somali prisoners off their hands because they had run out of room. He accepted some nomads and asked them, 'Why are you in prison?' The elder said, 'A bullock strayed to the edge of a high cliff and fell, breaking every bone in its body. It was dying in agony, so we killed it cleanly then butchered it. The Christians came and accused us of theft because it was on land that they occupied.'

Dad heard sobs outside his office. It was the youngest of the nomads, a boy. 'Shoot me, please.' Our father took him inside, gave him water and asked what happened.

'Each night, the English lieutenant came to the prison cell. He molested me. I want to die.'

'He is a criminal. I shall set you free. Nobody will attack you like that again.'

Dad could not hold those innocent people only to hand them back to the monsters. He released the Somalis. The English lieutenant barged into his office, swearing.

'Keep away from my desk,' Dad said. 'Sit on that chair in the corner. You raped the boy and are not a man. You are a criminal.'

The Englishman turned red and tore off his shirt. 'I will fight you for that!' Dad said, 'Step outside,' and beat him.

The UK complained to Addis Ababa. The emperor sent a helicopter, ordering Dad to fly straight there. He listened to his story and said, 'Raping children is unacceptable. Yet if we formally pursue a complaint, the judges will all be Europeans, mostly English. The fox will not convict a fox. Major, we must be diplomatic.'

'My king, you are telling me that paedophiles will not convict paedophiles.'

Ethiopia could not afford to clash face-to-face with the UK. Pretending to punish him, the emperor sent Dad to the remote west in Jimma. Before we left Harer, he promoted Dad to lieutenant colonel.

Corporal Wuro accompanied us. I was three.

Kaffa (Kefa) Province needed protection from smugglers and foreign cattle thieves. They came twice a year armed by invisible thieves from abroad – the UK controlled our neighbour Sudan. Dad set up a Border Security regiment from scratch and expanded it to form a battalion.

Kaffa included the original Bibika coffee and mango plantation with 100-year-old fruit trees that stood eight metres tall. Birds came twice each year from Arba Minch.

At the edge was a monastery with black-and-white *gureza* monkeys. Monk-like, they fasted, prayed with their palms upwards, listened to church music, and wanted more after midnight prayers. Younger monks fell asleep at sunrise under trees, so they shook them awake and climbed high to drop enormous mangoes upon them. They cleaned droppings and debris from drums and harps. When birds landed upon the harps' tuners, monkeys chased them off. Monks told newcomers, 'No need to tune any ceremonial instruments left outdoors.'

Lucy's People

In 2004, I would re-roof a Rift Valley monastery dwelling. *Gureza* dried the fruit of *wanza* and *shola* trees on roofs to plant in winter. They were known as mothers of plants.

Orthodox institutions did not harm any creature. Debre Libanos monks fed ants by chewing sugar cane for them. And nature protected monasteries. At Waldeba in Ethiopia's north, two youths raped a girl. *Gureza* chased them off with rocks and one gave evidence in court convicting them.

Ethiopian monasteries took in orphaned animals. By day, donkeys and horses walked free. At night they returned to be fed. Near the monastery of Debre Damos in Gondar, a horse stopped morning traffic. It refused to move off the road. A driver found a newborn by the side. The orphaned animal saved the abandoned child.

With Border Security established in Kaffa Province, Emperor Haile Selassie I built the Jimma Agricultural Institute. It was 27 kilometres long and took 3,000 scholarship students. The UK protested when 1,000 Japanese engineering students enrolled. Haile Selassie told them to back off. It was civil, not military.

The defence minister caught Scandinavian spies in boats with thousands of photos. In full Ethiopian dress, the emperor saw them off at the airport. He presented each with a set of traditional clothes. The Ethiopian handmade suits and dresses had embroidery known as 'wisdom'.

Forest surrounded the military camp. It was the habitat of wildcats and panthers. Wildcats puffed up their fur and latched onto children's necks. Stuck indoors, I learned to read and play chess with a giant soapstone set. Hefting the queen, I puffed, 'Ch... ch... checkmate.' Military officers nicknamed me Big Man.

Lieutenant General Aman said, 'No time for three chess games today. How about *dama*?' In three moves I zig-zagged across the squares and took his king. My eye father said, 'Do not tell the emperor.'

Dad taught me to tell the time with his Omega wristwatch, and how to use binoculars. They shared a shelf with other bravery awards and gifts: a golden revolver from Korea, Hungarian whisky service from the emperor, and a coffee pot and water canteen.

The wristwatch was from Korea. My father was a veteran of the war that ended in 1953. Ethiopian UN Peacekeepers served in three rounds. By the end Dad was a major and staff academic officer. He advised and trained South Koreans that started a permanent army.

As a two-star lieutenant under my eye father Lieutenant Colonel Aman, Dad was at the battlefront. 'Chinese soldiers came like a river with a strong current.' My sisters asked, 'Did you pray?'

'Well, I am Orthodox Christian, not Orit Orthodox like *Maye*.' He referred to Mum.

'Who did you pray to, then?'

'All of them. They saved me. I wore a wooden cross from your mother.'

Our maternal grandmother called Dad My Tummy. She said, 'My Tummy, come back from Korea or I will not be able to continue living.'

Ethiopians had photos in their tents. US troops did not. US General MacArthur visited a bunker. One of our soldiers stood chest-deep at the M1, his wife's photo behind its magazine. Her spirit and his desire to return to her helped him win. Family photos on desks later became trendy.

Under Lieutenant Colonel Aman, not one Ethiopian soldier was taken prisoner. He gave our men a delicacy: spiced raw meat. During battle they ate it. Chinese soldiers thought they might eat them and fled.

Ethiopian UN Peacekeepers did not receive their pay. In 2019, the Korean Government would compensate their descendants after veterans had died homeless. However, Dad insisted on UN and American post-command presentations for lower-rank UN Peacekeepers. In the 1960s, Korea gave bravery awards to Ethiopian soldiers with ranks from corporal to captain.

Generals tried to cheapskate lower-rank soldiers – our military had its belly-fillers. They gave them Seiko 5 wristwatches. Dad reported this to Colonel Aman who reported it to Colonel Kebede. He told Lieutenant Colonel Asfur and Colonel Tilahun. Led by my eye father, seven high-rank military men walked to Haile Selassie, who said, 'What has happened to my kids?' The officers saluted the emperor. Each took off his Omega wristwatch. 'My king, take this. We do not want division.' Removing their hats, they said, 'We served our country, Africa and the world. Imprison us or make us civilian.' For this, Haile Selassie promoted Dad to colonel. Others hammered him for the rest of his life.

Under Dad, the military built the Jimma 2nd Battalion training centre, mess, military base and depot. One year after our arrival it was complete. The opening ceremony and graduation were held together for the new brigade.

A fortnight earlier, a brigadier general—second in charge of Ground Force—arrived with a major general, who was second in charge of Airborne, Air Force and Navy. Each day they slaughtered goats and barbecued them, then drank martinis. One general could not reach beyond his belly to tie his 42-hole anti-fire, anti- explosive Airborne boots. The corporal did it.

Dad told Mum, 'Look after my children. I am going to kill those two pigs.'

'Do you want me to do that for you?' she said. 'Shall I clean your machine gun first? Tell Haile Selassie I did it. Your bosses will respect you for your wife's action. I will open their tummies and the big meat can be a gift for the next stupid general. Let the soldiers see how much he eats. If you have the guts, let me do it. You will keep your salary to bring up our kids.'

Other wives betrayed husbands to military police. 'He wanted to kill his boss.' When a major said, 'I am going to kill that general,' his wife reported the venting. He was imprisoned for two years. Their son was my best friend.

The emperor arrived with lords and chiefs, many of whom favoured European aristocracy. Dad refused to salute those traitors. Halfway through the flag-raising, Haile Selassie asked, 'Where is Colonel Tadesse? He built this.' To the belly-filler ready with Dad's report he said, 'You came ten days ago. Let him tell the story.'

Dad appeared armed to the neck in ranger uniform – Mum's idea. The emperor smiled. A chief said, 'Why is he not in ceremonial dress? It is disrespectful. This is not a war zone.'

Haile Selassie said, 'He is ready to defend us. The others wear uncomfortable clothes. Colonel Tadesse is a real soldier. Leave him alone.'

A week later, chiefs ordered Dad to report to Addis Ababa. Dad wrote back, 'You cannot order me. I am not a civilian. Go through the Ministry of Defence.'

They sent a helicopter. Colonel Aman said, 'Report straight to Haile Selassie.'

We packed two trucks. Corporal Wuro was now the 2nd Battalion's mascot. We farewelled him and left the birthplace of coffee production for our home in Addis Ababa.

---

1. Bahru Zewde, A History, 216

Chapter 3
Big Men

The truck driver wedged me between his seat and the machine gun tripod, canvas stretcher behind. Soldiers made me lie on it for rests.

'I am not wounded,' I said, 'Why put me there?'

The driver said, 'Hey, Big Man, mind if I smoke?' Big Man made up for the babying.

At Gilgel Gibe River, in Kaffa, we waited. Emperor Haile Selassie I was building a 319 metre suspension bridge and hydroelectric power dam. It was the largest in eastern Africa. He paid for it using his own money and gifts from General de Gaulle of France and others. The general had arrived in Ethiopia in military dress, lowered his sword and bowed. He apologised for the West's betrayal to Mussolini.

One car at a time got the green light to cross. A convoy of coffee bean trucks meant a two-hour wait. Floating cranes, construction towers and *trenta-cuatro* and *entre* trucks surrounded us. Ethiopian patriots had captured the Italian trucks during the 1935–41 occupation.

The UK then tried to take them to Kenya. Patriots refused.

'We paid for these with our blood, defending our country without your help.' The Ethiopian Coffee Corporation bought them.

Eight hundred metres below, the river surface was smooth and lamb-like. It controlled my heart and mind. Mum fed me two morsels for each one that she gave the others, including Dad. She said, 'Italians tried to cross Gilgel Gibe in tanks to get to our coffee. The current swept them away. Patriots stopped them from building a bridge.'

The fascists had dropped bombs. Many did not explode, wedged under boulders. Winter currents dislodged the bombs and they exploded, killing hippopotamuses. Ethiopians had to clear them before bridge construction. The UK had taken the post-World War II UN budget for that.

Ethiopia would build four dams on the Gilgel Gibe River. They had two hydroelectric power stations and eight substations. The Gilgel Gibe all but died.

Our sergeant major announced that we were going. My sisters were in a huddle. Dad had found a seriously injured, unconscious antelope. He put it on the front of the Wheelie jeep. The girls cried, but locals would appreciate its meat. I touched its huge horns and soft fur.

We stopped at a village. Mum covered her daughters with a shawl. She tried to stop me from witnessing the killing. 'Please, he is little.'

The military's body language differed. 'Leave him alone. He is a man.'

I ran behind the sergeant major to distribute the meat. Villagers queued to give me corn cobs, raw cow's milk, sugar cane and baskets of bananas. Women ran to the girls with a hair treatment, clarified butter. The corporal said, 'Stop. These are a colonel's children.' They then brought hand-painted wooden jewellery and 50 pats of butter.

From Kaffa, the river flowed through Welqite. This was home to Gurage societies. The land-conserving agrarians were peaceful and politically neutral. We nicknamed them Japanese Ethiopians.

In Addis Ababa, Wuro stepped out from the furniture truck. 'Miaow.' The sergeant major saluted him. 'Corporal Wuro stowed away from Jimma to Addis Ababa.' I surrendered to animals and their loyalty. The cat would live with us for another 16 years.

Dad was now military diplomat, military attaché and chief of INTERPOL. Ethiopia had co-founded The International Criminal Police Organisation. With General Yilma he proposed a federal police force, established it and taught recruits. General Gezaw, General Abiy and Dad designed and established Holeta Military Academy. General Abiy combined the best of military science from around the world. Dad wrote military science courses on logistics, hardware and Ground Force operations. He taught guerrilla warfare, riot policing, anti-terrorism and intelligence.

Ethiopia gained five campuses and one in Dare Selam. Tanzania transformed its system of police ranking from British to Ethiopian. My father also taught international forces for two decades. He told Haile Selassie, 'Ethiopia needs a permanent military force – not militia however heroic.' The Ethiopian military expanded.

Our emperor was pan-African, supporting nations in shaking off colonial rulers. He gave asylum to Kenya's 1950 Mau Mau resistance. Through him, Patrice Lumumba met Marcus Garvey. The US civil rights leader told him about Menelik II and Adwa 1896. Lumumba was the future prime minister of the Congo.

By 1952 the French had murdered 300,000 Algerians. They committed atrocities in Tunisia and Morocco. Haile Selassie protested; Europe ignored him. Dad trained freedom fighters in guerrilla warfare. He taught South Africa's Nelson Mandela or Madiba before his 20-year imprisonment. Dad trained other members of the African National Congress, formerly Oliver Tambo Abyssinianism Revolution.

Our Air Force was strong. Ethiopia trained pilots from Africa and the Middle East. She also taught Kenyan ground technicians and fighter jet pilots. The West opposed this without success. For 25 years it kept Ethiopia's Star of David off the flag of the African Union. Orthodox, it symbolised earth, water and stars.

I loved a song by Alemayehu: "Tikur Gisila".[1] "Black Panther" was anti-apartheid.[2] I read the news column Debub Afrika by Paulos Gnogno about South Africa. Its logo was a black hand tied with barbed wire. Paulos Gnogno fought for the powerless. Born in 1934, the year before the Italian occupation, he had no formal schooling and learned to read from train posters. Russia named a theatre in St Petersburg after him.[3]

Haile Selassie helped newly independent African nations. In 1963 the UK left Tanzania with no budget for maintenance of infrastructure. Our emperor paid workers' salaries for one year – administrators, teachers, bus drivers, doormen. Tanzania's Prime Minister Mualimu Julius Kambarage Nyerere named his grandson Tafari after him; he was originally Ras Tafari.

When the UK left Jomo Kenyatta's government in Kenya without a budget, he paid for health workers and the military. Few Kenyans remembered this.

Haile Selassie was friends with President Kenneth Kaunda of Zambia, who carried a white handkerchief as a symbol of peace and human rights. The UK sought the country's oil reserves. Kenneth Kaunda said that Zambia did not play cricket. He meant that the British Commonwealth was an exclusive club. Certain members were free to come and go. Others were restricted.

Kenneth Kaunda did not attend the queen of England's birthday party. The UK demanded to know why. He said he had not been invited. The UK imposed new taxes on the nation that it had impoverished. Economic independence for former colonies was a dream.[4]

Lucy's People

In 1969, US President Richard Nixon kept the emperor waiting at the US airport. After 45 minutes, a US mayor arrived. Haile Selassie said it did not matter if Nixon was unkind to him. 'He needs to be kind to his people.'

My father, centre, hand raised in a salute to the emperor in Arat Kilo. Imperial Ethiopian Government. Ministry of Defence, 1961.

Lucy's People

I played chess at Mekonnenoch, the military chiefs of staff club. Opponents were my eye father Lieutenant General Aman, Air Defence Commander Colonel Tilahun, Ground Force second in command General Gezaw, and the 'Illusion Colonel' General Kebede. He was second in charge at the Ministry of Defence. In the Korean war, he had been second in charge of Ethiopian UN Peacekeepers. For all three deployments he led logistics and intelligence.

General Gezaw would ask his driver, 'Can you bring Big Man? General Kebede will not smile unless Mesfine is here.' Mum checked my face and nose. The driver said, 'No need to do that.'

Two metre tall General Kebede would lift me onto his shoulder. He challenged me to games. I would say, 'I have to sit at the table like a man.' Helping roll up my shirt sleeves immaculate-military style, he whispered, 'Hey Big Man, do not beat me. Play soft.'

Afterward he would say, 'I let myself be beaten on purpose. How could I make this little boy cry?'

His driver laughed. The general glanced at him. He stood to attention. The officers had pooled their pension money to bet on my win. They saluted me. General Kebede opened his sterling-silver cigarette box and took out 20 *birr*. The officers won 40 *birr*, the weekly salary of a recruit. They bought me pastries and I vomited.

I once beat General Kebede three times in a row and laughed. He lifted me overhead to the ceiling. 'Do you have a machine inside your brain?'

General Gezaw asked Dad, 'What did Missus Tewode eat when she was pregnant with him? Tell her to let our wives know her secret. I have a house full of foolish children.'

My eye father said, 'Show me that move.' 'Work it out.'

Pondering the chess board, he stroked his chin and said, 'Stop swinging your legs.' 'Can I have a book while I am waiting?' He bear-hugged me. 'If I swallow you, Tewode will be cross.' General Aman ordered a martini and spiced raw meat. I left the room.

Invisible at gatherings, I stayed up after my sisters went to bed. One general always wore medal-bedecked uniform. None touched a morsel between meals, nor slouched, up to the day they died. General Mengistu's foiled 1960 coup d'état had killed our best, including Ras Abeba, the defence minister. During the resistance to Mussolini, he had led Shewa's patriots.

We hosted military leaders for dinner. Neighbour Itiye Aberrash welcomed each at the gate. She requested his pistol and put it in a basket which she gave to my mother. I asked Mum about it.

'This is not a military occasion. The officers want to dance and sing.' Patriot songs gave way to tears.

One evening, Dad walked in our backyard with three generals including General Gezaw, now chief of Ethiopian Ground Force and the military brain. They sent away the driver, bodyguard and radio operator. Mum locked us children in a room, but I glimpsed the four. All drank.

In the morning Dad was on the study floor, Bren machine gun mounted on a pile of books. He awoke asking for me. Mum said, 'I do not want to lose all my family. Men on my side died early, killed in war.'

The room contained military equipment, explosives and signal radios that went 'dong, dong, dong'. A world map had Italy and the UK marked in red. Dad said, 'Danger is fabricated there and spreads throughout the world.' All military houses contained radios, military-green with long antennae.

Colonel Tilahun commanded transport and logistics for Air Defence. He took ministry calls while at dinner, muttering asides. 'Stupid.'

We children joined shoe-polish tins with rope. 'Hallo.'

'Mumbo jumbo.'

'Yes? Sergeant Major?'
'Mumbo jumbo.'
'Stupid, stupid, stupid.'

One day, Colonel Tilahun went to his office at Mekelakeya, the Ministry of Defence. He put his pistol underneath his chin and squeezed the trigger. The emperor attended his full military funeral. The colonel's kids were closer to us than cousins. Itiye Minyishu, his widow, was Mum's best friend. She never spoke again. Was it an act to safeguard secrets?

As hosts, officers' wives wore the apron of the master of the kitchen; they controlled quantities of ingredients yet dressed humbly. Dad's medals spread across his chest, but women could remove his gun. Each man was the head of a brigade or leader of a battalion. His wife was above him. Our mothers could have spilled secrets but kept silent. Discretion stopped malicious gossip. It was an Ethiopian strength. Mum said, 'Save your words. It will save your life.'

Our leaders took part in senior-military training in the US.[5] Dad trained Ethiopians jointly with Israel, Sweden, Yugoslavia and the UK.

In Maryland, US, he trained ammunition factory workers. His officers taught 100,000 how to store and maintain our equipment. This was M16 Bren and 55-calibre machine guns for helicopters and jeeps. Ethiopia had adapted them so that they did not seize up in heat and humidity. In return the US gave Ethiopia twenty-five F5 jets.

The US military liked the exchange, but not Dad, saying, 'Why did you bring that colonel here? We do not want him.' Ethiopian Command had told Dad, 'Take your gun everywhere, even if you go to the toilet. Do not forget it when you go for a walk. Avoid groups of Americans in the military club.'

Twenty years previously, US soldiers had socialised with

Ethiopian UN Peacekeepers in Korea. High-ranking officers went shopping for something new at the Ethiopian camp. An Ethiopian corporal taught General MacArthur to play the Ethiopian violin. They risked court martial, but nobody enforced the rules.

In an army boxing spar, Lieutenant Colonel Aman floored General MacArthur. The general became wary of thin, bony hands. Americans never won a volleyball match or football game against our slight soldiers. US soldiers began to call them kind killers. If insulted they did not retaliate, but none dared touch them.

Americans ate beans straight from the tin while Ethiopians added spice, basil, onion and smoked meat from wild-caught fish and goats. US soldiers began taking rations to the Ethiopian seven-star hotel for improvement.

A researcher found that Ethiopians remained at the battlefront for long periods yet returned looking refreshed. They never ate junk, nor smoked or drank heavily. After battle, they rehabilitated themselves with dance and music. Our soldiers chatted while playing table games – *gebita, dama* and chess.

They travelled light. With heavy gear, Americans were slow to demobilise and escape attack. In battle, Ethiopians did not retreat. A short Ethiopian soldier fired his gun at three fleeing Americans. Shivering, they sat.

One became a war hero. He visited the Ethiopian twice in Addis Ababa and, later, his grave.

North Korean suicide missions detonated truckloads of explosives at depots. Lieutenant Colonel Aman told General MacArthur to dig pits and fill them with sand as traps. US soldiers had to stop boozing and bringing women to their camps. Hospitals and food, water and fuel depots needed to be top-secret, isolated and camouflaged.

White Americans gave African American World War II heroes no opportunity for leadership.[6] They segregated, slurred and abused them. In Nuremberg and Berlin, the US military served African American men meals after Nazi war criminals. US war heroes called Asian people 'goose' and 'rabbit' and African Americans 'hippo'.

General MacArthur said that the very word 'army' reminded him of Ethiopian soldiers, and that he was optimistic about the future of non-White societies.

Our soldiers served as UN Peacekeepers in Africa, North Korea, the Middle East, India, Pakistan, Kashmir and Indochina.[7] Dad was in charge of UN Peacekeepers in the Congo. He was one of 5,000 in Uganda where an Indian general put them in constant danger. Few acknowledged our UN Peacekeepers.

Most Ethiopian generals had friends in Belgium, South Africa, The Netherlands and UK. They gained luxury furniture, wrist-watches and cigarette boxes. Others became alcoholics and killed themselves.

Sabotage was rife from 1948 to 1970. The emperor survived attempts on his life by Turkish and US agents. His dog Lulu barked at a man in a palace queue. Despite the mild day, the man was sweating. When guards challenged him, he threw a bomb that killed them and himself.

A few belly-filler lords now owned Ethiopia's most fertile farming lands. By law they had to send peasants' children to school and provide medical services. Instead, they made them work as herders. They raised taxes as high as 75 per cent. Word of their corruption did not reach the emperor.

At court, those loyal to the emperor had a procedure done. Physicians inserted a product under the ball of the foot. After three days, they removed entry-site stitches by pulling on one end of the goat-intestine suture. At meals, the treated person gathered samples from their plate and let them fall to the floor. They placed their foot on top, lifted it and glanced down. Maggots meant that food had been poisoned.

The widow of Major Sihale—killed at the eastern border—was

a seer. Waking early from a dream, she hurried to the Ministry of Defence. Security admitted her to the office of General Kebede. She said, 'Do not go. Stop the flight.'

The general was scheduled to take the emperor to a meeting in Bale Province. They were travelling with two other Airborne Force generals in an Uzi helicopter. Made in Israel and Ethiopia, it was reliable. The men treated her warning as superstition.

Three hours later the helicopter crashed in dense Bale forest, its propeller broken into pieces. Cushioned by the tree canopy, it stuck. Explosives could have been planted. If tree branches broke and it fell, the helicopter would blow up.

The generals improvised a rope harness with which to lower the emperor. Then in his sixties, he was flexible and clambered out. General Kebede sent down the two other generals and co-pilot, telling them, 'Take Haile Selassie and run!' He passed them two machine guns for protection against wildlife. The co-pilot could help fly the emperor to safety when another helicopter came.

General Kebede, Haile Selassie's assistant and the pilot stayed behind. They drained the helicopter of fuel to prevent the whole area being burned in an explosion. After removing its radio, they contacted local Air Defence and Air Force, which rescued everybody.

The saboteur was a US ground technician, who serviced the helicopter. Tricking colleagues into leaving early, he removed the propeller belt. He confessed this and private investigators confirmed the story. The emperor detained him under house arrest akin to a hotel-cum-educational institute. Two years later he went home in tears. Eisenhower took him back.

---

1. Mr Mirkuzz, "Alemayehu Eshete"
2. Timkehet Teffera, "Chapter III", 96
3. Alfa Tube, "Uneducated Genius"
4. Mueni ma Wuiu, "Colonial and Postcolonial", 1318

5. Kasaye Chemeda, Yeto Meda, 304-5
6. Clark, "When Jim Crow Reigned", para. 8
7. Hussein Ahmed, Rete and Honey, 56-61

Chapter 4
Patriot

Our family treasure was a patriot's sword. During a raid the Derg stole four. After 10 years Mum got one back. It had a lion's head engraved in silver, the *Mo Anbesa*, and Ge'ez text that meant The Black Lion, the Root of Judaism. Now it was bent. My father's straight English sword was long gone. We were still missing two patriot swords. A short one was for long marches, and a long sword was for home defence.

I asked Mum, 'And Mama Teliqwa's sword and plumed helmet?' They were from an Italian general captured during the occupation.

'The government said they were in the National Museum. They are not there.'

Mum enacted family histories of those patriots' swords, striding about the house, children running behind. She said about the returned bent sword: 'When I am allowed to travel, I will take it to Rabbi Yusef.' He was an expert in metal work and weapons manufacture.

Others specialised in mining, clock making and the preparation of traditional medicine. Italian fascists and the Derg murdered many. Survivors downplayed manual dexterity, for this ability often matched skill in star counting or astronomy. Associated with reading the hearts and destinies of fellow humans, the Derg feared it.

Yusef lived in Mum's birthplace, Qur Amba in Gojjam. It was 700 kilometres north of Addis Ababa. Officials refused to give her a travel permit.

Mum was born Medhanit, which meant medicine. Her father taught her herbal medicine. She followed him, gathering herbs and roots.

She learned midwifery from her mother. They filled tubs with kettles of warm water to ease labour pain. Using iridology, they could tell if a full-term foetus had the cord around their neck. Mum placed the mother on a horse to fix this. The ride stimulated labour, saving the baby from gradual strangulation. Midwives also administered contraceptive leaves to women and female livestock.

Patriots presented her sword for service during the Italo-Ethiopian War. The Italians invaded late in 1935 when she was 14. They occupied most of Ethiopia until 1941. Mum fought at the front in Gojjam Province. She was a crack shot patriot.

For almost six years, patriots kept Mussolini's forces out of Gojjam, Kaffa and Sidamo. The forces did not plant one tent pole there. Women were essential to the resistance. Shawaragad was an undercover patriot in Addis Alem in the south. She enabled patriots to storm the Italian garrison.

Young girls like Mum pretended to be mourners. They smuggled medical supplies, food and weapons in coffins under the noses of Italian soldiers. Female patriots wore belts that wound around their waists three times. In these they smuggled scarce bullets.

Girls conveyed coded information. They wore green shawls to signal temporary peace, and red for imminent battle. When bombers were coming, they carried a wooden bird on a stick.

They drizzled water on their heads to warn of disrupted water supplies. An egg smashed on the road meant food shortages.

In 1937 there was only one machine gunner per 10,000 warriors. The sharpest shooter was 19-year-old Azalech. One morning Mum received a message from a runner. '*Maye*, come to the front. Azalech is in labour and will not leave her machine gun post.' It was her first child.

With two older midwives Mum left the base on foot. Italians had been bombing in the area, so the nurses avoided splashing at shallow crossings. Boosted with arsenic oil and mercury, mustard gas did not disperse. Near the front they crawled on their bellies.

Chest high in a trench, Azalech stood before her gun. The senior midwife said, 'Can we lift you out?' The girl did not pause. 'Brothers are dying. Not enough bullets for guns. I will stay.' She was shooting enemy bullets before they struck patriots.

The youngest and most agile, Mum climbed into the trench. She washed Azalech with water from a goatskin bag used for obstetrics and wounds. It was more sterile than metal or wood. The delivery was straightforward. Azalech did not hold her son. She continued shooting while birthing the placenta. Mum tied his cord with pampas grass. The older midwives suckled him until Azalech had time to let her milk come in.

She named him Tewod after Mum, who was now Tewode: the first Ethiopian man given a woman's name. His mother was the first Ethiopian woman promoted to colonel. With her long female-patriots' belt, she was buried near Mum at Selassie 'Trinity' Cathedral, Addis Ababa. Mum was later re-buried in Jerusalem, but her patriot, nurse and storyteller medals are in our patriots' museum.

Other patriots delivered their babies at the front, including the gunner Missus Zerfishiwal. She asked a warrior, 'Do you have a razor?' It would be unused, as he had a beard. He pulled it from his pack. Passing wild cabbage to him she asked, 'Can you sterilise it?' Above the battle noise, a cry came from the ground. There was the baby she had delivered. Zerfishiwal cut the umbilical cord. The warrior wrapped the boy in a jacket. They named him Igena, Hebrew for visitor. He would earn five degrees and become an adviser to the emperor.

At the end of her life, healthy yet ready to die, his mother walked into the bush. Two weeks later, Selassie Cathedral held her empty-coffin funeral.

In fertile regions, peasants and farmers defended lands against invaders. In Oromo regions, warriors owned several horses and a gun. North Shewa, Welo, Gojjam and Gondar Amhara owned a horse and at least one gun. Gondar and Gojjam families bought it when a son was born.

When this son was four, elders would stroke his back with the barrel end. The child then learned how to clean the metal parts and lubricate them. He polished the wood with honey wax to keep out termites. When he reached seven, he began to shoot. At 16 he received the gun, his to keep. He could not obtain a wife without skill in using it. A mark of prowess was to shoot through the centre of an orb-weaving spider's web without breaking it. I did this before the age of nine. A general whispered, 'You are ready for a woman now.'

Mum's brothers Andwalem and Beqalu were warriors in Gojjam. My uncles were undefeated in battle. Andwalem was in his early twenties. His name meant one world. He directly confronted two Italian colonels in their office. They fired. Andwalem killed both before dying. The fascists took his body to Asmara on the coast, claiming they had taken him alive. They hung up his corpse for three days in central Abbashiwele Square. In that square alone fascists hanged 311 patriots.

Beqalu was in his late twenties at the start of the occupation.

He would ride his horse into the middle of Italian troops or machine gun fire. Warrior and horse resisted bullets. However, he had no protection against Ras Hailu, the Gojjami traitor. The chief betrayed him to fascists who hung him in Bahir Dar, Gojjam. Locals said, 'If these men had lived, they would have accomplished more.'

Gojjami patriots engaged in two battles. The simplest was with Mussolini's fascists. The complicated one was with traitors. In the pay of invaders, they could be anybody. Traitors drove for fascists, and supplied them with stolen eggs, chickens and cabbage. They handed over anyone who supplied patriots with food. Traitors informed on patriots and sons of chiefs, and beheaded captives. And they led fascist torturers and murderers to civilians hidden in caves – mostly elderly and children.

Unable to shoot warriors, blackshirts got Ethiopian traitors to check them for surgical protection. Those marks could be disguised with tattoos. Monastic physicians inserted a product made from herbs under the skin. In the upper arm or eyebrow, it protected them from fatal gunshot. Beqalu and Andwalem may have had them; the emperor too. Haile Selassie I survived service at the front.

Forty years later the Derg stamped out this unique traditional technology. Remnants survived. In Awash in the 1980s, a poisonous snake stopped in a faint when it met a local with similar protection. Remote Kebre Mengist miners had it. On the upper arm, it protected them from malaria mosquito bites and eagle attacks. On the leg, it repelled snakes and scorpions. Long sleeves or trousers hid marks – no need to alarm visitors.

Mum's cousins were close like brothers. Warrior Belay Zeleq (Zeleke) was from Bichena, Gojjam. He had long hair worn in an Afro or Amhara style: braided on the head and free around the neck. Gojjami patriots called him by his horse's name, Aba Koster which meant Father Bold.

In 1935, at the start of the invasion, Belay was 23. He waged a new style of guerrilla warfare in secrecy. Only after their victory in 1941 did Ethiopians celebrate his achievements.

Belay fought the fascists in Gojjam, Welo, Shewa and Sidamo. He captured one Italian general and killed six. Early on, he ambushed a convoy. Patriots gained much-needed weapons. Never betrayed, the warrior and his horse survived in the thick of battle, bullets flying. He emerged through flames. This baffled Italians who called him Illusion. Yet he preferred peace.

Female patriots captured an Italian colonel. He begged them to kill him straightaway. The women found him attempting suicide. They kept him alive and handed him over to Belay's warriors. When they reached the camp Belay told the colonel's guards, 'Give him good breakfasts; cook his eggs how he likes. Let him read from a prayer book each morning, walk and think. Bring him to me later.'

The colonel wrote home, 'I am confident they will not kill me.' He observed the patriots' discipline as they prepared for campaigns. 'These barefoot men are more civilised than us.'

They took the colonel to Belay. He said, 'We will not touch you even though you have killed our children. You are free to go where you like about the camp. If you run, we will punish you. Our guards see far.'

For the first time in his career the colonel felt no pressure. In Rome he had always been on a deadline to design battles. He wrote a journal; it turned into a book. The colonel did not want to go back to the Italians, nor to Italy.

Ethiopians kept an eye on him. They treated him like any brother; he slept and ate with them. Patriots carried out kitchen and logistical work with him around. He marvelled at their preparation of battlefront supplies. Without refrigeration, food transported 1,000 kilometres did not spoil.

The Italian colonel asked to see their leader to apologise for what fascists did to his people. 'What do I do to ask his forgiveness?'

'Prostrate yourself at his feet and kiss them. If he is not ready to forgive, he will move them out of the way.'

He did this. Belay lifted him to his feet, kissing him on his shoulders, right, left, right.

The colonel wrote four books on Ethiopian culture and the injustice of the fascist invasion. The UK took him in and burned his books. For four years, it kept him cold in a London flat on two English meals per day. Back in Rome after the war, the Italians burned his latest volume. He tried to return to Ethiopia but died of stress-related illness.

Emperor Haile Selassie I made Belay Lord Protector of the Crown. He appointed him governor of Gojjam but Belay refused. 'I am a simple farmer.' In the lesser role of governor of Bichena he never involved himself in government intrigue. He did not benefit from rank. Others with official positions were unscrupulous belly-fillers. Thirty-three years of peace followed the fascists' defeat in Ethiopia. Feudal lords gained the upper hand.

Traitors had not vanished. Lord Belay declared that none should be buried on Gojjami soil. Its people had paid with their blood. This infuriated the feudal lords in league with them. Cronies in the city accused Belay of planning trouble. The emperor became wary of this most loyal of subjects.

The military placed him under house arrest with his brother Ejigu, the patriot Jembere and one other. Then they told Belay to leave. Fifty kilometres north of Addis Ababa, troops surrounded the four, accusing them of escaping. They fought back, killing a soldier. Officials did not identify Lord Belay's companions.

On 12 January 1945, they hung all four in the city's public square, Teklehaymanot Addebabay. Belay Zeleq was barely 33. Mum dressed in black, mourning him for a full year. Romans celebrated the execution with fireworks. Belay's family members are still wanted in Italy. His statue is in Bahir Dar, Gojjam.

At Mankusa in Gojjam, Mum's father Alemayehu was priest, Genius of Geniuses and head rabbi. He was also a seer, herbal medicine practitioner and *yeneta* or church-school teacher of Ge'ez and herbal-paint making.

In 1936, invaders took food, so he advocated farming on the Sabbath. Orthodox Christian clergy disapproved. With that as an excuse, traitor Ras Hailu trapped him and gave him to the fascists. They insisted he praise the Catholic Church before his congregation. He refused: 'Your cross is false; you've no respect for women and children. Your wives are mere property.'

South in Addis Ababa, General Graziani—Mussolini's right-hand man—tortured him with pincers, pencils and pens. He neither broke nor yielded the whereabouts of his children to his tormentors.

Graziani feared that he would turn into a fly or mosquito en route to Rome, so sent him 1,080 kilometres north to Eritrea. At noon Roman time, Askari-police conscripts hanged him in Asmara's Abbashiwele Square. They botched the execution and shot any who cried. After guarding his corpse for four hours, they took it down to dissolve in acid. Routine treatment of the influential.

Ethiopians named babies after grandfather Alemayehu. Our family renamed Mum Tewode; Medhanit was too painful a reminder.

Fascists captured Kes Alemayehu's nephew Wendson. He was secretary to the late *Pappas*. They tried to get him to endorse Catholicism; he refused. Fascists took him to Rome and imprisoned him until the end of World War II. A general's daughter fell for him. For that, torturers beat him relentlessly. At the same time, they attached a full bottle of water to his genitals.

After seven years Wendson returned home, his mind much less sharp. Mum's cousin had been literate in Hebrew, Ge'ez,

Amharic and European languages. Forever in a wheelchair, he was incontinent.

Many Ethiopians imprisoned in Rome never returned and did not have proper burials. Others came home on stretchers. Some remained after World War II. Human rights organisations and the UN did nothing to help. Italians returning home from detention in Ethiopia disembarked upon healthy legs. Ethiopians gave decent burials to captives who died.

Throughout the occupation, Mum's people said, 'Fear your fear. Do not respect him or he will become your owner.'

Abun Petros was the Orit Orthodox pope – *Pappas* of Ethiopia, Israel, Jordan, Yemen and Syria. The Abun held all humankind in his heart. When fascists sickened or were dying, he prayed for them.

He preached, 'If you accept the taking of your land, you are cursed. Sell your chickens and eggs to fascists and you are doomed. I have no sword. My weapon is my cross.' The fascists arrested him. General Graziani planned to civilise him. His subordinate challenged the Abun. 'Marrying once and remaining faithful is primitive. European women and men could go with anybody they liked.'

Abun Petros said, 'We keep not only the word of God but the natural order and balance of life. We cannot say that prostitution is natural, a part of democracy, belonging in civilised societies. Ethiopians create true love in the heart. Women in Europe have lost this. They have never received it.' The Italian said that, in European society, a man could go with his mother. He demanded a response to this from the Abun. 'Now you are warning me to pray deeply. You are right. A man can sleep with his mother but only if she is a virgin.'

He sent a message to General Graziani: the Abun was more civilised. Graziani read it over and over before bed. At midnight he awoke and wrote to his general. He told him to avoid the Abun or he would hand him his gun and tell him to shoot him. He might even shoot his fellow fascists.

The subordinate addressed Abun Petros as Father. 'Aba, I need to tell my children your history. Can you tell me about your mum and dad?'

'It is enough to tell my history. That alone will change a generation.'

Graziani ordered him to kill the Abun. He was to do it straightaway for Ethiopians make the most of every day.

His general executed the Abun by firing squad. Five Armenian residents shielded him. Graziani ordered them shot. That day, Italians killed 2,800 locals. Many were Greek and Yugoslav residents. Refugees from Mussolini in their homelands, they had sought asylum in Ethiopia.

Graziani asked locals, 'Are you with us or against us? Do you sympathise with this Jew?'

After they murdered our leader, fascists ordered a Greek ophthalmologist to dance. He refused. They shot him as well. General Graziani placed his foot on his body and ordered a glass of wine.

The subordinate sent his report then lost his mind. Back in Rome he died within a few years. Ethiopians named the place where fascists sought to eradicate our religion Abun Petros Square. His statue is there, machine gun underfoot.

Fascists bombed, burned or dismantled thousands of mosques, churches and monasteries. This included part of Selassie Cathedral. They pillaged Sidetenya Medhane Alem Sidist Kilo Monastery, stripping it of art and furnishings. A monk raced away with the Ark of the Covenant replica.

At the Rift Valley monastery of Debre Libanos, they massacred 10,000. It was an extension of atrocities begun in February

1937.[1] In 2004, a female monk would take me down the rocky path to monk caves. A mound contained human skulls and bones. This was the remains of 3,000 deacons, female monks, elderly monks, rabbis and circumcised boys and civilians from near and far. Blackshirts hurled holy ones 1,000 metres down a cliff. Many had Orthodox crosses on their forearms. Yellow robes contrasted with the black tattoos – visible to all. Catholic Italy's fascists were blind to them.

They destroyed the monastery. In 1951, Emperor Haile Selassie I would rebuild it for the seventh time in its 2,000-year history. Turkey's Grañ Ahmed had burned it twice in the sixteenth century; monks saved bibles from the flames. In 1937, they hid those.

Italians killed any Orthodox boy or man. They threw them from aircraft high above rivers. Others mutilated young boys. Soldiers hung the severed penises of children on their gun barrels as trophies. 'He is a hero; he has 11.' Fascists promoted them. They ordered boys to wear no trousers. 'Any circumcised boy has to be killed immediately.' Jewish mothers said, 'We will stop circumcision for now.'

They threatened to mutilate a patriot's four-year-old son if he did not surrender. He said that he was fighting for all children. Patriots hid the child in a cave. Blackshirts found him and cut off his penis, leaving him to die in agony. A monk rescued him. In a remote monastery the boy healed. He became Ethiopia's artist laureate.

Fascists took 1,200 Orthodox boys from Amhara to Rome. Some of the prisoners were only two and the oldest were 14. The English gave safe passage through Sudan. They knew what they were doing. Three hundred boys died on the way. The Italians took the remaining 900 to a stadium in Rome. Soldiers murdered each child in front of Mussolini. The Catholic Pope sat beside him. Today, in some areas of Ethiopia, the term Catholic is synonymous with murderer.

Itiye Aynesh cared for children and animals sheltering in

caves. Italians tore babies from their mothers' backs. Itiye refused to have children of her own. She closed the shutters whenever a neighbourhood child cried.

Our mother reacted to these atrocities differently to her sister. She and our father would have 10 children.

---

1. Campbell, Plot, 317-18

Chapter 5
Mama Teliqwa

Our grandmother Mama Teliqwa fought in the resistance. Her real name was Yuwagobesh Mirsha. This meant let people fight over you and forget horror.

When she was a child, Ethiopia triumphed at the Battle of Adwa 1896 with honour. The leaders were Emperor Menelik II and Empress Taytu, battalion leader Ras Mekonnen and Defence Minister Fetawerare Habte Giyorgis. His nickname was Aba Mela or Father Solution.[1]

Our empress and Aba Mela surrounded a vital water resource with warriors. Engineers diverted streams underground. This prevented Italians from spoiling water and deprived their troops of it.

Christian and Jewish warriors were fasting for Easter. Ras Mekonnen kept morale high. He flew the flags of the Lion of Judah and Saint Giyorgis. The emperor rode with troops and the Ark of the Covenant for 700 kilometres from the National Theatre in Addis Ababa. Musicians played.

Warriors had Ethiopian weapons: buffalo-hide shields, long spears, bows and arrows, homemade rifles and muskets and powder. Some had powerful rifles: the single shot 37 millimetre 'make you cured', and the semi-automatic 33 millimetre 'not lying' that never jammed.

There were two single shot 50 calibre rifles. The 900 millimetre 'shoot and tie up' was comparable to a twenty-first century rocket-propelled grenade. Emperor Menelik II's rifle was the 1.5 metre 'leg cutter'. Ethiopia developed her weapons over 3,000 years. During the reign of Queen Sheba (Saba), monks made a double-barrel shotgun.

Emperor Menelik II discouraged victory celebrations. People had died. Crying came from among captured soldiers. A youth said, 'I was pushed to war. Mum is in a wheelchair and I am all she has.' Immediately, the emperor sent him back to Italy. The youth's mother had died, rolling herself off a building. He wanted to return to Ethiopia and wrote to Emperor Menelik II. Welcomed back, the Italian entered a monastery, studied Ge'ez and became an artist.

Our emperor washed visitors' feet to prevent them infecting our soil with their fungus. They sneered when he repeated foot-washing upon departure. He said, 'You will not take away our goodness then return for more.' Italy was supposed to stay away.

Forty years on, it invaded again. The Catholic Pope called the Second Italo-Abyssinian War a holy war. Blackshirts called it a civilising mission. Mussolini's fascists had tanks, poisonous gas and bombers; Ethiopia had no military aircraft and used horses and mules for battle. Fascists immediately killed one million animals.

Europe denied Ethiopia ammunition and weapons. Marshal Tito of Yugoslavia supplied weapons later. Nevertheless, the fascists could not get far by land. Oromo warriors got close to tanks, disabled their chain-wheel works and captured them. Then Italians approached from the air. They dropped 280-kilogram bombs. Spitfire aircraft rained nerve gas, mustard gas and fire. Civilians and livestock had no defence.

In 1936, Emperor Haile Selassie I appealed for justice to the League of Nations.[2] Ethiopia was a founding member. The

League did nothing to stop the use of chemical weapons. Mussolini needed petrol to fuel his war machines, yet it did not stop supply.

Only New Zealand supported effective sanctions.[3] The UK and France led the League's betrayal of Ethiopia. West Africans reacted angrily. This was the beginning of pan-African militancy.[4]

In 1936, the patriots sent Mama Teliqwa to Addis Ababa as a double agent. Italians arrested her for crying as the Ethiopian flag was taken down. It had flown since before Moses. A general interrogated her.

'Why should I not cry?' she said to him. 'Your sisters, wives and mothers gave their wedding rings and other gold to fund your invasion.'

'Show respect or go before the firing squad.' The general left, returning later. When he had her name called, she did not respond. Guards used her second name, not her first. Mama Teliqwa said, 'You may not call me by my father's name and expect an answer.' The general let her go.

Patriot Yuwagobesh—our Mama Teliqwa—dressed in canvas leggings that held hand grenades, a Menelik hat and an ammunition belt made of wild buffalo leather. Wide and heavy, it wrapped around her waist three times, clasping at the front. Its green silk pouches had gold embroidery and held 336 bullets: 36 millimetre. The silk would be a bandage if she needed to dress a wound. It healed both soft and hard tissue and prevented infection.

She carried a metre-long *mozer*, a monastery-made rifle. Female patriots also had a round wooden lunchbox with a lining that preserved medicinal herbs and food. Younger women bore infants on their backs.

Mama Teliqwa left to fight in neighbouring Welega Province, west of Gojjam. However, Italians had brought flu with them. She turned around and walked back to Gojjam to tell her rabbi husband. He could deal with the health crisis.

Mama slept in caves stocked with food and water. Patriots kept children, the elderly and livestock there. Caves dripped water and bats produced toxic urine. Women entered, searching for orphaned babies to breastfeed. They did not distinguish any hungry child from their own offspring. The English called them milk cartons. We did not denigrate or belittle the feminine.

Drums and a long flute signalled the approach of bombers. Mustard gas blistered the throat and collapsed the lungs. It burned, blinded and disfigured victims. Survivors developed cancer of the lungs and skin. Orthodox monasteries cured some of this.

Returning to shelter, Mama Teliqwa applied eucalyptus oil all over people. Some had hats made from thick and spongey centres of false-banana leaves. Farmers had walked livestock through mud baths. This was the only protection they had against mustard gas attacks.

After bombings, crops and trees were on fire. Birds fell, stripped of feathers before reaching the ground. Monks neutralised lingering gases by burning a particular type of wood.

Some people covered themselves with coated paper that was shiny and reflective, which shielded them from nerve gas. It was impossible to protect animals. Wildlife and livestock bled copiously from their nostrils. People could not touch them. Millions of animals had to be euthanised and buried deep with quicklime.

Fascists bombed lakes. When animals drank, they died. People drank from wells, but some took water too soon from rivers. Birth defects followed – blindness, noses without flesh, missing fingers.

Mustard gas and incendiary bombs devastated areas controlled by patriots. In Gojjam's east, Italians obliterated Tana Beles bridge and poured mustard gas into the river Goa Tsion. This flowed through Welo Province and north-east Shewa. It continued to the Maji River of the Rift Valley. Future generations would be born blind. Mustard gas persisted in the environment for decades.[5]

Fascists aerially seeded a non-indigenous plant. Sharp stems and leaves cut people and animals. Any that ate it took three days to die. It took over endemic pampas grass which we used in baskets and soft furnishings. Monks restored the water with purifying plant. A branch placed into muddy water also cleared away sediment and water-borne disease.

Orthodox monasteries sheltered people, prime livestock, food, antiques and books. They hid them in tunnels. Monks dug new ones two trousers high – tall enough for people to stand; too low for war machines. Above ground, waves of invaders had destroyed our monasteries, churches and mosques. Tunnels conserved our people and heritage.

Wives and mothers prepared warriors' kits. They applied honey and butter to the skin to repel malaria mosquitoes and deter snakes. Women packed tea that alleviated the effects of chemical warfare. They transported meals to warriors in tightly woven baskets. *Injera* flatbread from organically grown *teff* was high in iron. With vegetables and spiced stew, it promoted immunity and stamina. For enduring long marches, hard times food contained barley, wheat, cheese, salt and preservative root. A small portion staved off hunger and slaked thirst. Patriots also drank a powder mixed with water. Women made it from roasted barley grown on pure land, adding salt and chilli.

Italians ate pork. They killed our cattle for steaks. Some gobbled 55 stolen eggs a day. Monks said, 'Do not kill all the Italians. Our eggs will do the job.' They passed so much wind that it betrayed their hiding places. Mama said, 'When they ran away, their farts were louder than their footsteps.

By night patriots moved to shelter under mountainous overhangs. Unseen from the air, they fired old guns at hundreds of enemy aircraft.

Mama Teliqwa cut her hair in an Afro like her sister's son Belay. In occupied areas she had come across human body parts. For sport, Mussolini's thugs apprehended Ethiopians with long hair, usually women. They tied them to tanks by their tresses, driving until only the victim's head remained.

After killings and attacks, a war-time singer would feign happiness with song. Patriots assembled musical teenagers. The girls created "Sheginawoch". It became the anthem of the patriots.

> Let the soil be lighter; let it comfort you like a
>   mattress
> May the stones be a pillow
> Do not feel you are burned from the air.
> Don't feel you are shot; don't feel you have been
>   dragged
> Don't feel you have fallen
> You are with us forever.
> I tell your story to my children to never stop
>   loving you
> But I need you to forget those devils
> I will never give them a chance to do the same
>   as what
> I have seen here, anywhere else on earth.
> I will stop the poison from being made
> I will make their hands and brains stop making
>   that gas

Lucy's People

I will stop them from killing animals
I will stop them from burning the beautiful forests
For I do not want to miss the whistling of birds,
    nature's music.
They do not only kill us
They kill our cows, goats, sheep, dogs, cats, birds
    and lovely jumping fish with which I love to
    swim.
All are dying; let us go bury them.
Do not forget to stop all these ways of the killers
This is the solution
We will carve this story in stone
Tell this story
That is the solution.

During my childhood, radio stations played the upbeat "Sheginawoch". In the 1960s, Missus Konjit, widow of the defence minister, made recordings. She grew seedlings for reforestation and gave one small tree with each audio cassette tape. 'If you plant this more birds will have life.'

Millions died during the occupation. Mum's people held onto land in Gojjami Mankusa, but in occupied provinces, patriots came from all over Ethiopia.[6]

Oromo people near Addis Ababa refused to kill Amhara people. Italians incited them to hatred.

'They took your land.'
    An elder said, 'We are from both regions. My wife is from Menz in Amhara and I am Oromo. We will not kill any Ethiopian.'
    'Give us your answer in three days.'
    The Oromo people brought a bullock hide and two

buckets of fine grain *teff*. One contained white *teff*; the other had brown. They spread the hide on the ground. Then they poured and mixed the grains.

'Separate the colours. We will return to see if you have done it in three days.'

For two days, 100 then 200... 300... 1,000 soldiers tried to separate the colours.

On the third day they had not succeeded and the community still refused to kill its neighbours. The Italians loaded everybody into aeroplanes and flew them 1,000 metres above Addis Ababa. They pushed them all out.

To support the resistance, Mama Teliqwa gave cash to patriots. Haile Selassie had entrusted her with it when forced to flee in 1937. She told the emperor that she had done it so that he could return.

In 1935, the UK sealed the border between Gondar in the north and Sudan. Galvanised, Mussolini's fascists invaded. They raided castles and monasteries. The UK had given them reinforcements: Muslim Indian conscripts. English generals in Khartoum ordered them to loot. 'Any fleeing cows, bulls and horses are yours.'

Blackshirts attacked the town of Deberg. They burned bamboo, huts and grass-thatched mud houses. Livestock barns were on fire for three days. Large bulls exploded like bombs.

After three days, Italian cannons did not work. Tanks broke down, stuck on roads. Patriots burned them. Seven thousand metres above sea level, the snow-topped Simien Mountains released hail: tennis-ball size ice stones.

Mussolini had received daily reports via Khartoum. Now he said, 'I will come'. His men warned him not to: 'The savage shawl dressers have an invisible power underneath their cotton wraps. They can stop steel chain wheels, rain hail, and blind you with windstorms. Then they chop you down. In our fine boots our feet freeze. We toddle. Frost does not hurt barefoot warriors. They catch us.'

A captured colonel wrote:

Patriots fed me. My wounds healed in two days. I had not expected to survive. They offered us the chance to collect corpses. We could not bear that, so patriots did it. They removed rank badges then placed bodies in neat rows.

Their second in command said, 'You will be given breakfast; we will not eat.' Ethiopians eat and drink only after the dead are buried.

I said, 'These are Italians.'

They said, 'They are human beings. Even in war they need proper burial.'

In Italy we drink wine, smoke cigars and place bouquets of white flowers on the coffin. Relatives enjoy sex that night. The following day we forget him.

A female patriot led laments to send the dead to heaven. She sang, 'Why are you cruel? Why do you start wars? Why take someone's green land, river and food?'

Gondar's people sang for the bereaved families of invaders. The boys had died for false beliefs.[7]

After the murder of her husband, Mama Teliqwa wore her ammunition belt for 40 years. It slept alongside her with the *mozer* rifle. She also lost a daughter, two sons and several nephews. Mama refused a mattress and went barefoot. 'I feel more connected with my sons and husband.' If she saw a mouse shoulder dancing she would not laugh.

Hunger was rife in Gojjam. Traitors plundered widows' resources. When she was away fighting, they took Mama's sheep.

They broke into her house to steal heirlooms including antique rifles. Italians would pay for their woodwork.

Five robbers returned, battering a hole in the wall. Mama Teliqwa was home and kept quiet. When the first poked his head through, she sliced off his ear and presented it on the end of her sword like a top hat with, 'Take your ear.' They fled. Mama called, 'Stitch it back on at the clinic.'

In February 1937, fascists murdered more than 41,000 unarmed civilians. These included the ill, the elderly, the pregnant and the underage. Their excuse was an attack on Graziani, though they knew Ethiopians were innocent.[8] They set fire to families in their houses, machine gunners outside.[9] Selassie's rabbis said they burned alive between 30,000 and 35,000 children. Italians attacked with spades and shovels, leaving the dying to hyenas. The 19 February monument in Sidist Kilo, Addis Ababa commemorates the atrocity.

Some got away. The resistance smuggled them to safety in the countryside. Tunnels, riverbeds and caves sheltered tens of thousands. 5,000 Italian troops refused to slaughter civilians. Some troops shut themselves in burning houses. Others threw away their weapons and fled. They surrendered to Oromo patriots at Ambo outside the city.

Patriots took them to the leader, Lord Geressu. The Italians told him not to drink mains water; General Graziani had poisoned Gifirse Dam. Fascists had burned Oromo families alive in their grass-thatched huts. For their warning, the lord pardoned the soldiers. He sheltered and fed them, ordering his patriots to eat once a day.

A married Italian soldier joined the patriots. Shewa patriot leader Abeba gave his wife armed guard for transit from Addis Ababa to Gojjam. For four years she hid in the community. She spoke Amharic and was baptised Orthodox. Neighbours stained her skin with charcoal from cooking pots. She went barefoot and dressed the same as them down to her silver anklet. At market she pretended to be mute. In 1941, UK administrators demanded that the emperor hand her over to the fascists. Haile Selassie refused. 'It is her choice to be Ethiopian.' She stayed in her adopted land even after her husband was captured and killed.

With Mussolini's defeat, some Italians who had surrendered voluntarily repatriated. In Rome, fascists murdered them. Emperor Haile Selassie I then had others stay on as Ethiopian residents.[10]

Sixty years later I visited the Italian War Memorial in Rome. Lord Geressu's name was on a list: WANTED. SAVAGE WARRIORS. How is clemency savage?

One fascist general was addicted to killing prisoners, two before dinner. With no prisoners left, he shot the cook. In 1939 in Menz and Jiru, a single attack killed at least 5,500 people. Ethiopians are still calling for reparations and an apology.[11] The Vatican did not manifest sorrow for atrocities in Libya and war crimes in Ethiopia. I met Italians in Australia who were proud of General Graziani. Germans dedicated memorials to Nazi victims. Those who acknowledged the Holocaust would not allow it to happen again.

After his return to Ethiopia, the emperor had given 600 oxen to the starving in Greece. Our people had nothing with which to make bread. By then, the English ran the Ethiopian police force. This was part of the Anglo-Ethiopian Agreement of 1942.[12] UK administrators forced peasants to give up wheat, high protein beans, oxen and rams for war-torn Europe. They sent livestock and frozen meat to the Red Sea for export. The French also stole livestock from Ethiopia's east and took them to Djibouti.

Patriots stopped theft of food. 'A second war has now begun with administrators and neighbouring colonisers. Do not put away your guns.' When the English changed our road rules they wrote to the emperor. He kept our right-hand drive.

One lord had sat out the occupation abroad. In Addis Ababa, he hosted a grand dinner for all who had defended the motherland. The dress code was shoes with traditional dress. Few could afford this. A guard turned away traumatised and hungry people. My grandmother wore hand-embroidered white cotton. An usher took her to the buffet. She scooped food and smeared it on herself.

The guard said, 'What are you doing?'

'Feeding my clothes. My clothes are invited.'

'Please stop.'

'Not unless you let the others in.'

After her night under house arrest, 20 patriots waited with breakfast for Patriot Yuwagobesh. The defence minister released her to prevent an uprising. The following year, all attended the banquet.

Each winter Mama Teliqwa travelled 700 kilometres by bus from Gojjam. She disembarked with Afro hair, bare feet, patriot leggings containing supplies and her ammunition belt. Out of loyalty to Ethiopia, locals scrambled to help though she was hands free. A small backpack held personal items. Her hand luggage was her *mozer* rifle. Once, police arrested her at the depot for bearing arms. Identifying her as a patriot, the chief chauffeured her home.

Mama had cargo: sacks of *gulo* silk from the waist-high angel's plant. She and our mother produced luxury garments.

Her favourite task was cleaning the patriot swords. She gave them pet names. *Mozer* and ammunition shone. Mama polished all the bullets, copper-green from lengthy peace. Our sisters filched her homemade leather-holster polish for their skin.

When I was six, the government installed a French-made

television set in our village of Arat Kilo near Jubilee in Palace. The location is now Africa Park, close to the African Economic Commission. Mama Teliqwa took us to watch a foreign movie there.

The whole village attended. We stood far from the screen. Mama stroked my hair, calling me Getahun which meant beloved. The movie commenced.

The star had a love interest, and there was a scene with what our grandmother called naked kissing. Mama Teliqwa took her rifle from her shoulder and aimed it at the television screen. She fired once. The screen shattered in tiny pieces. My sisters covered their ears and raced to tell Mum.

The police came. Mama told them she was protecting us from television's corrupting influence. 'We must not betray our children.' They apprehended her.

She growled at the officer who tried to lift her into the Land Rover. 'Do not touch me.'

He approached again and she pushed him away. 'Next time I will shoot you. Wait until I have sat down before you start the engine. I do not want to smell its dirty backside.' Mama hated exhaust fumes.

Mum contacted Dad. The defence minister had Mama set free with apologies. She had refused to relinquish her patriot's rifle. Bad boys in Arat Kilo nicknamed it *Aymire* – in her hands it never missed. Tilahun sang about it. From then on Arat Kilo's residents viewed movies containing scenes of questionable morality at 9 p.m. after Mama's bedtime. We hid our TV when she came to stay.

My tiny grandmother was the biggest person. She had fought war with war. Mama made fun of post-colonialist ambitions in Africa. She crouched like a ravenous fox fixated upon prey. Then she ambled on all fours, a bull with juicy balls that did not drop. Better for the fox to catch rabbits at home.

With work she switched on my brain. My brother and I processed her sacks of angel silk. Gojjami monks chanted about its dazzling whiteness. Burst-open purple bolls held seeds and fluffy silk. We separated them. Mum sold the oil-rich seeds for candle making.

Mama Teliqwa inspected Mum's fingernails. Her silk apprentice had to file them smooth. Mum spun thread then wove it on her mahogany loom. She sewed handkerchiefs and capes. For embroidery, Mum wove silk on a 50-centimetre frame. She dyed threads with sun dried flower petals.

I melted metal for Mum to make silver thread and polished it with iodine. In woven silver crosses, she incorporated bluestones that I sanded and shaped. Orthodox Christian lords bought her garments for palace events to impress the emperor. Haile Selassie would ask about the fine craftwork. Mum's customers would not mention her. To them she was evil eye.

Mum overcharged the belly-fillers. Upon their third order, they bargained. Mum said, 'You steal from the poor. Get out of the house.' Mama Teliqwa pulled the *mozer* on them. 'Leave or I will put a hole in you.'

'I am a second in command.'

'You are fat. I feel sorry for your wife. How do you sleep with her? She is missing a big part of life.'

Customers sent advance parties. They came if Patriot Yuwagobesh was out.

Our other grandmother complained to Dad: 'Tewode is turning the children into craftworkers.' The skill came from Mum's people in Gojjami Qur Amba. I would apply Mama Teliqwa's systems to budgeting and the home. Pure cotton clothing maintained the skin. Hand spun, its production did not harm the environment. Her dishes and woven baskets with precisely fitting lids decorated our walls.

I drew Dad's army cap, then his face. Mama Teliqwa said, 'The army never leaves you.' Glancing at me, Dad's mother said, 'The neighbour's corporal son died young.' Mama said, 'Say that again and you will die before my wee dries.'

From Mama Teliqwa I learned three types of silk cultivation. We grew silk plants that flowered purple in spring. Spiders and insects wove their white silk between jagged leaf points. It strengthened in the sun and we harvested it with scissors.

We kept the white maggot of a fly that reached three centimetres and pupated for 25 years. Shrinking as it aged, it made more silk. The maggot wove a silk case around a shell. When it got too large, my grandmother transferred it, still inside its shell, to a new home: the underside of an old bamboo coffee table. Adhering to the surface with a glue-like substance, it produced more silk: three frothy 600 millimetre square harvests per year. I scrounged coffee tables. Mama kissed my forehead – a rare gift from the bereft.

High-quality silk came from khaki spiders that wove a tent to protect themselves from flies, mosquitoes and bees. When we harvested the silk, none died. Mum sprinkled a cup of water on them daily and they danced, eyes roving in sunlight's rainbow. We fed them honeycomb and collard. Silk maggots preferred false-banana root porridge.

Our grandmother forbade coffee roasting near the maggots. Drunk on fumes, they would move to the garden. It would be impossible to get them out of thick mulch. I kept our sheep away from the spider, which would gorge on wool, then sicken and die.

Mama Teliqwa cleared away my two favourite plants from the silk cultivation area. Toxic detergent in soap plant killed both maggot and spider. Silk spiders loved the fragrant female pride flower. They would devour pollen and fatten until unable to breathe.

Children used female pride flowers as toy microphones. I added soap plant to rivers to filter them and the school gave me an award for reducing pollution. When I removed them from our yard, Mama Teliqwa gave me extra garden space.

Mama Teliqwa ate only after feeding poor people. She cared for the planet: 'Buy only what you need. When discarded, how many years will it take to break down?'

Young girls came to her. From behind a locked door Mama shouted, 'You are a woman! Respect your body.' The girl would depart with a remedy that safely terminated early pregnancy. My grandmother did not agree with Catholics and other anti-abortionists. Why bring more troubled citizens into the world?

A youth sprinted into our yard after my sister. Our 158-centimetre grandmother grabbed him by his manhood, lifting and trapping him. Her patriot's knife glinted; he vowed never to return. She taught my sisters the technique. 'Bend your knees. Grab him quickly. When your hand is full, dig in with your strong fingernails. If he collapses, step out of the way.' Mama educated my brothers and me about respect for girls. We fell asleep in her arms to tales of Mother Ethiopia and the deeds of women.[13]

Mama Teliqwa gave us music. 'Let us have some of this.' Eyes twinkling, she would do a shoulder-dance move. This turned into a patriot drama. On cue we chorused, 'Hazar!' We hid the *mozer* rifle under the bed. What if Mama got carried away? She still had her holster and curved sword.

She joined a monastery. The *mozer* and ammunition belt retired. Mama Teliqwa became Mama Mowe (a monk). A century old, she faded away into the bush, body never found.

Her funeral was at Selassie Cathedral, no tears allowed. The Ethiopian flag covered her empty coffin, criss-crossed by spears. Patriots placed a curved sword and shield on top. They lowered it with a 21-gun salute.

Patriots performed a Maori-style *haka*. Its ending was from a classic poem.[14] 'The children of Ethiopia sting like a bee.'

---

1. Evangadi Production, "Tilahun Gessesse"

Lucy's People

2. Haile Selassie and Ullendorff, My Life, 134
3. Peters, "New Zealand's Attitudes", 89
4. Asante, "The Italo-Ethiopian Conflict", 302
5. International Agency, "Sulfur Mustard", 2. Cancer in Humans
6. Levine, Greater Ethiopia, 215
7. Melaku Tefera, The Diary, 153-63
8. Campbell, Plot, 243-45, 288 & 324
9. Pankhurst, Ethiopia, 542-48
10. Priselac, Habesha's Adventure, 140-43
11. Gashaw Ayferam Endaylalu, "Mustard Gas", 512
12. Bahru Zewde, A History, 174
13. Baye Speedy, "Filfilu. Biharu Kegne"
14. "Children of Gojjam", 518

Chapter 6
Arat Kilo

Mum liked the emperor less after January 1945, yet she enrolled me at his school when I was five. Jubilee in Palace School was across the road from us.

The three storey building had a workshop, gym and art rooms; each class had a nurse, who was a mother figure. Three Ministry superintendents at a time observed our lessons. Haile Selassie visited and tasted meals to ensure the food was nutritious. We put on overalls and went to his classic car garage. Mechanics taught us how they worked and about the various types of motor oil. We children used grease guns.

Emperor Menelik II had established national education. In 1906 he built the Menelik Preparatory School for Higher Education. According to Dr Aklilu Lemma, former president of Addis Ababa University, he made 270 speeches on education.

Around 1930, Emperor Haile Selassie I started the Ministry of Education. Schooling was for all. Dr Aklilu said it maintained high standards. After World War II education across Ethiopia was limited.[1] Fascists had murdered teachers. They bombed, took over and closed schools. In 1942, children had none to return to.[2] Ethiopia's texts survived thanks to church-school teachers.

They had preserved resources by hiding them in caves and tunnels.

Those supreme teachers worked only to see people armed with knowledge, helping mother earth and each other. Without education a human being can grow into a dangerous animal. At Haile Selassie's school we thrived in their classes. Each lesson, we sat in the same places. Quick students were at front to prevent callouts. Our teachers respected children who were slower to learn, while extending gifted predators of knowledge.

By Grade 3 all of us were literate and multilingual. We read and wrote two scripts: Ethiopian Fidal and the Roman alphabet. Most spoke Oromigna, Tigrinya, Amharic, Ge'ez and English.

All children knew their multiplication tables. It was an Ethiopian innovation to have them printed on the back covers of our exercise books. Our only calculators were between our ears. Ethiopian arithmetic used Ge'ez numerals. I still do.

We studied agriculture, land care; morality or right and wrong conduct; social equality; meditation and self-management. Church-school teachers gave us thrilling Ge'ez language lessons that included church chants with dance moves. We played drums worn across the body and beaten at both ends; also, the harp and hand-held sistrum that sounded like bells.

Reading early, I skipped baby stuff and gardened or did construction. If I hit my thumb with the hammer or cut my hand on the planer, I never cried. At home my sisters hid my toolkit. Dad said, 'By using it he will learn not to hurt himself.'

One day I broke Dad's favourite wooden stool. He spanked me. I refused to cry. 'Don't you like me?' I asked. 'Why hit me? You are big and I am small. You are not a man. I am a man.' Furious at the big punishment for accidental damage, I built another at school, took it home and gave it to Mum. Dad cried.

At elementary school we learned circus skills and entertained the Peace Corps. It dug trenches at schools and cleared undetonated bombs, saving kids at plays. Volunteers were Greek, Yugoslav, Armenian, Yemeni and Mongolian. They were grateful for asylum from Ethiopia. Monastic masters of dyking rivers and stonemasonry guided them.

I walked down steps on my hands and rode a unicycle, balancing a lit candle on my lip. We had egg-in-spoon sack races. The shows raised funds for the emperor's other schools. He had made education free and provided uniform, lunch and fruit for the poor and children of patriots with war disabilities.

Monkeys, antelope, mountain goats, a crocodile, lions and a cheetah shared the grounds. In a grassed area we played with dogs around white columns. Haile Selassie kept black-headed lions. The alpha male Mola stood at attention for morning flag-raising assemblies.

We played in the grounds of Jubilee and Menelik II Palaces. If any child had a runny nose, staff would ask, 'Have you eaten?' A nurse checked their ears and tongue and served them barley bread.

Nearby was Jembere School for patriots' children from the country. Their parents were in the final stages of illness arising from war. Those kids showed us how to live. I followed them up sky scraping trees to shouts of, 'Come back, Big Man!'

In July and August, we sheltered from thunderstorms inside Inkulal Bete. This was Menelik's egg store where not a sound entered. Its three-storey walls were made of local river sand, clay and hydrated lime. 'Emperor Menelik II' was worked into the stonemasonry. Mama Teliqwa said that after the Battle of Adwa 1896 he was financially stressed – he had funded Ethiopia's defence. Menelik II developed high blood pressure. A physician advised him to drink aged red wine. He built the Egg Store as a cellar, but meat kept untainted for a week and unwrapped lettuce stayed fresh.

I roamed Arat Kilo with its birds, tortoises, wildcats, a rushing river, mountain forests, and *warka* trees 100 metres tall and 50 metres wide. We called valued elders *warka*, which meant big shade. People chiselled dead *warka* trunks into dwellings and built boats. Emperor Menelik stopped commercial logging of living *warka*.

One species had a fruit called *shola*. Singers likened it to girlfriends and wives. The size of an apricot, it was round, honey-coloured and shiny. Inside, it was like a fig. *Shola* trees grew near monasteries. Buttress roots descended into the earth and re-emerged like arms.

The superstitious said, 'Cemeteries provide fertiliser. Do not eat the fruit.' When I picked it, they said, 'He is a devil because he is not dying from eating *shola*.'

From Selassie Cathedral, I also collected leaf litter and dry leaves for our vegetable garden and cooking. It was home to unique tortoises. One species was vegetarian. The other ate worms that grew big on bird droppings. *Anir* wildcats hunted there yet perched on tortoises' backs without harming them. Tortoises waited for *shola* fruit to drop and *anir* caught fallen birds' eggs. I told Teacher Yewobnesh, who asked me to give a talk.

We put on a patriots' drama for parents. My props were a shield that I could barely lift, and stick of the volunteer for throwing. Moved by my performance, Lord Tilahun had a chain with a medallion crafted. It had an intricate patriot scene.

A decorated patriot, his nickname was Father of the Forgotten. He helped poor workers, walking 10 kilometres on Saturdays to identify households with newborns. Lord Tilahun gave them food coupons and arranged for delivery of dairy products from his farm. Its peak season produce filled 10 trucks daily.

His son Henok took me home and his mother Azalech became my spare mother. They had 20 horses. The corporal would stand to attention, front hooves together, nose in air, nostrils dilating. At a signal, he flicked his mane from left to right overhead.

Henok's father also founded Mo Anbesa Shoe Factory in

Piazza. He held a design competition for cobblers. The winner chose its name and became technical manager.

Friends and I organised winter vacations. Six of us stowed away on the train from Addis Ababa to Djibouti. Our pockets held a 1-*birr* note, pocketknife, water and dried food: our luggage. Removing our shoes, we attached them to our belts and climbed onto a train roof. Then we sprinted from railway police, who called, 'We will come on the slow train to Dire Dawa and catch you.'

Boys ran along compartment roofs, mothers inside praying not to have children like us. They called through windows, 'Come down. We will give you biscuits.' Leaping carriages, we plunged into the cargo compartment. It separated from the rest. We lounged on cotton sacks and stole biscuits from boxes.

At Dire Dawa in Harer Province, Security caught us but let us go. 'My son cannot tie his shoelaces. You travel across the nation evading detection for 347 kilometres.'

Harer mothers looked after us during our week's stay.

'Do your mums know where you are?'

'Yes.'

We collected frankincense and river pebbles as gifts for them. Back in Addis Ababa we buried the treasure. By Saint Gebriel or Kidane Mihret, we swore to unearth it together, sealing the promise with the Orthodox symbol of unity. Each grasped his own left wrist with his right hand, and his left hand grasped another's right wrist. The UN adopted the shape as its logo and the US for its weapons. It charged us with confidence.

Our mothers embraced us delightedly, then whipped us before not letting us out of their sight for a week. I made Mum laugh, which spread to others. 'How did you get into the cargo compartment? What about the guards?'

Mothers used stinging leaf, so we rubbed our skin with broad leaf, making it leathery to dull pain. We had to pretend to suffer during the punishment. 'Ow! That hurts.' One boy's mother overheard him boast of it and told the others. Mum realised we used broad leaf. After the next vacation they said, 'In the shower with you.'

Those escapades boosted us, but we started out admiring old trains. Pictures showed the *Zegamba*, built for Emperor Menelik II with his portrait on its exterior in bronze, and Amharic for 'M'. The emperor had made it available for the public, teachers and health workers. As World War II ended, the English took it to Mombasa in Kenya.

I was inspired by the Royal Haile Selassie train to his boyhood home in Dire Dawa. To gain access to its interior we used teamwork. One feigned collapse. The watchman ran to him calling for help.

On board we drank in its glory. From top to bottom in the dining carriage, lounge, library and reading room, all was gold, silver and ivory. The dining tabletop was bluestone and marble framed with eighteen-carat gold. Its legs were ivory lions' paws. Ivory handrails had lions' heads. Qedamawi Haile Selassie was carved into the head and foot of the emperor's bed. It had three Stars of David, and Lion of Judah in Ge'ez.

The Derg would abandon it outdoors like some cargo freighter. Young Samual was never to see and touch it.

Each August, we caught the train 60 kilometres south to Debre Zait. Locals left offerings on the shore of one of its seven volcanic lakes. Departing at night, we rolled up blankets in bed. My brother left a giant-sized roll.

At the lake, we barbecued sheep or goats and loaded up with goods. We would need one hand free for the rail on the train, so I chose small items: 'mother and daughter' garlic liqueur, handmade scent and clarified butter. My Addis Ababa customers would pay well if I held sales back for a few days.

Companions carried roosters by their legs, like handbags – awkward for boarding the train, but guards, who were reservists, supported our initiative. Boys needed to beware of blundering into a horse compartment. In Addis Ababa, I conducted training sessions. The Addis Merkato group did not attend and had the most mishaps.

Our second youngest brother was too small to go. Furious, he told on us. Mum called uncle Gebre Kristos, who rewarded him with a drawing book and pencils – best gifts for an Ethiopian child. The brother returning from Debre Zait got his whipping over with. I kept them all waiting. Stashing my loot inside the fence, I went to the soccer ground.

Neighbourhood mothers gathered: Itiye Lomi, Itiye Messelo and Teacher Yewobnesh. The two aunts left early, not wanting to see me cry.

I bargained with Gebre Kristos: 'How much if I pretend it hurts?'

'You have to cry.'

'Fifty cents.'

Dad once gave me the severest punishment. He took me to the palace to be locked in the lion's cage. Removing the canvas cover from his jeep he drove wildly.

I gripped the M16 tripod pole.

'Sit properly.'

'I like it here.'

Mola needed a bath and his cage reeked of meat. He put his paw on my shoulder as though saying, 'You are small. Welcome.'

Lions are not ridden like horses. I sat on his shoulder and he gave me his paw pad to rub. He rolled over like a puppy for me to scratch his belly.

The sergeant major took him to the river. When Mola emerged, he shook like a dog. Soldiers had to change their uniforms. Then he sunned himself on his wall. People skirted it to leave him in peace.

Children picked fruit in mountain forests. Asko was four hours away, and Mount Entoto two-and-a-half. Rangers tied ropes around our waists connecting us all. They checked our shoes, running a thumb over the tread. If it was smooth, they sent us back because moss-covered tracks edged cliffs all year.

Sliding downhill we raced eagles. We feasted on ox-salt leaf, mulberry, mango and Yeka Mikael – the winter fruit that looked like a pepper. And tree sap like honey. For homemade scent, girls picked flowers: yellow spring and female pride. It stopped heavy menstrual bleeding. Boys ate many mountain bush carrots and vomited. Intensely sweet, they were dark red and the size of our middle fingers. We pounded and mixed them with grass as a gift to newly delivered cows, to make superb milk. Endemic to Addis Ababa, Eritrea and Gondar, urban sprawl and bombs would destroy them.

We took home small monkeys. Soon tame, they sat on our shoulders checking us for head lice or gazing into our faces. At the butcher, we begged ten cent kidney or liver and diced it with stones. The monkeys licked their chops all day.

During Pagme, Ethiopia's short 13th month, the porcupine moulted. We collected its decorative quills. Craftsmen used them in jewellery making, monks filled them with ink for writing on goatskin books, and people used them as bookmarks and page holders. They said, 'Mind your eyes. Porcupines shoot spines.'

They fed on termites and flies. Their skin produced fragrant oil, an ingredient of hand-made scent. Around monasteries they were not to be touched. In the forests panthers preyed on them. One would leap over and another would follow. With the porcupine off-guard, they turned it over and ripped its belly. Panthers did not harm children that didn't follow them.

At Jubilee in Palace, Henok and I visited the lions' enclosure. We found a half-full honey wine flask, drained it and fell asleep. A crowd gathered. One of the lions was asleep, partially on top of us. What might it do if we stirred? How about the harm to a five-year-old from alcohol? The keeper was asleep nearby, empty flask in hand. He coaxed the animal back to its cage.

A toddler strayed from a wedding party in the palace grounds. She chased butterflies then fell down a steep slope Below was a river. A black-headed lion pulled the unconscious girl to safety. He returned to his cage and roared until the keeper came.

Henok and I ran around the top of the Menelik buildings. We held spitting competitions with Prince Gedion. Then we sprinted under scudding clouds, placing bets on which would travel the fastest. One day we were playing with a high-ranking officer's son and another prince. From the palace wall, I took a curved sword. Partially dragging it, I said, 'Let us fight the devils below.'

A network of tunnels extended 20 kilometres north. They ended at the late Empress Taytu's medicine factory. Italians had used them to store booty and chemicals. They kept influential prisoners and interpreters there – Greek and Armenian merchants who understood Amharic.

Henok said, 'Bougainvillea!' We followed it to the entrance of a tunnel, air fresh from the creeper. Rounding the bend designed to stop fire, we entered a chamber from which sound travelled upwards. Those above heard our voices and the sword scraping on rock.

Guards tracked us down. An official removed his son and the princes. He left Henok and me sitting on a chair. After 15 minutes he returned. 'You are the ringleader and are to be taken to Haile Selassie.'

'Am I to be hung in the square like Belay Zeleq?'

The official smiled.

'Can I see Mum first?'

The emperor gave me strong shoes and scout's shorts and shirts. He said, 'Do not steal.'

Court officials said, 'He will not live past 20.' A neighbour gossiped that I was born supernaturally with an old man's brain and had few years left. Mum brandished her patriot's gun, but a monk would have used reason. It cleaned brains effectively.

Tunnels and caves could kill you or make you rich. Fleeing invaders abandoned bombs and gems. In a cave, a poor classmate found a chest with gold coins. I ran to Dad who sent soldiers to carry it out. Haile Selassie rewarded the helpers and gave the boy's father a ten-acre farm with a 500 square metre house. He had sold boiled eggs on trains for a living.

Any adult who caught us near the Kebena River spanked us. Parents backed them. We hid in dense bush to listen to the current on rocks. Chickens, goats and dogs washed down. July rains could send a donkey. When river waters swelled, white horses rose up to take children. The river's other name was man eater.

On the banks of the Gion River we grew vegetables, mostly collard. We caught fish by hand or with bush bean, deadly to humans. If a fish swallowed a single bean, its flesh could kill if eaten. We sandwiched our catch raw between wild ox-salt leaves. First, we scraped away the sandpapery coating and stripped fish, discarding bones so that other fish would not choke on them.

Boys leapt from a bridge into white waters where a tributary flowed in. We walked on our hands along its rails. Girls applied butter but we knew where to fall. We snorkelled with trumpet flowers. Eddies, whirlpools and the current meant that we could neither stand nor tread water. We had to swim constantly in order not to be pulled downstream.

If we went home with wet shorts, we would be belted for all rivers were dangerous. Girls lined the bridge. 'Come on, you have to come out. Your strength is nearly gone.'

Our arms ached as we tried to stay in the water. We dived, squatting low before up-ending ourselves to retrieve a river stone. Stronger swimmers brought up decent sized rocks. 'Quick, pass it!' An accurate thrower aimed low under the bridge. The splash caused a diversion. A boy ready to sink scrambled up the riverbank. Others followed, shivering sideways toward their clothes. Passers-by teased, 'It will not bite!'

No child today would be able to do any of this. In the 1970s our waters were clean. The emperor had made one ministry for water, sewerage, drainage, and roads. He combined departments so that they worked together. No system compromised another.

The Derg split them into separate ministries. This led to pollution of urban rivers. The Gion became shallow, choked with rubbish and supported no life. Children born after 1988 did not learn to swim. Those who lived near monasteries climbed through fences to swim at waterfalls. They used plastic bottle floats.

Kids born into the Derg era never went to Scouts. Then the TPLF took their soccer grounds. Soccer was our favourite organised sport. Between the ages of five and eight I played Number Ten Attack. This was for Giyorgis Soccer Team at Qedamawi Haile Selassie Stadium. After matches the monarch's guard took us to the palace for dinner.

Friend Melaku and I started a team for younger kids. We trained them, organised matches and washed soccer shirts. With firewood sales, we bought the cheapest shoes at 4.50 *birr* a pair – the price of 25 kilograms of corn cobs.

When I was eight Mum treated a new mother for mastitis. Friends and I cared for the baby. He began crying because his nappy needed changing.

'They show it on television.' 'I know how.'

I brought water and cloths. The others tied sofa protectors around their faces, backing away. Baby soon smiled. His mother raced to our home whenever I was arrested.

Patriots stayed with us. Mama Teliqwa's nephew Tibebu described 1966 crop failures in Amhara Province and later ones in Tigray and Welo. The UK had sent wheat that harboured locusts. Local crops self-sowed and locusts re-emerged.

The emperor had shipments burned at the dock. The English declared them free of charge. Haile Selassie said, 'Do not pretend you are not snakes. They never change skin colour and pattern.'

Our emperors gave international aid. Haile Selassie I sent food, livestock and cash to the UK during a drought in Ireland. When the UK divided Biafra in Nigeria, civilians starved. He sent twice-weekly shipments of maize flour. Emperor Menelik II had sent famine relief to Norway when it froze over. During an 1890s drought, he shipped gold, silver, trees, livestock, prepared food and wheat, herbs and bamboo to Australia.

Girazmach Alemayehu, another uncle, came in winter. He was governor at Sirre Awraja in Arsi Province where Oromo farmers produced butter and cheese so economically that they fed it to animals.

Alemayehu had two UN medals. He saved the patriot Lord Geressu in battle. Covering him, he made him gallop to safety. The lord later protected Italians that defected from fascist atrocities. And with two generals, Alemayehu saved civilians from 19 February slaughter. General Graziani advertised a reward of two million lire for their capture.

Our uncle then served with another patriot, Lord Gara. They held a mountain in Harer against the invaders. Brumbies lived at the top with its pure water. Hidden by cloud, patriots picked off enemies below.

Like a brother to the emperor, Alemayehu was never sycophantic. Belly-fillers told the emperor, 'He does not respect you.' Haile Selassie said, 'So what? He is good for the country. That matters more.'

Gash Alemayehu prayed at 4 a.m. and refused food and water from fridges. 'Get me the room-temperature stuff.' He lived to 105. The Derg got to his third son Mesfin. It tortured the boy for activism. After both parents were gone, he took his own life.

Dad's relative Gebre Kristos Desta visited. His Genius of Geniuses rabbi father was a renowned poet. He had pioneered the planting of *teff* grain in the US. The Derg passed him over for work.

Gebre Kristos drew a woman asleep. Her abandoned pose signified her trust in the man she was with. He sculpted a patriots' trinity: two men and one woman, my grandmother. The Patriot's Association paid for the bronze and locals supported him. He sketched an ox sharing the yoke with a man. A European, whip in hand, drove them. I explained this artwork to a classmate. He replicated the drawing. Derg cadre took the child away. We never saw him again.

Gebre Kristos would flee the Derg to Germany. By then, he had a brain tumour from electric shock torture. His work is exhibited today.[3]

When I was seven, Gash Gebre Kristos gave me a 1-*birr* note. *Mother India* starring Telly Savalas and Anthony Quinn was at Cinema Adwa. Emperor Menelik II built it. The interior was all river stone and mosaic. Movie and cinema delighted Henok and me.

We stopped outside. A man was crying. 'My name is Tulu. I have lost my five donkeys. They transported produce: firewood, aromatic rushes and corn cobs. I sold it all today and treated myself to the movie.'

'Where did you leave them?'

'Tied to a parking metre in Piazza near Adwa Theatre. They slipped their ropes. I did not realise *Mother India* was so long. Can you help me find them?'

We retrieved three and reported the others as missing. At the police station we helped Tulu fill out the form. Then someone handed in two stray donkeys.

Tulu had to pay a fine of 25 cents apiece. This was the cost of a pair of children's shoes. We told the constable his hard luck story and he ripped up the form. Tulu left town and the police took us to their canteen for treats. They drove us home in the police bus. We were free, yet all adults kept an eye out for children.

A decade later, the police journal published our tale as "Mother India and the Five Donkeys." It was in memory of police officers who were honest and caring. By then the Derg had destroyed Cinema Adwa.

---

1. Library of Congress, "History"
2. Pankhurst, Ethiopia, 539 & 551–52
3. WikiArt. Visual Art Encyclopaedia, "Gebre Kristos Desta Center"

Chapter 7
Revolution

When I was fourteen in 1974, low rank military guards took control of Ethiopia. They de-throned Emperor Haile Selassie I. He broadcast that Ethiopians needed to look after the country, the world and the powerless people. On 12 September, revolutionary forces detained him. They put Mola the lion in the zoo where he died.

The previous year Henok and I had visited dense forest. It was three kilometres from the entrance to Addis Ababa. We gathered plants for rope, harvested beans, ate wild peaches and admired a striped bird.

In a clearing we saw walking skeletons. There were starving people with crying children. Dropping everything we ran to tell Henok's father. Relatives surrounded us. They shook us by the shoulders. 'Tell us what you saw.'

We shivered. Henok cried. 'I saw Satans.' He had no words to describe human beings with huge heads and protruding ribs. The adults cleaned our faces, put us in a Land Rover and drove toward the city entrance.

'Which way did you go?'
'Through the bush.'

We found the clearing. The driver and bodyguard shielded our sight with seat cushions. Suffocated, I peeked out.

It was Lord Tilahun's turn to cry. He jumped from the vehicle. 'Lord, Lord!' Drawing his long- muzzled revolver he ran toward the guards.

'Did you give these people water?'

One man cried and dived down at his feet. 'I cannot bear this. Remove me or kill me.'

The lord told the driver to take him home with us. Henok's mother gave us a cold shower and milk and put us to bed. I slept for a long while. Ever since I have never accepted this kind of catastrophe.

Women volunteered in Azalech's kitchen. People delivered meat and milk. With Scouts, I took food to the famine survivors. It killed many. Food tore the insides of their throats. They needed minute amounts of thin porridge.

Henok's father said, 'I talked with My Badge.' This was his nickname for Dad. 'He warns you not to tell anyone about this. My Badge will not whip your arse. He will shoot you.' The lord held his pistol at our heads. Henok cried again. His mother laughed, 'This foolish one is afraid of a little gun.'

Lord Tilahun said, 'Azale, take these kids out of my face.' The adults sent us to the springs at Sodere, 280 kilometres from Addis Ababa. We had seen too much.

Dad said, 'Those stupid feudal lords have eaten those people alive. I am going to tell Haile Selassie.' Feudal lords had long contributed to the disaster that was killing those people. Drought was only one factor. Farmers once owned the land that they worked. Now a single lord controlled one-third of Ethiopia's fertile farming land.

When feudal lords abused their power, soldiers backed them. Peasants stopped growing food. Then belly-fillers did not report to the city that over 300,000 farmers faced starvation in Tigray and Welo provinces. Babies died in the womb and at the breast.

Poisoned waterways may have killed livestock – containers

dumped by former occupiers could have eventually leaked. Whatever the cause, starvation in Ethiopia was to continue. Tilahun would sing of it and raise funds.[1]

Henok's father begged Dad to move the famine survivors to where they could get help. High-ranking generals and princes could not hide the plight of the people. Dad was still head of Border Security.

The only road from the clearing to Arat Kilo was protected by 16 metre Mama control towers. Guards with Bren machine guns were at each corner.

My father gave a pass code to Lord Tilahun. This gave safe passage at checkpoints. His labourers disseminated it among the famine survivors. The lord worked the whole 24 hours prior to the transfer. Dad told police that defence forces would be undertaking training. This would be in the nearby mountains. It involved a bush investigation exercise, climbing, searching and shooting. They could expect troops passing along the military route that night.

The throng went by cover of dark. When challenged, men called out the code to Border Security. Guards let them pass. Starved people unable to run moved along the military route.

At first light they appeared in Arat Kilo near the palace. A monastery, B'hata Monastery, rang the tone reserved for invasion and disaster. The next took it up. Soon, all monasteries rang their bells at once. The emperor awoke to tens of thousands of starving people. It was the first he knew of the extent of the catastrophe. Chiefs, princes, decent lords and generals realised that the crown had been betrayed.

For every nine famine victims, two reached the outskirts of the city. Officials stopped truck drivers from giving them lifts into Addis Ababa, keeping them away from advisors and officials loyal to the emperor. Truck drivers relayed the news to others, infuriating students.

Foreigners hastened the downfall of the Imperial Ethiopian Government. None cared about the cost to our people. British producer Jonathon Dimbleby made a documentary. It juxtaposed footage of the emperor with images of famine victims. The Derg used the documentary to foment hatred of the royal family. It depicted them as feasting while our nation starved. By 1974 we were under the Provisional Military Government of Socialist Ethiopia.

In 1971 Haile Selassie had addressed the UN in Geneva. Its hall had 20 microphones, all selective. If an African dropped a little air in his pants, the news made Western newspapers. When Europeans broke ivory tusks off African elephants, it went unreported.

A land reform movement had begun in Gondar in the north. General Jegama ought to have been advisor and negotiator for rural regions. Distinguished retirees took on such roles. The general would have alerted the emperor to land grabbing and dire hunger.

The monarchy was absolute. However, in theory the system supported justice. Emperor Menelik II had established a parliament and Haile Selassie built it. Ethiopians could appeal for justice to the Public Court, the Patriots Civil Court and the Court of the Crown.

The lower court awarded a discarded de facto wife no alimony. The woman appealed to the emperor. He multiplied the amount paid for the first night by the number of nights together. She received that.

In another miscarriage of justice, the judge had decided a case in favour of the woman involved. She was his mistress. The wronged man stopped the emperor in his carriage. Haile Selassie said, 'Let the case be judged by priests.' They found the judge to be corrupt.

In November 1974, the Derg arrested my father and other senior military. Dad was paying for his humanity in helping the famine survivors. This had infuriated foreigners. They had the ear of the communist leader, Mengistu Haile Mariam.

For forty-four years, the palace grounds and their botanical gardens were neglected. Then the new government of the Federal Democratic Republic of Ethiopia would re-open sections to the public. Indinet Park included a black-headed lion habitat. Was Ethiopia's black lion back? As for Menelik's library, where were the antique volumes?

On 25 November 1974, a sergeant major, who had been made dwellers' association chairman, stopped Mum and me in the street. 'I have good news for you, lady. Your general was killed last night.' Lieutenant General Aman filled the whole village with army jeeps when he visited us. Locals knew what my eye father meant to me.

Mum pretended that this was the first time she had heard the news. I maintained silence.

'Why is his face white and tear streaked?'

'I do not know. He has been playing soccer and sweating.' Mum excused herself.

The man blocked our way. 'Did you see it on television?'

'Our TV does not work, and we have no radio.'

'Your son's eye father tried to return the country to imperialism. We defeated him last night. So, why are you sad?'

'I am if anyone dies, even you.'

Lieutenant General Aman had formed a committee on land-tenure reform.[2] Mengistu promoted conflict that kept citizens too busy to overthrow him. My eye father opposed war.[3] He refused to surrender to low-rank Derg. 'Let me die with dignity.'

Mengistu sent tanks to his villa. Ten Russian T55s with chain wheels loomed. Lieutenant General Aman defended himself, shooting from windows. The Derg killed him. Tanks crushed the housemaid, dresser, cook, chauffeur and program co-ordinator.

His wife had escaped. The Ethiopian Democratic Union rescued her. It tried to do the same with Lieutenant General Aman. He told it to get lost: it was formed from the remnants of feudal lords. Their cruelty to peasants had brought down the monarchy.

Itiye Misiraq had taken in war orphans. She taught them knitting, weaving, and embroidery with silver and gold thread. A speech therapist, she was the first African to take literacy to Djibouti. She established the Menelik School there.

Some maligned Mum and her for being *Falasha*. Misiraq said, 'They do not accept us. So what? Let us accept them.'

The Ethiopian Democratic Union tricked her, sending her to Sudan instead of Israel. In refugee camps she taught children from Kenya and Sudan. Refusing re-settlement in enemy countries, England and the US, her lifespan was reduced by camp deprivations.

At home came a radio announcement. The Derg had shot Dad. Itete fainted. She was preparing food and clothes to take to Kerchele prison. He was only 56. I wished that I too had died that day. Whenever we looked out the window, we expected to see Dad in the garden talking to the birds.

Losing a father is long pain. For months I barely talked or read. I sketched all day. Only visitors cheered me. My loss was small compared to our mother's.

Daily, the Derg shot prominent prisoners and announced the names of 59 of them by radio, television and newspaper. It concealed the identity of seven others to prevent all-out revolt. Dad was one of 66 murdered high-rank military, senior administrators and princes.

The communists interred them in clothes or pyjamas without coffins, dumping bodies into a two metre pit. They covered them with chalky-white hydrated lime and soil. Twenty years later, the

TPLF government moved some to Selassie Cathedral. The African Economic Commission funded a memorial with 59 names inscribed on it.

Most of the 66 had given a lifetime of service to Ethiopia and the international community. Our family friend General Kebede was trying to retire. Prime Minister Dr Aklilu Habte-Wolde was a former foreign minister. Nominated as UN Secretary General, he spoke French, Russian, Persian, German, English, Amharic, Ge'ez and Hebrew.

The Derg took apart the Mekonnenoch premises that I visited, converting them into a socialist-ideology school. With few senior military officers left, the sight of a disciplined straight back hurt me.

Mengistu retired the minister of defence, General Gezaw, who had worldwide diplomatic immunity. The masterful military designer had set up the Ethiopian Ground Force. He commanded our father at the Military Science Academy in Harer. The Derg ensured his living death, placing him under security day and night. Cadre removed his military signal radio and prevented him from coming and going from the city. Despite this, General Gezaw helped families of the murdered 66 and gave us food.

The Derg First Command came to our home in the afternoon. Soldiers vandalised it and stole antiques. They were looking for powerful weapons. The Second Command came later. The Derg locked the children in our rooms. Then it arrested our mother without charge. Mum had to leave behind our three-month-old brother. She never held a funeral for her husband.

The Derg imprisoned Mum in the palace prison. This was under the Throne Room. Then they put her in Kerchele. It incarcerated wives and children to humiliate them. The widow of one murdered prince became paralysed during 18 years in prison. The youngest of the emperor's grandsons was only four. He was imprisoned until the age of 22.

Politicians said of my father, 'He was brainwashed by the lord.' The Derg put Dad to death swiftly. He must have been betrayed. The West never wanted Ethiopia to have a strong military.

Mengistu had an uncontrollable temper. He had been unable to complete military studies in the US. Easily goaded, he now engaged in a bloodbath.

My father with senior officials. Left to right: Colonel Tadesse, Foreign Minister Aklilu Habte-Wolde, Governor of Harer, Chief of Staff General Kebede Gebre & General Haile Baykidan. The Derg murdered all except for the Governor of Harer. Imperial Ethiopian Government, Ministry of Defence, 1963.

Mengistu's version of Hitler's Himmler was a single-stripe corporal. His name was Legisse. Early in August 1975, Mengistu and Legisse murdered the healthy 83-year-old emperor. They smothered him with a pillow. [4] 'I have killed the *Yehuda* envoy,' said Mengistu. Emperor Haile Selassie I was the last king descended from Salamon or Solomon.

Corporal Legisse murdered people with a handgun in front of Addis Ababa University. He cackled on the sidelines during tortures. The TPLF would eventually imprison him for 21 years. Then it released him on good behaviour. In 2019 he died in hospital.

Ethiopian emperors were Orthodox. Haile Selassie had converted prior to coronation. Gossips about *Falasha* picked on him. He could turn into a fly, bee, bird, cat or fallen leaf. 'Do not let him escape by transforming into something else.'

A guard was punching flies. The emperor asked, 'What are you doing, son?'

'The boss told me you might turn into a fly and escape.'

'I am here.'

'It could be a trick.'

Mengistu feared that the emperor would resurrect. He relieved the stress this caused him. At night he visited the high-security prison at the palace, now Derg headquarters. He killed or ordered the killing of a prisoner in cold blood – someone esteemed by Ethiopians.

The Derg leader closed B'hata Mariyam Monastery. He took it as his office. Mengistu buried the late emperor underneath. He put him five metres below a reinforced-concrete slab. Outside the monastery he installed towers with guards.

Mengistu did not maintain the building and grounds. One night he went outside for a cigarette. The earth collapsed. In the dark, a soldier, lifted him out of the hole.

The Derg leader said, 'Tell anybody this and I will kill you.'

His unwitting saviour replied, 'If I tell anybody what I have just done, one million will kill me.'

The dictator often enjoyed a few beers. Afterward he would hold peeing contests on palace garden beds. He shot any man declining an invitation to join him. Mengistu also ordered anything well-made to be removed FOR ETHIOPIA. Students joked that Mengistu told one officer, 'Yours is big.' The officer said, 'Please, it is the only one I have.'

The world barely uttered a whimper for Haile Selassie.

At a factory's opening ceremony, he shook hands with workers and families. A ten-year-old held out her hand. The emperor missed it. When he learned this, he invited the child and her parents to the palace. 'I was careless and greeted everybody around you, forgetting you.' He lifted his cape to bend and kiss her feet.

The child's parents said, 'No, lift him.' Haile Selassie said, 'This is for your dignity and my stupidity. What is the price I need to pay?' 'Ten *birr*.'

He paid 10,000 *birr* into her bank account for her education. The girl did not achieve university entrance. The emperor obtained a skilled tutor for her. She gained a place at university, studied journalism and became the first African to work for news network CNN.

In Iran she observed the exclusion of women during menstruation. In Ethiopia, the term for menstrual periods means monthly flower. The journalist had restrooms built with Flower Ladies on the door. Middle Eastern countries and France copied this.

The world wanted Ethiopia's wealth. When Emperor Haile Selassie I left Ethiopia in 1936, he took 111 boxes of gold and silver. The UK charged him for exporting it. In London, it overcharged him for all purchases.

After 1941, the emperor reserved gold from Ethiopian mines. In event of a third world war, his people would eat. Each year he deposited gold into banks in London, Zurich and New York: 200,000 Ethiopian weight units. In 1975 the total value was 9 billion US dollars. He also had the 111 boxes and personal savings of 250 million US dollars.

Backed by the UK, Egypt supported the Derg. Mengistu killed the emperor the following year. Then came stealing. In the 1980s, Ethiopians starved. We asked foreign banks for our money, but our national reserves had vanished. Fortunately, Emperor Haile Selassie I followed an ancient tradition that Emperor Menelik II had revived. Into Barclay's Bank in Israel, he deposited gold nuggets. The bank held 200,000 pots of gold. When the UK and US pressured Israel into returning them to Ethiopia, Israel said the emperor had used it all.[5]

Lord Tilahun became a vegetarian. He stopped listening to music on the radio and never went near a court or church. His philanthropy continued.

The Derg wanted to look good to its supporters. In 1978 it murdered Tilahun. His lord's title was the excuse, although he was awarded it for heroism, for serving as a patriot and saving our country from fascism.

Cadre seized the Mo Anbesa shoe factory. They changed its name to Darmar to hide their crime. The Derg also snatched Tilahun's farm and horses.

During a raid on our house, a thug ripped his medallion from my neck. He pushed me onto my knees. 'Son of exploiter!'

Africans lost good leaders. In 2018, Ethiopia had spent 5 billion US dollars on the hydroelectric power project on the Blue Nile River: Grand Ethiopian Renaissance Dam. Shoe shiners' taxes paid for it. Somebody murdered the project's chief engineer. His killer remained free.[6]

If Africans thrived, foreign agents provoked violence. Social media fomented negativity. The West called it ethnic violence.[7]

Ethiopia completed the dam project at the end of June 2020. Traitors in the pay of outsiders set to work. They murdered popular singer Hachalu Hundessa and a mayor. Rioters destroyed schools, clinics, farms, food depots, factories and businesses. This added up to a billion US dollars of damage.

The attacks were meant to seem ethnically motivated. Traitors slaughtered hundreds and devastated the industrial district of Shashamene.[8] Descendants of Jamaicans shielded monasteries. Christians defended mosques. Victims refused to retaliate.

In Addis Ababa, a truck dropped off piles of machetes every 100 metres. At German Square, somebody left three bundles of machetes in the traffic roundabout. Ethiopians did not pick them up. They were not having Rwanda redux, with millions hacked to death.

Ethiopia caught the criminals. The West made a fuss about their detention and said nothing about pregnant *Falasha* women run over.

In late-2020, a fanatic arranged the murder of 88 people in Ethiopia's west. Intruders murdered 56 in Welega District, mostly mothers and babies. A member of parliament cried, 'Life is over for me.' The world was silent.

Within days the Tigray People's Liberation Front declared war upon the Ethiopian National Defence Force. It killed soldiers in the middle of the night. Stationed in Tigray District for 21 years, those soldiers belonged to the community. They had fought locust plagues. TPLF stripped their brothers in arms, then shot them.

For four days the TPLF left their bodies to the sun, vultures and hyenas. Foreign human rights representatives in Addis Ababa asked to investigate. Ethiopian National Defence Forces transported them under guard to Tigray. The TPLF then murdered tens of thousands of Amhara Jews. Europeans kept silent about it .

National Defence forces arrested TPLF soldiers. Egyptian,

Turkish and Syrian mercenaries had already fled. The Air Force destroyed missiles and weapons. The West complained of excessive force by our Air Force. Ethiopian monasteries and mosques prayed for the world.

---

1. "Tilahun Gessess."
2. Cohen, "Foreign Involvement", 2
3. Hamlin and Little, Hospital, 2509
4. Hamlin and Little, Hospital, 2564
5. Ababa Welde-Tensay, Asidenyaki, 110
6. Abdur Rahman Alfa Shaban, "Shock"
7. Mueni ma Wuiu, "Colonial and Postcolonial", 1325
8. Arefaynie Fantahun, "Ethnically Motivated Attacks"

Chapter 8
Advisor

Neighbour Itiye Beti fed our baby brother Samual. Itete and Mama Teliqwa cared for us. Servants tried to help while expecting nothing in return. In 1975 we had no income. Neighbours gave me spare land to grow vegetables, and I shared half the produce with them.

The whole of Ethiopia began to starve. We dreamed of bread like diamonds. Boys raced to the government bakery for leftovers. Guards beat them back. My brother and I took turns to stand in all-night queues. A clan of hyenas once grabbed a child from a line. Hyenas harassed children gathering firewood, which soon ran out on the ground. We climbed trees to cut dead wood, fuel for cooking hard beans and cheap cuts.

Friend Melaku and I walked to dark, green Yeka Girar Mountain to gather more wood. Sacking padded our spines underneath forty-kilogram bundles. On the way home we were bent over parallel to the road surface. We left some wood by the road if it was too back-breaking. Thugs robbed us after we had borne the firewood to the city. The unscrupulous tried to cheat us.

We toughened into *yerada lijoch:* smart and self-sufficient supporters of the helpless. When we left tight bundles of kindling tied with bark in the city streets, Mothers took them, throwing down coins for us to collect later. If they could not pay straight-away, they waited for me on my way to school. Then they ran and stuffed my pockets with extra coins. No person haggled.

In September we sold dry eucalyptus for burning at the ceremony of the True Cross. We bought shoes, exercise books and school bags. The Derg later cleared Yeka Girar, selling timber to the European Eastern bloc.

Our menu was a slice of bread with tea and a banana for breakfast; bread and apple for lunch; and bread for dinner. The best was bean stew with *injera*. I was thin with an unhealthy pallor that lasted for years.

The Derg stole our late father's service revolver and clothes. They also took our best memory: his bronze bust inscribed in gold. Squads helped themselves to our clothing, carpet and furniture – needed to sell for food money.

One day my brother removed his last pair of trousers and threw them onto the truck. 'Here, take these. You will not need to come back.' The driver bundled them with extra garments and threw them down to him.

Communists imposed a domestic animal quota: two sheep and two goats per household. We kept one sheep and one goat. The Derg took the tortoise that had been our pet for generations. She died in the Derg zoo.

When a squad stole our sofa, it was about to rip our front door off its hinges to fit it through. I said, 'Its legs can be unscrewed,' sparing us alpine nights without a door. The sergeant major labelled me invisible devil and evil eye. My ideas were beyond a child's, whispered into my ear by a Satan.

Mum pawned her gold earrings to pay the maintenance fee for high school. In years 9 and 10, I had been the youngest and smallest. Our enormous teacher of botany and ecology had a victim in each class: a malnourished bright boy. 'Beware of all small things. They are dangerous.' I put up my hand. 'Stinky goat?' 'What about bees? They make healing honey.'

The following day the botany teacher hauled me out front. 'Shitty goat, describe three small yet beneficial things.' 'Bees that make honey, worms that aerate the soil, and the silk spider.'

'Sit on the floor!'

'I will not. Even the biggest elephant can be killed by the bite of a tiny snake.'

The man slapped me on the face. I sprinted to the office, chalky hand mark visible. Our director told him to leave me alone.

The teacher then got students to turn on me. They forced me to do their assignments. One night I fell asleep after completing three. I did not do the fourth, which was for a 15-year-old twice my size. She slapped me. I saw multiple colours.

The abuse continued for two years. Then I scored a goal at soccer. Three boys came for me. One grabbed me by the throat and lifted me. He punched me in the face. I punched him back and he dropped me. All ran crying to the guard, who laughed while they quaked behind him. Students left me alone and called me Big Man again.

The School Council and Ministry of Education sacked the botany teacher.

When I was an adult, he approached me in a bar. The troll was knocking back shots of gin. Swearing, he racially vilified my Japanese girlfriend. He declared to all that I behaved like I was his professor when in school. Roaring drunk, he challenged me to a fight. I said, 'I will see you outside,' then felled him with one punch. Patrons and bar workers said that he tripped and fell after drinking too much. This satisfied the dwellers' association.

The Somali Democratic Republic invaded. A coalition of enemy forces came 800 kilometres inside our eastern border. It took over Jigol Mikael. This was an Orthodox Christian church and the oldest in ancient Harer Province. The invaders stole its gold cross and gilt books. They put them in Jigol mosque with its seven gates and miracles galore.

The Somali coalition raised its own flags at the mosque's gates and changed the name to Haji Umerah. It wanted to shift Haj from Mecca to there because it was the site of the prophet's remains. The town of Jigol was older than Mecca in Saudi Arabia. Followers of the prophet Muhammad had taken refuge there. Ethiopia's Orthodox ruler said, 'Settle here as if you were in your own country.'

Somalia destroyed parts of Harer. They included churches and monasteries, the modern city of Jijiga, and the border towns of Farfar and Abwarre. Invaders got within 360 kilometres of Addis Ababa.

They reached our strategic point: Gara Muleta Mountain. Dogfight pilots trained there. Patriots had held it during the Italian occupation. Its name would be changed to Kara Mara, meaning won empty-handed or the patriots' mountain.

Old patriots fought with farmers. They occupied and held the mountain. Hidden by its permanent cloud, they surveyed the entire area. Before a fast bomber came near, they spotted it. Anti-aircraft picked off the Tornado or other craft. War veterans stopped the Somali forces. The invaders said, 'The land is eating us.'

Somalia had invaded five years previously. It formed a coalition with countries keen to wipe out Ethiopia. This was despite diplomacy by Emperor Haile Selassie I. He had negotiated the UK's departure from their land. Lieutenant General Aman was in charge and my father led Ground Force. It captured weapons. They were manufactured in the UK, France and Turkey.

Realising who was behind the invasion, Aman recommended pushing the invaders back. He wanted to go all the way to the

Somali capital Mogadishu. The emperor stopped this. He did not want Ethiopia counted as an invader. My eye father warned, 'They will return.'

At the start of the Somali War 1975-77, the Ethiopian National Defence Force had collapsed. This was due to Derg killings. In one night, the president had five generals murdered. He imprisoned bright officers of the Ground Force. Foreigners knew that Ethiopia now had only a few strong Air Force officers. The Soviet Union and Middle East armed Somalia's President Mohamed Siad Barre. He was backed by Egypt, Iraq, Qatar, Oman, Bahrain, Saudi Arabia, Turkey, Pakistan and Indonesia.

The Derg sought help from a patriot. Mengistu had tried to destroy them. For a while he took over their eight- storey building.

Mum's cousin Tesfahun was Chairman of the Patriots' Association. He was a member of the Jerusalem Ethiopian Association. During the Italian occupation he had been a messenger for the Ethiopian resistance based in Sudan. He imported tents, ammunition and weapons.

Tall and bearded like Cuba's Fidel Castro, he had an Emperor Menelik II tattoo on the back of his hand and resembled the late Belay Zeleq. Mum and he were decorated for war service, then Tesfahun studied in Yugoslavia. He excelled at modern military science, intelligence, and radio coding. Speaking French, Arabic and Serb, he then worked for the Ministry of Defence.

In 1974, the Derg retired him. A year later, it sent a jeep to his home. Soldiers took him at gunpoint to the unqualified Defence Minister, Major Tesfay. Tesfahun became unofficial adviser to disaster bringers, to prevent the destruction of Ethiopia.

To the defence minister he said, You people will destroy this country. We will pay with blood. Tell that to your friend Mengistu. I have a short walk to my grave. Here is some practical advice.'

Tesfahun showed Tesfay what Ethiopia had bought from Russia: rusty World War II guns, spray-painted and sold as new.

He said, 'The Soviet Union wants to control part of Africa, the Red Sea and the Middle East. By buying its arms, Ethiopia will be in debt for generations.' He told the Derg major about Turks selling faulty weapons during the occupation. The Portuguese sent poisoned rations via Sudan. Only Greeks and Yugoslavs had helped.

In 1975 few supported Ethiopia – only Cuba, Israel, Zambia, Yemen and the German Democratic Republic. Ethiopian Ground Force had 50,000 soldiers. They were joined by 80,000 veterans with walking sticks and 34-year-old injuries. The elderly patriots went unregistered. 'Do not count me. I will die for my country.'

Ethiopia was battling one million invaders, who had hi-tech weapons. Defence at ground level with tanks was impossible. The only option was Air Defence. It had 20 military aircraft: retired US F5 fighter jets and slow Swedish and Ethiopian jets. Somalia had modern Soviet jets: MIG25 and MIG29.

The West blocked Ethiopia from arming itself. Ethiopia paid the US for guns and bombs for use with F5 fighters, then President Carter cancelled the order. The US refunded our money five years later, and bribed Vietnam not to sell F5 weapons to us. It was part of the coalition to destroy our country.

Tesfahun gave Major Tesfay strategical advice, which he followed. Ethiopia rained whatever bombs it had on Somali coalition military resources. It destroyed the sugar factory and petrol depot at Berbera, the food store in Chisimaio (Kismayu) and Mogadishu's port. The petrol depot burned for 28 days.

Old jets flew 700 kilometres. They had to refuel in desert sands, loaded with missiles and bombs. Ethiopia's 20 antiques bombed the Somali air force and naval base. The Soviet Union had aircraft carriers there – Ethiopia destroyed those as well. Egypt and Turkey had supplied Somalia with submarines for launching missiles. They fled, Somali flags flying.

Tesfahun said, 'Do not give the enemy any breathing space.'

Patriots had done so to Mussolini's fascists. They had no bombs. At Menelik's Air Force and Air Defence airport, they burned charcoal. This produced no visible flames, but Italian logistics craft exploded upon touch-down. Now, Ethiopians drove T55 tanks driven onto runways and set them alight. They destroyed brand-new Soviet jets. Our soldiers placed remote-controlled bombs around the perimeter of bases. As aircraft landed, they detonated them.

The UK called the strategies terrorist tactics and suicide missions. This was the first use of the terms. Ethiopian attacks appeared suicidal because of the low numbers of craft in the sky at any one time. Our Air Force had just over 10,000 pilots. They did not die. Sweden said, 'Never before on earth has there been such Air Force mastery.'

Ethiopia stopped the Somali coalition from rebuilding its bases. We took Berbera on the Gulf of Aden, Chisimaio on the Indian Ocean, and the capital Mogadishu. The UK said, 'Ethiopians have a hidden army. They spoiled the environment and demolished the port of Mogadishu,' and of our defence, 'Excessive force'.

The UN had never reacted when Ethiopia reported that invaders were 800 kilometres inside our borders. None in the West wanted the Ethiopian flag in Mogadishu, but our soldiers planted it. In the city's centre, they built an Orthodox monastery, Mikael. Today it shelters Somali orphans; citizens guard it, searching red- bearded or swathed Ikhwan for incendiary devices.

Neighbouring Yemen split like Germany. Sana'a was Western and Aden socialist. Ethiopian UN Peacekeepers were stationed there. The Soviet Union had really wanted Somali Mogadishu and Berbera. They were strategically located on the Gulf of Aden. The Russian leader Leonid Brezhnev called Somalis and Arabs pussies, and came over to our side. Soviets armed Mengistu with modern weapons that he used on us.

The Derg defence minister accepted advice from a retired

employee of Haile Selassie. Major Tesfay was promoted. Gash Tesfahun continued to teach him everything he knew.

The military had conscripted 300,000 for Ground Force. Farmers downed shovels and axes for AK-47; and Chinese-donated *chichi* – automatic rifles originally made by Josef Stalin. Nobody grew crops, so 300,000 Amhara people starved, and city dwellers lived on rations. Farmers remained near Somalia as Border Security guards; others fought near Eritrea. Conscription continued: twice yearly, governors went to farms to take any boy who could hold a gun. Lands were untouched for eight years. Famine prevailed.

By late 1976, Mum was home. She had an arthritic knee from two years on prison floors with barely any drinking water and food. Mum had buoyed the other women. Their gaoler was a corporal helped by Dad. He jeered, 'Now you will see life.' Feet swollen, she said, 'I love life. Before you were born, I was a fighter, a freedom fighter for you all.'

The Arat Kilo community welcomed her. One man walked on his knees to our compound, singing, 'Tewode, you are mother to your own little children, yet you are *Maye* to us all.' Our toddler brother was confused: who was his mother? We had many. Able to mourn properly for her husband, Mum dressed in black.

The Ethiopian Democratic Union approached her. It promised asylum in the West; she refused. Ten children left behind in Ethiopia would die of starvation. The Union wanted to benefit from her profile as widow of one of the 66 slaughtered. Those belly-filling feudal lords overlooked that our mother was a patriot.

Our street of retired generals and army widows had one belly-filler. One day, I was picking up leaves outside our home. A man sprinted downhill. 'Hide me, hide me.' Dropping everything I took him to shelter. Soon, Mum stood beside me. 'What is it, son?' The man said, 'Eight of us did roof maintenance work for the lord. He did not pay us. We went to ask for our money, and he chased us away.' The lord had set his creatures on the man and co-workers. He had four dogs, and two overfed, brain-dead guards.

Mum settled the man at the back of the house. She took down her patriot's rifle and grabbed a shawl. Another worker lay bleeding in the ditch. Mum tore her shawl into strips, applied a tourniquet and dressed the wound. Itiye Aberrash from next door took him in until he could be moved. General Seyoum sheltered the one who had run to me. He had five children and not a cent in payment.

Neighbours begged Mum not to confront he lord. He had police connections. She said, 'I have been a patriot and know his kind. The army into which I married never tolerated it.'

Ten years later, the lord's epitaph would praise his generosity toward the starving.

Meskel Square in Addis Ababa was now Revolution Square, where Derg fed us Stalinism. Dignitaries visited: Russia's Brezhnev, Cuba's Castro, Romania's Ceausescu, and the Cambodian Khmer Rouge's Pol Pot. Mengistu hurled bottles of blood.

In 1977, when Ethiopia's population was 29 million, students joked about our president.

Three Stalinist leaders were flying over Addis Ababa.
Fidel Castro of Cuba said, 'If I throw 100 *birr* out of this aeroplane, I will make one hundred people happy.'
Leonid Brezhnev of the Soviet Union said, 'If I throw 200 *birr* out, I will make two hundred people happy.'
It was Mengistu's turn. 'If I throw out 3,000 *birr*, I will make three thousand happy.'
The pilot said, 'If I throw three of you out of my aeroplane, it will make thirty million people happy.'

Tesfahun would collect me in his jeep. I drove him 85 kilometres to Sendafa Military College. One day, we discussed a *Newsweek* report on protests in London against overfishing of the Amazon and Blue Nile. Ethiopians took what they needed. We fasted weekly, not eating meat including fish. There were also extended fasts before Easter and Ethiopian Christmas and for Ramadan. Fish were safest around us.

Lake Tana, source of the Blue Nile, was rich in fish. They cleansed the water of bacteria with their exhalations via gills. This kept it pure. Monks would be angry if a person took too many. 'How many families are you feeding?' they would say. 'How many tummies do you have?'

Gash Tesfahun said, 'Europeans are trying to regain control over Africa's attractive tourism areas.'

'Why complain so often?'

'Our defeat of fascism in 1941 heralded the end of colonialism in Africa.'

During World War II, Mussolini's forces had bombed and poisoned 250 of our rivers. They wrecked our infrastructure: roads, bridges, dams, pipelines, sub-stations, hospitals, schools and places of worship.

Ethiopia claimed £184,746,023 for damage to infrastructure.[1] The UN ordered Italy to pay 800 million US dollars in compensation. We saw nothing of it.

Using its power in the UN and position as administrator, the UK gave itself contracts for rebuilding. Ignoring skilled Ethiopian workers, the English brought in unskilled workers from colonies.

They managed the Koka Dam irrigation and hydroelectric power project called Koka ina Gifirse. The name is Oromigna for bubbling sprinkler water. It was 160 kilometres from Addis Ababa in the upper Awash River Basin. Construction was bungled, so engineers investigated.

The UK had colonised our drinking water. The dam looked like a giant cup of soup. It was full of an introduced species of parasitic snail. When cattle drank, snails lodged in throats, sucking blood, growing and reproducing. Livestock could neither chew nor swallow and suffocated. Snails also harboured water-borne diseases dangerous to humans.

The biological warfare could have destroyed our agriculture. Scientists countered with bush bean and water purifying plant. Calling somebody parasite was a criminal offence.

Other sabotage continued. English vets injected livestock, and unique animals stopped bearing young. Each family had a war horse that knew its owners anywhere. One breed was an excellent guard. And the brumby would roll to survive battle fire. It could travel 200 kilometres daily on little food and water.

A couple went to court after one called the other English. That warranted prosecution and a fine.

At the end of World War II, the UK and US demanded that Ethiopia send 35,000 workers to rebuild Europe. The emperor refused; they moved to impose economic sanctions. Haile Selassie said that they were racists, fascists and Nazis. They had sanctioned atrocities: children thrown from aeroplanes, and mustard gas that stripped animals' hides while they were still alive. Ethiopia faced many enemies while Europe had only one. The Soviet Union used its UN power of veto against the sanctions. Without them, the UK and US could have invaded. Troops were still in the area and Africa was in the hands of colonisers.

The emperor presented two faces to the UK. He pretended he was ignorant of some of its deeds. Using diplomacy, he juggled the West and the European Eastern bloc. He obtained rebuilding support from both.

The West did not want development in Ethiopia. Nevertheless, for money, the UK contracted with the UN to rebuild the bombed bridge at Goa Tsion River in east Gojjam. It made a footbridge. The Ethiopian lord overseeing construction was a traitor. He gained a European-style house in Addis Ababa and a pedigree dog. Most of the bridge money went on him. Protest was futile and sabotage of compensation projects continued.

The emperor promoted him to minister, which kept him in the city. He worked alongside palace archivists, records managers and spokespersons. Haile Selassie made him food and ceremonial dinner minister. The man ate and drank until he weighed 100 kilograms with high blood pressure.

Ethiopia's poet laureate said, 'Fascists cut throats and throw boys from aeroplanes. Haile Selassie kills you by feeding you honey wine and gourmet raw meat. He turns you into an elephant.'

The emperor also took the Gojjam traitor Ras Hailu to Addis Ababa. Winston Churchill visited. Ras Hailu showed him around.

Of a *gelada* baboon Churchill said, 'That monkey looks like you.'

'Ah yes she does,' said Ras Hailu, 'And your face looks like her bottom.'

---

1. Pankhurst, Ethiopia, 549

Chapter 9
Red Terror

During my May 1991 downtime, Samual asked, 'Help me with the garden .' We took buckets and stainless-steel scoops to Selassie Cathedral. Monks made *warka* mulch and compost in 1.6 metre drums. It had a sweet smell that attracted tortoises.

It was free, but we needed four lots, so did chores around the monastery. Samual cleared spiderwebs and cleaned printing workshops. They produced book covers and processed paper. Monks felt my biceps, smiling. I treated a hide with salt, and ground leaves with flour to make ink. Then I sharpened chisels made from wood and basaltic stone.

We worked the compost into hen house refuse. Rain settled it and runoff from the chicken run soaked the garden. It would grow onion, garlic, chilli, corn, tomatoes, herbs including Ethiopian basil and *tenadum*, potato, carrot and thick-leaved collard weighing five kilograms. That went well with lamb or goat ribs cut 50 millimetres thick with little meat on them.

Samual and I bought charcoal. Then we filled jerry cans with water for the supply could be cut.

We did the same for my part-time parents who lived nearby. Gash Birhanu had been our late father's colleague. Dean of the Police Academy, he had worked for INTERPOL. Retired Colonel Birhanu said, 'Our sons!' and called to Itiye Messelo, '*Maye!*' They hugged us as they would do real sons and asked if we'd eaten. We did our chores. Then Itiye served aromatic bean-paste and *injera*.

Itiye Messelo brought a jug of water and basin for us to wash our hands. We exchanged morsels. Itiye looked us over. 'You need to eat. You are too thin.' She loved to take charge of young ones.

When I was 12, I tore a toenail at soccer training. Itiye disinfected and dressed it before belting me for having carelessly hurt myself. Children could not help being barefoot on the bald, stony ground that served as our soccer oval.

I became the couple's part-time child. At Sabbath I stayed with them and received better food than usual. They washed my feet so tenderly that it put me to sleep. I pretended not to notice when they came in to cover me at night.

Samual said, 'Five-thirty. Better head home.' Curfew was soon. Itiye stretched out her arms and we hugged. I felt only her heartbeat.

Fifteen years previously, our armed forces had repelled the Somali invasion. The Derg then attacked Ethiopian civilians. It killed more than one thousand in a single day in Addis Ababa. Ethiopia turned into a slaughterhouse.

Itete hid three of us boys in the chimney. The death squad came. Our sister convinced its leader we were elsewhere. After three days she smuggled us to Mum's sister.

Henchmen went to Colonel Birhanu's house. 'We are taking your sons for registration.'

The seven-year-old was asleep under the table with his homework. Itiye Messelo said, 'Take him too.'

The Derg murdered all six of their children the same night. The couple went to the morgue to retrieve the bodies.

'Look for them yourselves. Try that pile. Ha ha ha.' They found three. Hyenas took bodies after squads left.

'That will be three hundred *birr* for each.' In 1977 this was equivalent to 150 US dollars. Engineers would earn only 700 *birr* per month in 1989.

Born in the same month, Colonel Birhanu and Itiye Messelo's fourth son Girma and I were firm friends. When I visited, Colonel Birhanu accidentally called me Girma. 'Sorry that I live and your friend has died.' We cried as I weeded his vegetable patch.

Their home became forever silent. They covered the piano and put away the bamboo flute. No more compulsory concerts and music lessons for the village's children, who always longed to go and kick the soccer ball. Happiness evaporated from kids like summer clouds. Colonel Birhanua would live bereft for 23 years.

In 1977, Mengistu started Red Terror. The Derg president wanted to destroy opposition in the rural north. Anybody anywhere was at risk of summary execution. Military leaders went to gaol.[1]

Mengistu formed dwellers' associations with unrestricted licence to search and kill on the spot. No questions afterward.[2]

The most dangerous were guardians of the revolution.[3] Full of self-importance, they planned massacres. In our village the association's chairman was one.

One afternoon he left the pub and took a shortcut across our soccer ground. Kids did not notice him until too late. There was no time to run and hide in Selassie's cemetery. The drunkard attacked. 'Out of my way!' He bore down on us. As I faced him, rock in hand, he was almost upon me. I threw it and hit him.

Friend Azeze ran to tell his father, who was rabbi. 'Come quickly. Mesfin is beating the revolutionary guard. He'll kill him.'

All the mothers hurried to the ground. Mum took her patriot's rifle. The rabbi said, 'Run,' and hid me under his office table at

B'hata Mariyam Monastery. I received delicious food from various mothers throughout the evening. They took the chairman's wife chicken stew and cash. 'Give your husband the best meals.'

Afterward, the chairman and I avoided each other. In the street we turned off 20 metres before coming face to face.

At Entoto, north of the city, another guardian of the revolution beat a young girl. Her brother confronted him. 'Why beat her? What has she done? She is little.' The bully refused to answer. The youth went home, took a large stick and returned to beat him. That afternoon the guardian machine-gunned locals crossing at traffic lights. One was the shoemaker on his way home from work.

It was impossible to confront Mengistu. He could be anywhere in a convoy of 500 vehicles. Each had eight machine guns. Nazi-style, he drove out of the palace escorted by blue motorcycles. When he went to the airport, all remained indoors. Early in the preceding afternoon, city blocks would close. This shut down business. Nobody could get to work or school.

Any time he passed citizens had to plaster their faces against street walls. We froze, feet apart and arms in a high V. A friend named Wegel was deaf. Security shouted at her. She did not plaster. They sprayed her with machine gun fire. Another friend had the habit of scratching his ear. He did this when a convoy passed and the Derg shot him.

Cadre made youth swear allegiance and update their student ID cards with party membership details. The Derg called those who did not comply right-wing. Mengistu's Security machine-gunned them down in the street from motorcycle sidecars. Squads executed youth by firing squad, afterwards placing signs on their backs saying RED DEATH and leaving them strung up in the sun until midday. Families had to pay for the bullets that murdered their children.

Driven by personal, ethnic and political motives, the communists killed 750,000 innocents. Most were very young. Some

Derg human rights abuses were legally documented.[4] The Derg murdered 119,000 in one period. Elders said, 'In our lifetime, children are more disposable than animals.'

When any child died, all mothers wore black. If they could not afford new clothes, they dyed what they owned. During the Red Terror, the mothers of Ethiopia did this. They mourned the country's youth. Mengistu banned it and women defied him. He imprisoned them; guards set them free. There was not enough room for the whole female population. Our mothers would not let fear push them around.

Priests intervened. 'Heavy sorrow in mourning dress is inviting more disaster. You continue to pay to collect your children's bodies. They are still murdered in the streets. As of today, do not wear black.' Mum threw out her black clothes though Colonel Tilahun's widow stuck with it.

Bereaved fathers stopped the first wave of Red Terror. With no avenue for justice, they killed those responsible for their children's murders. The fathers became bandits: prepared to survive outside the law and their communities for 25 years. This was equivalent to the Ethiopian life sentence. After one year, there were so many that Mengistu had to declare an amnesty.

The Derg killed many of my peers. B'hata Mariyam Monastery had been home to Miheda, a classmate. She was a soccer player in the first African girls' team Itu Mela Mechi. Haile Selassie set it up. Its name meant my dear sister, find a solution. Security caught her handing out pro- democracy pamphlets. A firing squad executed her. The Derg labelled her RIGHT-WING EXTREMIST. It displayed her body until it changed colour in the afternoon. Only 17, she was wearing her school uniform.

Miheda's father was Rabbi and Head of Geniuses at the monastery's school for clergy. The Derg murdered him at a military camp, evicted his family and closed the monastery to the public. Thugs killed most of its priests and monks. They castrated young deacons.

Aba Gunina had survived the atrocities. He slept outside the monastery gates. Dressed only in a wrap, he had dreadlocks down his back plus a beard. Apart from one daily meal, he accepted nothing from locals. He remained in perfect physical health.

We visited him. When it rained, he remained dry as did the ground about him. After some conversation he would smile before dismissing us. 'Grow well my sons. Go home now.'

Mum would look into my face. 'Have you been bothering the monk again? Here, take him this stew.'

One day, without moving from the spot, Aba saved two lives. A Derg death squad chased two youths escaped from prison. Aba Gunina said, 'Stop. Sit here with me.' 'We will be killed.' 'Sit down.'

The squad sprinted past them toward Saint Gebriel Church. They could not find their quarry and left. The boys got up to leave. Aba Gunina said, 'Wait.' Moments later the squad returned with reinforcements. It scoured the area and the entire church. Soldiers searched male and female monks' rooms.

The teenagers remained outside B'hata Mariyam with the monk until 4 a.m. Their smell betrayed their presence to all except the death squad. They sat in their excrement. The squad then left to search in Piazza.

One of the youths moved to Uganda. He wrote for a university newspaper with Gunina as his middle name. Ethiopians living abroad would tell this story as eyewitnesses.

Derg Security forced Aba Gunina to move onto the roadway. It expected that he would be killed. When that did not happen, it drove a Mack truck to within centimetres of him. It tipped over onto its side. Mengistu had him arrested, imprisoned and chained inside an underground cell at Central Police Station. A fly could not escape. But when the Derg leader came, Aba had vanished.

Guards had no recollection of the night before. The few who survived were too afraid to give interviews, except for one: 'That night outside the monk's cell, I awoke as though returning from some place elsewhere. I reached for my AK-47 to find that its shooting mechanism had dissolved into a mud-like substance.'

A barefoot, unarmed monk barely covered in rotting rags had defeated a dictator and twentieth-century weapons. This was non-violent action from a spiritual being. He never touched money or expensive gadgets. Aba had triumphed over disaster bringers: those who enslave, exploit and put others down physically, morally and mentally.

Abun Tekle Haymanot was *Pappas* at Debre Libanos Monastery. The Abun was first to use the Ge'ez term disaster bringer for Derg. He cited our bible: the mother of idiots would bring disaster. His driver and I were in prison together for a while. He told how the Derg had sent the Abun to Leningrad to align with the Russian Orthodox Church. The Russians offered gifts: gold shoes, a black cape and a rabbit-fur hat. Though it was minus 36 degrees Fahrenheit, the Abun refused.

The driver said, 'I vomited with the cold. The Russians wanted to check his temperature. Slender, vital and barefoot, Abun Tekle Haymanot told them to look after themselves.' He would not shake hands with the Soviet leader, Mikhail Gorbachev. In Ge'ez he said his hand was not clean, warning the Russian clergy not to touch it.

Back in Ethiopia the Abun refused to shake Mengistu's hand. He imprisoned him in an office area at Bete Mengist. Eight armed guards were outside, yet he vanished. Mengistu punished the guards personally, killing three.

Abun Tekle Haymanot handed himself in. 'Do not kill these kids.'

Mortified at having been the indirect cause of three deaths, he did not eat or drink. In 1987 or 1988, he died weighing 27 kilograms.⁵

A second wave of Red Terror came in the 1980s. More death squads conducted house-to-house hunts. One brother hid in our chimney from the dwellers' association squad. He emerged days later looking non-human.

A death squad murdered one of our team. Girma was a football artist. He danced on one foot on the ball. A graphic artist, he painted graffiti: SOCIALISTS ARE FASCISTS.

His cat found him in Piazza, chest ripped open. It made Girma's mother follow him there. Both howled so loudly that the red guard fired his AK-47 into the air to drown them out. He then roared at the mother to put down her child's body. She had to wait until after midday the next day to retrieve it from among a pile before paying the fee.

Girma and I would walk home together after soccer training. We dribbled the ball. After his murder, I stopped that habit. Unblinking, the cat would come out to watch me. Mum had me help Girma's mother in her yard. I could barely stand the pain in her eyes. But stopping the visits would have been worse for her.

The Derg arrested and detained me without charge a dozen times. Sometimes it called me anti-revolutionary. When I was a young teenager, I followed my parents to prison underneath the palace Throne Room. Friends and I had once played in its grounds. Gash Tesfahun demanded my release.

During another imprisonment, guards chained me at the ankles. The Derg kept me in prison for months with other starved adolescents. Older prisoners had been there for years. To stay sane they kept a routine, so I did too. When let outdoors I tended a vegetable patch on the prison grounds. This was the beginning of my never giving up on life.

Inside, we became ill. The prison hospital director said, 'I have never seen Ethiopians do this to children.' He resigned after having us freed. Locals rescued us, cared for us and fed us for a week. They contacted our families.

Itiye Messelo had become so ill with worry that she lost the use of her legs. She went south to Debre Libanos Monastery for 15 months. Cured, she returned to a community welcome. *'Ulelelele!'*

Little more than a child, I addressed a girls' school assembly. 'The Derg does not like young people and will not let them speak out. It murders them. If your parents are Derg, do not like them.'

Security came with rifles and bayonets. I ran to the kitchen. Friend Melaku emptied sacks of charcoal on top of me. The soldiers glanced in and left.

One afternoon our puppy barked. Two children were hiding in our banana tree – a brother and sister aged ten and eight. They were strangers; poor, innocent and afraid. Mum coaxed them down and took them inside. She calmed the dog. Then Derg Security banged on our gate.

Mum said, 'You can search the back.' Soldiers looked around the compound without stepping indoors.

The children said, 'Anti-government people gave us pamphlets to drop off in Piazza. We could not understand the writing, but they paid us – all 17. One was seven; the oldest 14. The soldiers shot everybody.'

Mum sent her own children to their rooms. Then she let them believe that the pair had gotten away. She told the fugitives, 'I will care for you. Nobody will hurt you.' For three days she hid them in a honey wine barrel. She kept them under her bed for another four. 'Stay quiet until you hear the school bell. Then we will continue our board game.'

Mum contacted their mother to let her know they were safe. The woman tried to kiss her feet, but Mum stopped her: too dangerous. Their mother made arrangements to get them to safety, and ours co-ordinated their getaway.

On the pre- arranged evening, she wore a floor-length dress and shawls. The children hid under them. In tandem they walked to the main road where charcoal was dropped off. Sacks landed on the footpath as a taxi came. The driver picked up some along with the children. Then he drove them to family in the country.

Our mother waited ten years before telling this.

Derg tried to teach us to spy on spouses, siblings and neighbours. In communist Europe people felt they could not trust anyone, fearing betrayal to authorities. Ethiopian families of all religions including Animism had visiting soul fathers. They ensured fair treatment for all members of a household, so they stayed loyal to it.

Arat Kilo wildcats or *anir*, the size of small cheetahs, shunned flesh. They killed only to lap up blood. Endemic to B'hata Mariyam, they lurked on our roof and in our juniper.

One brother kept hens to sell eggs. Two layers of chicken wire could not withstand the onslaught of the *anir*. They pulled the wire out, then stalked and killed poultry all night. Mum kept us back. 'Do not go outside. You cannot save your chickens. There are always more than two. If you try to save one hen, another cat will attack you.'

Females were dangerous, never retreating if people threw stones. They puffed up and became fiercer. A man lost an eye when he confronted one. After work in the pub, he drank honey wine. Hot from the alcohol, he then tried to save his chickens from attack. There were five cats and one went for him.

Mum lit firecrackers. *Anir* were afraid only of fire and their fur was sensitive to smoke. Our tiny sister would say, '*Abat.*' She was under two when he died. Dark like him, she had silken hair that obscured her eyes. She remembered Dad for his firework displays in our compound. We made firesticks: balls of compacted, dried eucalyptus leaves or juniper needles on sticks.

I scrounged strong mesh from a construction yard and built a double-layer fence around our three hen houses. Wildcats could not penetrate or dismantle it. Sometimes our roosters refused to enter their coop at dusk. Mama Teliqwa said, 'Goodnight. You will be dinner for the anir.'

Locals queued for me to build stronger coops for their poultry. Cadre viewed our yard. 'Did your father bury gold here? How did you get that?' I said, 'If you want one, I will charge you double.'

One day we heard chanting from Selassie Cathedral and B'hata Mariyam Monastery. Neighbours said, 'It is for the *anir*.' The Derg was wiping them out. Soldiers strung popcorn explosives in *warka* trees even though they housed many other species of wildlife.

Mengistu also sold *anir* to the European Eastern bloc in return for weapons. Soon there were none. Every living thing belonged to the communists.

Of *warka*, people said, 'If this tree disappears from the face of the earth, there will be no fruit – *shola* music will be all that remains.'

---

1. Kasaye Chemeda, Yeto Meda, 253
2. Firew Kebede Tiba, "Trial", 164
3. Bahru Zewde, A History, 243
4. Firew Kebede Tiba, "Trial", 168–70
5. Debre Libanos Monastery Museum Tour, March 3, 2020

Chapter 10
Books

Empress Taytu had said, 'If you want to grow, work hard and co-operate with others.' The Derg appropriated this in Mengistu's name. It made it into a sign atop the Ministry for Education. We could read it kilometres away.

From 1975, the Ministry shut our history away. School libraries closed; public libraries burned. Students could not afford books, but we had community elders. They were storytellers. Pocketing pencils and brown paper bread bags for note paper, we visited them. We cleaned their houses and gathered firewood, then they taught us.

Elders had used the national library at Emperor Menelik II Palace: Menelik's House of Books. I had been inside it while at Jubilee in Palace School. It was for everybody. The Derg closed it. Our national library would remain a sleeping beauty within 40 hectares of neglected gardens.

Under Emperor Haile Selassie I, it had 15,000 books: 7,800 with basalt or soapstone covers; 5,100 with wood from *warka* and ancient *girar* trees. The rest were bound in leather. Mostly handmade, they were between 500 and 1500 years old. Many were illuminated. The library loaned them at no charge.

Priest librarians came across as ordinary. Each was multilingual, literate in five or six languages, and specialised in a subject. Patrons would leave with a perfect book for one month. Library staff did not record personal information: no name, contact, place of work or address. Priests instead stamped the inside of borrowers' wrists with indelible ink. The shoe shiner or footpath vegetable seller would notice it. 'Ah, you have a book from Menelik's House of Books.'

People commented when rogue patrons kept books for longer than a month. 'The mark is two months old. Why not return the book?' A son said, 'I will return the library book tomorrow.' His mother said, 'Until you do, no food.'

If stamp marks remained, community members could take library patrons to the police station, with, 'By the justice of God.' The utterance could stop the flow of river water. It would make a king step down from the throne to address mundane business. A street sweeper could arrest a prince or official. The police then took the delinquent borrower to the library where staff accepted returns wordlessly and without a fine. The patron had to look away while a priest took a leaf from an opaque jar replenished at midnight. With it they made the wrist mark vanish painlessly.

What about those hyena-like people who cut pages from 1,500-year-old books? Priests handling returns could not detect this straightaway: some had 1,200 pages.

Instead of copying out an appealing article, these people kept it. It could be a recipe for beer or honey wine, the formula for treatment of hepatitis A or a How To on magic spells and witchcraft. A patron might have wanted to learn mineral exploration. They needed a tract on soil types that went with deposits. Then they required instructions on how to mine gold, diamonds, bluestone or uranium and extract and wash the ore.

Weeks later the library patron would be at a community event, perhaps the theatre. There would be an announcement. 'So-and-so has cut a page from _____, a book from the National Library.'

Their wife would run away and file for divorce. Nobody in the community would speak to them. They had to return to the library. The Master of the House of Books was called, heard their case and decided the punishment. It did not include imprisonment for nobody is infallible. No kangaroo court for the rich to bribe and hire expensive lawyers; nor a military court martial with one-size-fits-all punishment.

Masters of empathy, priests put themselves in the patron's position. There would be excuses.

'I was stunned by that illustration.'

'I wanted to know how to get rich.'

'*The Song of David* beguiled me. The book made me a fool. I am a mere human. Its craft and knowledge are in a world of their own. It made me do it.'

The guilty one burst into tears. The master could see through a sob story. Monks would bring tea and continue to listen, reading the offender. Then they posed unexpected questions. Psychologically disarmed, he would confess to having made up the story. No soldiers, guns, no waterboarding or torturing upside down, no starvation or solitary confinement.

The patron awaited the library court's decision. It did not judge people as equal. Some might have a mental disability. Others could suffer economic pressure to prospect for gold.

Penalties depended on the age and rarity of the vandalised book. Judges would sentence ordinary workers to three or four hours of daily community work, lasting between three and six months. This could be street sweeping, toilet cleaning or tidying the workshops of the disabled, especially the blind.

When wrongdoers completed community service, they were exonerated and returned to society. Nobody mentioned any crime. Futures were not affected by the serious yet one-off error. For their next loan they needed a guarantor. The library permanently barred prominent members of society who vandalised books. Given the chance, what would they do with public funds?

Mum tantalised us with titles held in the National Library: a Ge'ez book dated from before the twelfth century. *The Love Book* provided guidance for when passion died. Advice even worked for cattle and goats. I had read the 50-year-old classic by Haddis (Addis) Alemayehu, *Fikir Eske Mekabir* or *Love Unto the Crypt*.

Dr Haddis was former Vice-Minister of Foreign Affairs. He had been a friend of our late grandfather. When he visited he called Mum my lady. He greeted her by kissing her knees. Hands clasped behind his back, he waited until we formally invited him in. We took his hat, jacket and cane.

Originally a teacher, he served as a patriot. He was in the battalion of a prince: Leul Ras Imru Haile Selassie. A coalition of Italians, Egyptians and Indians captured Leul. Ethiopians could not escape the occupiers. France and the UK held territory at all borders. In the north, Egyptians captured patriots and handed them over to the English for slow death. The UK had encouraged Mussolini to manufacture armaments and poison gas. It was an invisible fascist.[1] France stopped Ethiopia from buying medicine from Iran, India and Armenia. We were all meant to die.

The prince's warriors said, 'Let us scatter like popcorn.' Some hid inside Sudan, but UK soldiers were at the border stealing Ethiopian cattle, petrol and food for the fascists. The English apprehended the patriots including Dr Haddis and took them to Italians in Massawa, Eritrea. 'We look forward to hearing of the beheadings.'

General Armando commanded Massawa forces. He said, 'Why not kill them yourselves when you capture them? We are not your knife. These are prisoners of war.'

At Massawa it was above 40 degrees Celsius (105 degrees Fahrenheit.). Captives died. General Armando shifted them to semi-desert at alpine Hamassen near Eritrean Asmara. Then he engineered the escape of one thousand. He said, 'These people were in their own land, never invading other countries. We gave them no chance to breathe, not even to run away.' Atrocities in Africa sickened him. The UK, France, Italy and Germany committed most of them. Italy waged war upon Ethiopia for the UK. Back in Massawa, General Armando dressed in civvies, then took his life shunning fascist uniform.

In prison Dr Haddis began writing writing *Wenjl Danya* or *Criminal Judge*. The novel was about the crimes of ruling classes. He likened their world to that of animals in which there were no scales of justice. Foreigners would dub him THE HERO OF THE PEN.

In the 1950s, the UK would ban him from entering England. No former UK colony let him visit and he could not fly to current UK colonies. It did the same to Nelson Mandela and Oliver Tambo of South Africa. Trinidad and Tobago refused entry to Foreign Minister Dr Aklilu.

Emperor Haile Selassie I told the UK prime minister, 'Dr Haddis is not a citizen of any colony of yours and has done nothing wrong.'

'He agitates colonial African youth.'

'Based on abuses of Africans, we could ban many of your people from entering Ethiopia.'

My first passports had a stamp: NOT PERMITTED TO ENTER SOUTH AFRICA.

Addis Ababa University's Department of History published a textbook about Leul Ras Imru and his battalion: *Kayhut Kemastawisaw* or *I Am a Witness to Much*.

In 1936, General Graziani took over the prince's home in Kechene, a suburb of Addis Ababa. Leul Ras Imru's dogs and pet *gureza* refused food from him. The monkey descended only for Ethiopia's flag raising. He would not come down for the fascist flag. Dogs were the same. Graziani killed the handler, dogs and *gureza*. He burned our flag on top of their corpses. The mound remains today in front of the house.

The general said that Jewish dogs had their owners' blood. From his new residence in Sidist Kilo, General Graziani ordered the killing of Addis Ababa dogs. But when Italians gave them poisoned meat, they did not take it, for our dogs refused food from strangers. Soldiers slaughtered them with axes.

England announced a new breed: the Abyssinian dog. No such dog existed. From 1941 they would lay poison baits, but cats and birds took them. English hatred turned Europeans against our pets.

The prince's heritage house in Addis Ababa survived. In 2012 the TPLF would try to sell it. Protesters surrounded it and the TPLF gave up. It handed it over to the Ministry of Culture. The house had unique Ethiopian technology, including ventilating windows and doors. Their termite-proof wood was highly durable. It was the oldest in Africa, from 15,000-year-old *qararo* trees. Re-opening in 2020, it housed a *Falasha* women's pottery with kiln: Insara Yeshekila Ma'akel. The entrance was pink and green granite. It led to a show room with a sea of black-glazed, hand-painted traditional pottery.

For 27 years the TPLF had banned the potters from working together. It sold their wares in Europe without crediting them. Artists were not permitted to add an Orthodox motif to pottery or national clothing. No cross, Star of David or Queen Saba images.

The UK embassy in Addis Ababa had racehorses, five golf courses, a tennis court, firewood plantation and a lake. The TPLF pushed Ethiopians to slopes that had no water supply. They presented irresistible produce on blue tarpaulin. Around 2015, a pair of embassy workers visited them.

They quizzed locals about their lives. Gaining the trust of youth, they made a video of them. A few young men described suffering under the government of the TPLF. Security confronted the community with footage. They arrested 11 men. Two vanished. Five years on, wives searched for them. The others were tortured in Ziway. One survived. He feigned insanity and was released.

The Derg was holding an election. Wanting to read about voting, and unaware of a ban on all movement, I walked to the municipal library. Soldiers seized me and threw me in the air. I landed in the tray of a three metre high truck. They took me to prison. The captain looked at my student ID. At 14, I was post-secondary. He took me aside: 'Let me do the talking. Do not speak. You are mentally disabled.' Thugs came for me, I remained mute, and the captain intervened. I walked free after leaving home 12 hours earlier.

Unable to afford textbooks I studied in the campus library. One afternoon before exams I forgot the curfew. I camped under a tree in the college grounds to wait out the night. Home was too far.

At 7 p.m., midnight and 5 a.m., Derg Security was vigilant, hoping to catch astronomers at work. Mengistu stamped it out.

Two men in army garb found me. Not comprehending my Amharic, they took me to the police station. Calling three others, they beat me. Mengistu formed the Security Force from diverse groups. They were unfamiliar with each other's home languages as well as Amharic. He drove them to commit violence. Their victims were usually multilingual and bright.

The station supervisor noticed my student card among the contents of my riffled pockets. 'We had better not let him die here. Dump him on the roundabout.'

Two blue taxi drivers came along. With a third, they lifted me into a cab and took me to hospital. Bruised and swollen everywhere, I was unrecognisable. After five days I could walk with crutches, so nurses phoned home. My sister fainted. Mum came with herbs for shock and bruising. Five days later I went home. I gained high marks for my exams.

Under Haile Selassie, Lord Kebede Mikael (Michael) was director general of the Ministry of Education. He then became advisor while Dr Akalu Werqnaw was minister. The author of more than 24 books, he planned multilingual curricula, both traditional and modern.

His famous work was on technological progress: *Japan Indemin Seletenech* or *How did Japan Modernize?* His works were published in European languages, Amharic and Ge'ez, but his English language publications are scarce.

I read his rhyming moral stories for children.[2] His year 10 and 11 textbooks criticised the conduct of the UK in Ethiopia and elsewhere in Africa. Those have vanished. The lord had enemies outside Ethiopia. He stood up to the Orthodox Christian church. It controlled fertile land, grew powerful and involved itself in state affairs.

Lord Kebede became vulnerable within the country. The UK used its influence to remove his teachings from the school curriculum. When the revolution came, it told the communists, 'He is a friend of Haile Selassie.' He was a relative. The Derg took away his paid work and land. He ended up in a four-*birr* Shewa hostel. Youth lost access to his historical texts. Derg decision makers were unqualified in education.[3] They dismantled our system. For 44 years Ethiopians were to educate themselves.

The communist régime shut part of the Theological College in Addis Ababa. Emperor Menelik II had established it. It incorporated a science institute because Ethiopian theology and science were aligned. Mengistu sacked, imprisoned and killed most lecturers at Addis Ababa University. Ge'ez was integral to many courses; he banned its use. The School of Law was taught in Amharic; it closed. Haile Selassie had set up the university.

Mengistu closed Jubilee in Palace School. He turned it into a residence for 52 African heads of state. Sacked school staff was forced to work there. The senior school nurse cleaned rooms. Once she found many thousands of US dollars in a toilet used by a visiting dignitary. The Derg removed years 11 and 12. It stopped courses in foreign languages and Ge'ez. Cadre said, 'Ge'ez is the language of evil.' Today in Addis Ababa, one Ethiopian per square kilometre understands the language of Ethiopian liturgy. Our rich curriculum and pedagogy ended with the mid-seventies.

My least favourite school textbook had a red cover with hammer-and-sickle motif. Cadre forced technical stream students to attend Political Science Studies. They sat at the back of classes. Some walked around lecture rooms; snoring students disappeared with teachers. Switching off, I read science and seismology. For a test I scored 3 out of 100. My teacher had me re-sit. 'I will tell you the answers. Memorise them now.' For the repeat I received 97 out of 100. This saved me from communist re-education.

Teacher Mesmur was named for church music. Blind, he saw all. A student would draw on the chalkboard. Teacher Mesmur held his ear to it and described the image. He could tell if any of us pretended to be someone else. Walking in the grounds, we would hit our heads on overhanging branches. Not him. Preventing a boy from falling down an uncovered manhole, he said, 'The workers are showing their dissatisfaction; perhaps not paid again.'

With him we studied piano, guitar and *Ato Sax*. On the five-tiered Ethiopian piano, his music was river, wind, rain and birds. He would never call himself pianist, saying, 'I am a student of piano. My performance today will be forgotten within two years'.

At a monastery, a barefoot monk played with angels. Birds came to the roof and windows, *gureza* monkeys descended from trees, lions lay down quietly. That was a pianist.

Mengistu purged teachers with so-called Western- imperialist values. He called this movement Stalin's Stick. Teacher Yewobnesh was Unit Leader at St Joseph's, my old school. She taught junior secondary General Knowledge. I memorised her lessons. This helped classes flow smoothly from the end of one to the start of the next. Before I left for high school, I made her a goat horn lamp in the form of a fish with a light for its eyes.

She volunteered weekly at Berhanena Selam Printing Press. It produced school textbooks. The Derg filled them with Soviet propaganda. Teacher Yewobnesh refused cadre orders to devote textbooks to Lenin-Marx-Engels. Children needed to master basic skills.

One Friday in 1977, she kissed her students' foreheads. 'Stay well until Monday, Beloved.' She was on night shift at Birhanena Selam.

Security thugs came and put her against the wall across the road. It was outside the Corruption Control Office, formerly the Baptist Church. The Canadian Peace Corps had taught friends and me piano and guitar there. The Derg machine-gunned her. It displayed her body until noon. At the morgue, cadre made her family pay the usual 300 *birr*. Teacher Yewobnesh was a mother of four and six months pregnant.

There were between 16 and 20 children in my elementary school classes. In 1982, there were 102 children in Samual's Grade 3 class and Derg schools operated in shifts. The first started at 7 a.m. when kids were barely awake. The third lasted from 5 to 8.30 p.m. My youngest sister Miserat had that, so I taught her the Ethiopian script Fidal. By mid-1991, Grade 1 classes had 150. After the National Examination at the end of Grade 6, rural children dropped out to farm. Under the TPLF, students would stay at school longer. But 15-year-olds performed inadequately.[4]

TPLF would undermine Ethiopian literacy and culture, forcing parents to give babies monikers like Tony, Margaret and Helmut. Some schools suppressed Amharic even after the change of government in 2018. In 2020 a child could be fined 12 *birr* for uttering one word of Amharic. For most it was their home language. Any teacher who slipped up had to pay 30 *birr* (one US dollar). If a child could not pay the fine, classes jeered at them in English. 'Stupid. *Clap- clap-clap.*'

The Derg destroyed or locked away monastery books. Monks hid some goatskin books in caves and tunnels. They saved archives dating from the fourth century BC. Archivists inscribed them on horn, waxing them annually and storing them in limestone boxes. Twenty horses moved them. Records managers had secret instructions for joining the horses. The boxes unlocked with a code on a tiny scroll inside a locket that any rabbi could wear.

Monasteries provided goods, services and education. Monks grew, harvested, sun dried, and prepared ingredients for *berbere*. Abroad, the spice mix is known as *peri peri*. They prepared Ethiopian beer and honey wine. Each monk and rabbi had a specific occupation. Monasteries were busy, so some opened to the public a few days per year.

There were thousands of monastery schools in Gondar, Gojjam and central Shewa around the Alps. Rabbis taught farming skills. Because of them, peasants knew how to count stars to time the planting of crops. They stored water without it souring. In backyards they grew medicinal herbs. When a sheep or cow fell ill, nomads took it to veterinary monks to be treated while rabbis improved the literacy of the animal's owners. The communists declared monastery schools the education of alien demons and shut many.

The Derg destroyed 29 monasteries. It shut an exquisite synagogue in Gondar. Mengistu feared Orthodox. With each closure or destruction our nation lost productivity. Communists could not abide inventive genius, initiative and the marvellous.

Dr Aklilu, former president of Haile Selassie I University Addis Ababa, said monasteries were centres of excellence. Ethiopian scholars influenced those of other cultures. They exchanged knowledge with Ancient Greece and medieval societies. The destruction of any Orthodox monastery was the world's loss.[5]

Monasteries specialised in engineering, music, medicine, agriculture, veterinary science, astronomy or linguistics. The *pappas* would teach advanced scholars, perhaps astronomy nightly for six months after midnight prayers. Veterinary and animal husbandry students would learn how to give roots to cows so that they delivered in minutes. A monastic education took decades to complete. Scholars dedicated themselves for life; it was a calling and an honour.

Teacher-priests decided where students needed to go for specialisations. It could be thousands of kilometres from home with a goatskin bag, shorts and bare feet. When they passed through a village the community fed them. Farmers packed food for six months. They could be on their way to complete an assignment for a medical course. It might take them deep into the forest that abounded with butterflies and bees. The insects spread pollen through the air, which helped human lungs pump oxygen and survive pneumonia.

Many bees had a serious sting. Scholars applied a protective wax; some were even nicknamed Bee. In Gondar, they became invisible to lions, cheetahs and tigers.

The TPLF would seize land to sell. Unable to sell monasteries, it burned them. Developers from Saudi Arabia, Qatar and United Arab Emirates wanted to wipe them out, so the TPLF bulldozed the ancient highland Waldeba Monastery. Dozers all tipped over. In 2018, Turks and Arabs invaded our north, throwing elderly monks and rabbis down cliffs. In the east at Jijiga, Somalis burned clergy alive and destroyed 11 monasteries. Militia had UK weapons.[6] The world kept quiet. All our religious leaders prayed together.

During the second week of May 1991, our little sister Miserat arrived. Eight months pregnant, she had travelled 800 kilometres from Sidamo in the south.

Miserat said, '*Gashe*, come and stay with us until things calm down... all of you.'

Hewan said, 'Still no word of Dad. Will we ever see him

again?' He was at the Eritrean war front. With her family mast gone, why stay?

Rebels had taken Gondar in the north, bombing bridges that connected regions, dams and water supply substations. They burned food and energy depots, elementary schools, kindergartens, hospitals, banks, churches and mosques. The TPLF stole thousand-year-old bibles from Orthodox monasteries. One volume would burn all night keeping rebels warm. Some were handmade from silk, linen, hemp or bamboo. Most were goatskin.[7]

They burned bushland and blew up *girar* trees with TNT. Each would have been between 500 and 800 years old. Many had exquisite landscaping at the base. A 3,000-year-old specimen stands at Queen Sheba's Baths in Aksum. It bears leaves. The *girar* is a metaphor for a vast bank of history.

Samual cried. He told Hewan that he mourned the trees. However, our brother was staying in Addis Ababa for the animals and Mum. We would separate because married women in Ethiopia had the last word. Hewan and I were leaving with Miserat.

My youngest brother Samual in his thirties. Mesfin Tadesse, 2010?

Lucy's People

Hewan packed our bags. I was taking my B52 fighter jet pilot's boots from the US. Fireproof and buoyant in water, they were wonderful for both land and ocean.

How had Mum provided school shoes for us? Derg took anything we were not wearing. We had one pair or none at all. Some of us perused shoe soles for holes. Mum would say, 'Do not worry if your shoes wear out. Some people have no feet.'

---

1. Nigatu Kifelaw, Somali Lands, 27
2. Kebede Michael, Tarik, 3
3. Library of Congress, "History"
4. Young Lives, "Round 5", Key Findings 5
5. Library of Congress, "History"
6. Ostego, Haustein, Fasika Gedif, Kedir Jemal Kadir, Muhammed Jemal, and Yihenew Alemu Tesfaye. Religion, Ethnicity, and Charges of Extremism
7. Solomon Nigus, "Ethiopian Biran Mitshift"

Chapter 11
The Bean

The high school director sent a letter to my parents. He invited them to a meeting. Itiye Messelo accompanied Mum. The director asked, 'Who is his mother?' Both said, 'I am.'

He consulted the receptionist and smiled. 'I wish I was Mesfin, having two such mothers.' I had won an academic award: trophy, uniform and shoes for a year and 100 *birr* (50 US dollars). The two split the cash. Itiye Messelo borrowed the trophy. Protecting it from rain under her long dress, she showed it off at coffee morning. 'See how he has come good since I took him under my wing.'

I sorted mail at the post office. In winter I planted trees for the Ministry of Forests where I became supervisor and then carpenter, making seedling crates. My pay reached four *birr* per day, then five – my education fund. Ravenous, I watched collard grow four times daily and sometimes at night.

My brothers worked. One bought magazines and local newspapers wholesale and retailed them. At 15 he had his own bank account from which he paid his school fees. To help feed the little ones, he sold cigarettes, lighters, matches and chocolates downtown and at Cinema Ambassador and National Theatre.

Recognising him behind his mask, some said, 'The African Star's son. How he has fallen.'

That brother kept hens to sell eggs for school stationery. I fed roosters wheat, corn and popcorn, and bathed their feathers. At six months they weighed five kilograms and sold for three *birr* each – the going rate was 35 cents. My brother left to study journalism in Prague where Czechs pioneered the free press.

City people dressed in clean clothes but had empty stomachs. Inside their houses they starved. My classmate was the eldest of six. His father was a driver and the family lived in two rooms. My friend studied in a monastery and was at risk of failing. Mum invited him to stay with us during the week. He passed his exams.

Classmates asked for help with study. In Year 12, one student thanked me with a cassette tape of his mother Hirut. The Derg had imprisoned her for refusing to praise it in song. Cadre caught me with it and accused me of accepting bribes. At a school assembly one beat me up.

'Who else has been bribing him?' they asked. A peer put up his hand. 'I offered him a notebook and pencil for helping me with math.' I had rejected the gift, but the cadre gave it to me. 'He uses those whose DNA did not make them clever for his own profit.'

Girls offered facial tissues, though I had not cried. Those students had begged for tutoring. I stayed home for a full week to recover. Mum was puzzled because I kept silent. After three days she went to the school.

'What has he done wrong?'

'Your son is a Western imperialist.'

The market for firewood remained. Those who had food did not like cooking with gas. Poor women carted branches from eucalyptus plantations on a mountain outside Addis Ababa. Torsos parallel to the roadway, they balanced 2.8 metre bundles on their backs. Wrinkled faces framed by head scarves lifted toward the city below. After each kilometre they leaned exhausted at the edge of the road. GDR trucks forced them to the edge of ditches. None offered any a lift.

In the church of Tekle Haymanot the congregation chanted, 'Our women have become beasts of burden, like donkeys.' The Derg shut the church, then burned it, denying culpability. Ethiopia's 2018 government talked about alternative work for firewood women, but they continued the carting.[1]

Woman represents Ethiopia, our spiritual mother. Mum told me an allegory. It dated from before Aesop the Ethiopian Philosopher. We called it "The Bean".

> A wizard gave a pregnant woman a bean. After she put it in her mouth, he told her not to swallow it, not hold it in her mouth nor throw it away. Whatever she did, the consequence would be disastrous.
>
> 'If you swallow the bean, your baby will die. The future generation will not be.
>
> 'If you hold it in your mouth, you will die. The next generation will not grow up beautiful although it can be made to survive.
>
> 'If you spit it out and throw it away your husband will die. You will lead a half existence, forever sad without the love of your life.'
>
> The woman could not choose. Woman is the umbrella of the community on whom all depend. If she dies so does part of our society. She prayed.
>
> God answered, 'You have shown that you are responsible. Caring equally for your husband and unborn child you will not selfishly sacrifice your own life. The community will not be deprived of its wonderful member. You have passed the test. All will live.'

God made the bean vanish and the family lived in peace and health.

Mum kept her beliefs. She said, 'The dark side of life cannot be avoided. Put it away. Make your daily life full of spice. Do not waste life.'

Our family faced starvation. We made contact with a sister in the US. She sent cash through go-betweens, who took their cut. We were left with 100 US dollars. With thrift it could feed 12 for two months.

I collected the money on the other side of town at Addis Merkato. It was the largest market in Africa. Though I had a secret signal, I had no precise location or name. Somebody silently put an envelope in my hand containing the cash.

To save the bus fare of 25 cents, I walked home. Half-way, a prison truck appeared. The Derg now conscripted youths and older boys. Few men in their prime were left. A soldier pointed his gun at me. Two others lifted and threw me into the tray. Its wheels were three metres in diameter. It would be hazardous to jump off even while stationary.

The GDR-made machine sped off at 100 kilometres per hour to the city's outskirts. Some boys jumped. They died upon impact with the tarmac or oncoming traffic ran over them. I thought of doing the same, of this way out of meeting death at the battle-front. The cash in my pocket would be buried with my body. Young family would starve.

We stopped in the Awash River Basin near a military training camp. Soldiers forced us to jump down. They herded us onto a soccer ground packed with other youth. 'You will stay here tonight. In the morning you will be selected for the services.' We had no blankets, water, food or toilets.

If I was selected, my family would likely have no idea of

where I had gone. After three months of intensive training, I would die at the war front. They would not get the money in time. I would feign disability. Knowing none of the other prisoners, I remained silent.

Officers arrived at sunrise to choose boys for ground, air or sea forces. A naval officer stopped in front of me. I did not speak, acting as though I could not understand him because I was deaf and mute. The officer said, 'He should not be here. Send him home.' A soldier took me to a row of boys under 14, who should never have been grabbed. The Derg carted us back to the city.

At home I handed the envelope to Mum and gulped water. I awoke on the kitchen chair to Samual's grin. '*Ga-se,* your tiny brain is worth more than 25 cents.'

Late one night I was completing a college assignment. I ate a couple of potatoes. Toddler Samual awoke crying because he was hungry. Mum had saved the potatoes for him. Next morning, she gave me 25 cents for school lunch. Barely enough for a snack, I refused it.

Mum told a fellow patriot, the musician Asnakech. She came that weekend and made us her red onion stew. The dish had substance, like her songs. After lunch she played her *krar* (Ethiopian lyre) and sang.[2]

Her music challenged the Ethiopian establishment, also foreigners. Assassins from the Middle East came to her home and fell in love with her. Asnakech never locked her door. 'I am the willing prisoner of the Ethiopian people, not of materialism.'

Neighbour Bizunesh also sang. She kissed me. When I wiped it off her husband laughed and told Mum. She said, 'Give it to him again.' He gave me stationery and drawing supplies, and was the only one in our row not from the military.

Derg widows were not allowed to sell their houses. In Arat

Kilo, residents had built their homes. Yet they officially belonged to the communist government. Mum still paid municipal taxes for civic services. This included septic tank suctioning. The dwellers' association refused her. 'You own the house. Pay for the septic tank truck yourself.' It cost 60 *birr*. Most lived on less than this each month.

Our full tank stank, which happened around the neighbourhood. The next-door neighbour wanted to help. Mrs Aberrash was another Derg widow, not supposed to have money. Her late husband was a retired general when murdered. He had advised and trained the navy. Because of his high profile, sympathisers abroad may have helped his young family.

If she paid for the service herself, Mrs Aberrash would be found out. The association would know if she gave cash. Mum's tiny children could innocently mention their neighbour's generosity to the wrong person. The Derg would imprison and kill both.

Mrs Aberrash had a son the same age as my brother and told him, 'Phone your friend and ask him to come over to play now.' She left money on the footpath outside her gate. My brother walked past it.

She called out, 'You dropped something. Go back and pick it up.'

'Huh?'

'That money on the ground. It fell out of your pocket. Pick it up. That is yours. Give it to your Mum.'

Mum and I continued with silk production. Lords who survived the revolution lived it up. They had become mortal. Others never bowed to them and none would visit their graves. They demanded Mum's luxury garments. The belly-filler who set dogs on roof workers came as a customer. Mama Teliqwa caught him. She slapped him twice, left, right. Three of his servants witnessed this. The lord bribed them not to tell anybody.

Mum treated neighbours, clearing up teenage acne and handling blood pressure problems. She prescribed specific cuts of meat including liver. Knowing that she was helping others for nothing, the butcher packed extra for us.

A patient thanked her with a gift of a goat. In Ethiopia, only male livestock is killed for meat. He was meant to become soup and stew. Samual cried and clung to the legs of the man supposed to slaughter him. The goat wagged his tail at coffee ceremonies, sipping up spilled popcorn.

Mum fed birds with table crumbs brushed into her shawl. She saved scraps for stray dogs, and left milk with linseed for pregnant cats to shorten their labour. When horses, donkeys and cows gave birth, she took them salt blocks to lick.

Samual took food to Mamite the dog rescuer. She had been sacked without a pension from her job with Emperor Haile Selassie I. Her son was conscripted and returned from war minus a leg and eye. Mamite had nothing. By caring for strays, she prevented them moving to rural areas. If any had untreated rabies, they could infect Ethiopian wolves. People stoned and cursed our brother when he helped her.

The death squad came and shot her dogs. The dwellers' association had said she was too poor to feed and care for them. They killed two German shepherds owned by Colonel Birhanu and Itiye Messelo. When a friend walked his dog on the leash, the squad shot it.

A Derg governor in the north had a nightmare about being chased by two dogs. He ordered the execution of every dog on the streets. In two days, special forces killed 5,000 across northern Ethiopia. A soldier was photographed with tears streaming down his cheeks. He could have been court-martialled and executed.

On the third day, a monastery bell tolled by itself. When soldiers went to fire their guns, they would not work. They handed them in. The next day, the governor's leg swelled and he died in the night. At his funeral the coffin would not descend into the pit of his grave. After priestly intercession it sank 30 metres.

Earlier, Mengistu stole 200 dogs and sent them to work in

Soviet mines. He gave 2,000 horses to the military. In return he received painted-over old military hardware. Soviets fed our horses processed food, killing 1,200. They had only ever eaten barley, soft grass and salt blocks. Others did not survive minus 20 degrees Fahrenheit. Gorbachev returned 300.

In Arat Kilo, boys secured pet dogs inside compounds. We exercised them together at the soccer ground or river, the highlight of the week. Before sunset, Derg prime time, we returned home.

In the morning, we cleaned yards, lined chicken coups with pine needles, and made compost. Boys removed cobwebs and mopped and dusted the house with herbal disinfectant. My sisters pounded it to extract the cleansing juice. We laundered clothes with purifying plant. The girls gave me the largest pile. 'If Mesfine washes them they will be clean.'

Mum relied only upon her patriot's pension. She said, 'Poverty is in the brain.' Using pure ingredients, she made everything from scratch. Disease rarely visited. Mama Teliqwa appeared to grow younger, her skin smoother.

A child wandered outside a monastery. A Somali war bomb had cut her brother in half. Mum put her under wing, soothing her with silken hair. We gained a sister. There were a dozen children in the house.

No neighbour or relative spent two hours in bed ill, young or old. Bone broth made us strong and fast. It helped relatives injured during World War II: all had them.

Patriot Gash Adal was missing his nose, upper lip, teeth and part of his jaw – sliced off by a fascist bomb explosion. He came from Harer to stay. Mum knitted masks for him and gave him bone broth.

Mum and our sisters made soaps and perfume. We pressed olives, linseed and black seed or cumin for cooking oil. Our family did not eat canned, processed food. We went without refined sugar though it reduces hunger.

It was impossible to get all ingredients, but we ate traditional Ethiopian food. Our gardens thrived. Ethiopians did not eat ducks, which ate snails. We did not eat rabbits and they ate our leafy crops. Cats hunted rabbits. Nature kept its balance.

In cities, dwellers' associations supplied most groceries. Each household had a ration card. Cadre doled out cooking oil, sugar, soap, wheat, sorghum flour and *teff* grain. Meat came only from the association butcher. Panadol was exclusive to Derg pharmacies.

Locals lost their self-sufficiency. In Harer, they had kept beehives, polishing floors with wax as a deterrent to termites. They made candles and lights. To store potatoes, they wove bamboo baskets. I made something similar for bees. In Addis Ababa, women sang of Lenin and Stalin, hands unoccupied by knitting, sewing or spinning. What was there to wear and eat in winter?

Mum did not actively support the dwellers' association and cadre, so they refused to supply any items to us. Revolutionary guards abused her. 'Leftover bourgeois imperialist... Exploiter.'

Derg oil was bad for the health. The Derg imported cheap, unhealthy Russian cooking oil, harmful to arteries, heart and immune system. Ethiopia exported edible oils to the Soviet Union and eastern Europe. When my brother studied in Prague, he found BLUE NILE linseed oil in a pharmacy.

We were spared another hazard: Soviet refrigerators or Lenin's Boxes. Government workers had to buy them out of their salaries. They suited Russian diets of cheese wheels, litres of bear's milk yoghurt, and kilos of ham, pork and turkey. Not for us. We ate fresh vegetables and some fresh meat.

People with fridges got flu and diarrhoea. Motors roared when nearly empty, which was usual in our homes. They kept children awake and made them cry. We never slammed doors or banged windows shut. Families switched off the affronts and used them as wardrobes.

On the doors, owners had to display a transcript of Mengistu's speech on Marxist-Leninism. Revolutionary guards randomly inspected homes for compliance and sent the remiss to political re-education.

In 1976, I witnessed a marvellous cure. A friend caught the bus with me to college. His father was at the front in Asmara. Pay took four months to reach home. The family was as poor as mine.

My friend preferred standing to sitting and asked, 'Can you look at my lower back area? There is a lump.' 'Have you told your Mum?' 'No. It is in a bad place.' He was referring to his bottom. It had a tennis-ball-size lump.

Within the wider community were monastery trained traditional physicians. Not rabbis like my late grandfather Alemayehu, they were highly skilled.

I said, 'Why not see one?' He objected to the cost. 'Do you want to risk the Derg hospital?' I said. 'We will take your school report to show you are a high achiever and worthy citizen. They will not charge too much.'

We walked to an area near Medhane Alem. Long-legged brown sheep chewed pruned twigs. In front of a mud house fragrant female pride bloomed beside a false banana. Around an old Volkswagen, *tenadum* herb thrived. Underneath an awning, female hands wound spun cotton.

The physician's house was scrubbed and uncluttered. We gave him my friend's report. He said, 'I do not need that. If he needs help, he needs help, but he must stay overnight.' From the backyard, he gathered leaves, and prepared a drink. He dosed my friend and put him to bed.

He pulled me aside. 'He needs to stay because he will vomit, and the lesion will bleed a lot.' I left to tell our mothers that we had to stay behind for a college project. Then I collected three *birr* and returned to my friend.

He vomited. That soon stopped and his lesion bled. The healer tended and comforted him throughout the night. The bleeding ended before morning. I made the healer take the money. He killed a rooster and cooked stew. The patient ate well. Then came the final stage of the cure.

White threads discharged from the lump in small balls like knitting wool. The physician said, 'Each ball is the beginning of a new tumour. They would have started spreading through the rest of his body.'

After another night my friend was fit enough to leave the traditional physician and return home. His life was barely interrupted by the permanent cure of a life-threatening condition. The healer carried it out without chemotherapy and invasive surgery. He handled it inexpensively, humanely and with dignity. The humble man was one of the world's best healers.

For forty years, such helpers of humanity would be at risk. The Derg tortured one and imprisoned him for a total of twelve years. In the 1990s, trouble renewed during the AIDS epidemic. Then in 2020, French and US embassy cars squeezed through the narrow streets of Addis Ababa's *Falasha* area. They stopped at a physician's premises. The Europeans accused him of treating COVID-19 infections. Locals got rid of them, but they continued the harassment.

Rebels made Ethiopia's non-stop famine worse. To get the world's attention, they attacked farming communities in Tigray and destroyed crops. Meanwhile, the Derg ousted traditional land management geniuses. Fertile farming land lay fallow. In return for Russian weapons, the Derg exported goats, sheep, chickens and cattle, depriving famine victims.

In 1984, Somalia invaded Ethiopia again. Italy and Russia

armed them. Anti-Ethiopian forces from Ethiopia and Eritrea joined with Somalia. These were the Tigray People's Liberation Front (TPLF) and the Eritrean Liberation Front's Shabiya. Both Ethiopian and Eritrean rebels belonged to Shabiya. They fought their own country and families. Ethiopian People's Revolutionary Party forces were supposed to be on our side, but shot militia in the back. Old soldiers said, 'Your enemy is at the front; your own children are behind – enemies too.'

Gash Tesfahun was still advising the defence minister and Ethiopia repelled the invaders. Amhara youths did most of the fighting and 120,000 died, so the permanent famine then worsened in their homelands. Welo (Wollo) was hit the worst with 300,000 deaths.

One of our brothers worked as a surveyor in Amhara. He volunteered to take food to the Welo Region. People died with their pet dogs, cats and livestock. Ethiopians never ate domestic animals. Oxen that pulled ploughs were family.

A non-government organisation provided canned meat soup because famine victims were too weak to cook raw ingredients. Germany had donated pork and Sweden horse meat, both never eaten by us. The starving refused the canned insults. 'Those animals are not food. And we cannot eat food that has been imprisoned in cans.' They died and cans had to be transported and disposed of in Ethiopia.

The UK offered seed to Ethiopia for the best sorghum and wheat crops. It was fast-growing with quarterly yields. The Derg accepted four shipments, each greeted by singing children. When planted, the seed released locusts. They flew all over Welo.

After the insects died, people became ill. Eyelashes and body hair fell out. They bled from the nostrils, corners of the mouth and fingernail beds. Fungus grew on tongues. Some developed stutters. Deaths from this went uncounted and unregistered. Monasteries treated many sufferers. Rains came and wiped out the pestilence.

Eastern Europeans provided powdered milk from areas

affected by the 1986 Chernobyl nuclear disaster. Ethiopia accepted no food donations afterward.

Mengistu expelled *Médicins sans Frontières* or Doctors Without Borders for exposing the famine. However, with Derg ascendancy, the world forgot the misery of our people.

Thirty-six years on, Ethiopia would export 300,000 animals each day, some live with others already slaughtered. This was more than the combined exports of 13 other African countries. The TPLF would allow the weekly export of thousands of donkeys to China for meat. Ethiopians do not eat donkey meat. Meanwhile, our organically produced meat supplied European childcare centres and hospitals while our own children remained malnourished.[3]

In November 2020, after the TPLF declared war on the Addis Ababa government, farmers continued exports. They sent live bulls to China, Japan and the Middle East.

'We send our bulls. You send the TPLF guns. We will not stop sending our cattle. You will not stop sending guns. But you will not destroy us.'

In mid-May 1991, soldiers stranded in Addis Ababa said, 'Gojjam has resisted the TPLF, but rebels have reached northern Shewa. They cannot fly helicopters and fighter aircraft. That will stop them from bombing us. They also cannot operate ZU-23 anti-aircraft mounts. We disabled Panhard tank guns.'

Hewan, Miserat and I did not want to meet them. We were going to the Rift Valley. The Awash River watered it. From the centre of Ethiopia, it flowed thousands of kilometres before desert swallowed it. Fertile soil, a moderate climate, and alpine air nurtured our civilisation.

It was home to the fossil of an early humanoid: Australopithecus *afarensis*. Archaeologists discovered her in 1974. They nicknamed her Lucy. Lucy was 3.2 million years old, yet her skeleton was remarkably complete. Ethiopians called her Dinknesh, a woman's name meaning, 'You are marvellous and unique'.

She had lived where Hadar is today. It was in the Afar Region of central eastern Ethiopia. Queen Nefertiti, wife of an Egyptian pharaoh, came from there.

People in the Shewa Alps believed the tiny Dinknesh to be their ancestral mother. To Ethiopians, she was a symbolic mother. Hers was a story of miraculous survival. So was ours.

---

1. Abiy Ahmed Ali, Twitter Post
2. Ethio Pentatonic, "Asnakech Worku"
3. Young Lives, "Lessons", Findings 2

Chapter 12

Heritage

From 1978, the Derg sent young teenagers to battlefronts. It was the first modern government to do so. In Addis Ababa, soldiers stopped minibuses to look for conscripts.

Oromo mothers would call, 'Quick! Come here!' They hid boys under long dresses. Countless times they saved my brothers and me.

Youths ran up to them in Piazza. '*Maye*, thank you for saving me last week on the transport.' The woman had saved so many that she could not remember each boy. The Derg took years to find out. Security forces apprehending buses said, 'All mothers, stand.'

Our high school history teacher had opposed war. 'Cruise missiles do not distinguish fighters from the elderly, children and pregnant women.' Of the Red Terror he said, 'If you survive, tell of this.'

Ethiopians told foreigners about the unspeakable acts committed upon youth. They went unheard. In tolerating Mengistu, the West was waging an indirect war upon Ethiopians.

Teacher Girma said our last direct war with England was the Maqdala Campaign in 1868.

Emperor Tewodros II then ruled from the north where Gondar is today. He wore Amhara braids and was vibrant. Each afternoon he said, 'May I have my leggings.' He ran alongside his horse, not riding him. For his pet lions, he built a sunning platform and groomed and fed them.

His senior military officers could remember the names and addresses of 10,000 people and their relatives. The best warrior was Kagnazmach Geberay, second in command. Third in command was Girazmach Aleme.

In 1862, sixteen Christian missionaries arrived from England. They carried bibles and wore robes and shiny crosses. 500 Portuguese Catholics, English Anglicans and Protestants and German Lutherans followed.

The Orthodox emperor was religiously tolerant. For more than 3,000 years, the cross had symbolised the temple, life and resurrection. Christians adopted it later.[1] Thousands of years before John the Baptist, they celebrated baptism. Now, all Ethiopians celebrate it together.

Emperor Tewodros II gave the 500 diplomats' visas. He told his people to show them around. 'Treat them like family.' *Aba* Yohannes was advisor and counsellor to the emperor. Portuguese Catholics and Greeks had once preyed upon our children. He warned, 'Do not let them go deep into villages.'

The visitors spread throughout the countryside, too interested in our science and technology: food storage, water supply, reservoirs, hydrogeology, aquaculture and bad day fishponds, beekeeping, veterinary science, disease prevention, meteorology and astronomy. The emperor told Kagnazmach Geberay, 'Provide around-the-clock on this lot. Avoid street justice. We will arrest them if need be.'

Husbands had gone away on business, and some of these visitors tried to rape their wives. The women told Kagnazmach Geberay. Should they respect their emperor's guests or shoot them with their husbands' rifles? Other villagers kept silent about abuses. The emperor's right-hand man had to hold back.

Corpses of children appeared by rivers. Geberay said he could not go on. Tewodros made him bite a double-knife blade with him and swear, 'I will never betray you until my arm becomes my pillow.' He would not take his own life.

Aba Yohannes said that he could survive in the desert with scorpions and snakes. He respected their territory and they his. Missionaries carried large crosses like walking canes. The tops held knives with which they killed girls after raping them. Soldiers caught them with medicinal leaves, bluestone, and body parts serving perverts: eyes, and a girl's severed hand.

In Ethiopia, girls and women walked with confidence, not constantly fearing rape. It was rare. Child sex abuse or paedophilia was unheard of. Orthodox said the power of Mariyam's tears restored Christ. Our country, the moon and the sun were female. The emperor did not negotiate regarding motherland, mother, wife, sisters and children.

Tewodros removed the mercenaries' robes, crosses and bibles, and threw the worst offenders off cliffs. Detaining some in his palace, he gave each a servant and teacher. He made them study Ge'ez and learn true Christianity. Tewodros believed that life turned some bad.

Queen Victoria of England sent 1,200 British, Egyptian and Turkish soldiers to bring back her envoys. They destroyed surrounding lands. For fun, they killed sheep, goats, dogs, poultry and wild birds. They murdered young and elderly people.

Ethiopians hid in caves and bunkers with domestic animals. Military engineers made false villages. Inside termite chimneys, they placed a spongy material containing phosphate. Once lit, it smoked for several days. The English used up their ammunition on unoccupied areas.

On a cliff top, a Scottish child soldier pushed in front of captives. 'Me first. I want to die.' Three high-rank English officers had raped him. Emperor Tewodros II sent them off the cliffs.

Girazmach Aleme arrested deserters, putting the fit to work in mines and teaching them to build cannons. Egyptians later named boys after him for strength. Visiting the cannon workshop, the emperor heard sobbing and asked, 'Who is crying?' 'A young white soldier.'

Tewodros had the 15-year-old brought to him. A monk interpreted: 'I miss my mother.' Older soldiers had made him clean for them, and worse.

The emperor rescued 317 child soldiers from Egypt, Scotland and Ireland. He took them to the palace. Aba Yohannes counselled them to give up cigarettes. The boys mixed with Ethiopian youth. They sang, learned languages, swam, and picked fruit. Tewodros never referred to them as prisoners.

He transferred them to the Red Sea port. Germany offered to take them to Europe. Ethiopia would have to accept 20 missionaries, so Tewodros refused.

He wrote to the King of Portugal. It was cruel to cut a rosebud before it bloomed. Those boys needed their mothers. The body and brain did not grow at the same pace. If the young took part in the horrors of war, they would do worse at home.

Portugal took the youths to Lisbon. Then the ship's captain quit. He removed his anchorage rank and returned it to the king. 'Europeans are savages. Most of the children no longer wanted to go home. Two threw themselves into the sea.' One was a 14-year-old corporal from Scotland. The other was an Egyptian aged 13.

In 1868, Queen Victoria sent more than 36,000 UK troops. General Napier put 15,000 Indian conscripts with elephants out front. England enticed 100,000 Ottoman troops. 'Why not destroy the real Christians?' Traitors showed invaders the swift way to the heart of Ethiopia.

The fiercest fighting was at Moto, a farming area with water from the alps. Medhane Alem Monastery had attracted the invaders. It specialised in silver and gold smelting, diamond and bluestone cutting, crown manufacture, bible production, and processing of titanium for medical equipment. Titanium pots stored herbs indefinitely. More than 100,000 non-UK conscripts and volunteers died there.

Tewodros fought with his hide shield and curved sword. The coalition overwhelmed his forces. He farewelled his wife and son and freed his lions. UK troops captured a loyal lion; pining for Tewodros it died. A soldier shot his horse Satenaw to spare him capture.

Emperor Tewodros II shot himself, dying like a man. He was 49.

General Napier cut off the emperor's braids. He removed his possessions: gold-and-diamond ring ornamented with night lightning, gold-and-diamond tool belt and buffalo hide shoes. He stole his crown, chalice and prayer book.

UK forces ransacked the area. They defiled the corpses of Ethiopians, removing teeth, hair and tattooed skin. Soldiers loaded elephants with antiquities including books, crosses and robes; and built bonfires from what they could not carry: goatskin books and scrolls dating from AD 800 and earlier.

From peasants they stole health-giving toothpicks made of titanium and silver. Those doubled as tweezers. In 2005 a UK museum displayed them in bulletproof glass cases as CHIEFS' POSSESSIONS. Troops even stole sewing needles. England returned them 150 years later, rusted through. It kept the best stuff.

The UK looted the monarchy's sacred text *Kebra Negast* or *Glory of the Kings*. In 1872, Emperor Yohannes IV wrote to England asking for its return. Ethiopia would continue until today campaigning for the return of stolen heritage.[2]

Napier removed seven-year-old Prince Alemayehu. Queen Victoria asked Napier, 'Where is Tewodros? I did not ask you to bring his child.' The boy begged to go home. His mother died. Queen Victoria kept him until he died in England's cold north at 18.

The UK had spent 300 million pounds on the Maqdala Campaign. Queen Victoria said to Napier, 'Where are the Indians with horses, donkeys and elephants? You do not know how to read what you looted. Take it to the museum.' Scottish troops had run off with many books and scrolls.

From then on, England only ever engaged indirectly with Ethiopia. Within three years Queen Victoria advocated for Italy's presence in the area that is now Eritrea.³

One of the 88 books of the Orthodox bible foretold colonisation. This would happen to parts of Asia and most of Africa. There would be a pattern. Emperor Tewodros II discerned it in the colonisation of India and surrounding areas. In a letter to Queen Victoria, he described what Europe had done to Hindustan Raj. It had applied a formula consisting of six stages.

> In Stage 1, missionaries would go to a country. Beatific and calm, they sent home weather reports. These would cover the environment, climate and economy – and when and where people did mining.
>
> Weather and wealth were important to the English. If these were attractive, the missionaries would report on religion and culture. They would list door-openers: manners that locals appreciated.
>
> Stage 2 commenced. Consuls would arrive from Europe. They would bear gifts that influential community members loved. Respectful behaviour towards elders

always helped them befriend leaders. Taking their time, they would gain the leaders' confidences.

Stage 3 would flow from this. Consuls dropped hints. Why was the community friendly with neighbouring tribes? Those people ate weird food and had bizarre beliefs. They were not good for the consul's friends.

The consuls would remain patient. Within a year, fighting would break out between ethnic groups. Oh dear, they no longer felt safe. The consuls needed protection.

Stage 4 would begin with, 'We have to look after our consuls.' Soldiers then arrived to guard them.

Stage 5 would come with prisons. Locals would have no words to describe what was being built, nor what would be done to them underground.

Stage 6 was enslavement. The coloniser controlled a broken people. They would serve its interests in Africa.

By 1868, Queen Victoria had amassed the people of Hindustan Raj to send as slave-soldiers to Ethiopia.[4]

With Emperor Tewodros II, Europeans did not complete Stage 1. Ethiopia's people did not become an endangered species. We did not share the fate of the Indian tiger, South African white rhinoceros, our Simien fox or ancient *girar* and *warka* trees.

As General Napier departed Moto, an alien species of fly arrived. The fertile land became useless for many years. Farmers refused to plant on lands of blood. They would do the same 70 years later in Menz following fascist massacres during the Italian occupation.[5]

Teacher Girma said, 'We do not know where the next war will come from – west from Sudan, north from Egypt or east from Somalia and the Arabic nations. But we do know that the same enemies are behind each invasion and assassination.'

In the nineteenth century, Egyptians, Arabs, Persians, Indians and European so-called sailors smuggled Ethiopian manuscripts and wares. Some Orthodox priests enabled this. They did so out of hatred for Emperor Tewodros II, for he had ended their exploitation of peasants.

Aba Yohannes told Tewodros that he needed to stop the trade. Girazmach Aleme said, 'Queen Saba's shoes were stolen because you are too soft.'

Girazmach Aleme and 112 undercover agents rounded up 10,000 smugglers and border breakers. The emperor put them in a hall that he ordered set on fire; they burned to death. He then established Ethiopia's first Border Security Force. Girazmach Aleme commanded it.

Ninety years later, my late father was Commanding Officer of Border Security. At the Djibouti border he stopped smugglers of ivory, animal body parts, and illicit drugs. A French journalist alleged that Dad stole an army vehicle and changed its number plate. Dad challenged him. 'Do you believe everything you hear? Do you believe it when I tell you I slept with your mother?'

During the 1935–41 occupation, Italians stole whole structures. These included a small rural bridge, and fixtures from B'hata Mariyam Monastery in Addis Ababa. They took its golden lion statues. With a crane, the fascists also removed the monastery's 24-carat-gold roof dome that weighed 27 kilograms. Later, they gave Ethiopia a 9-carat replacement dome. From Aksum they took the largest stele, eventually returning it broken.

Fascists raided B'hata Mariyam for its Orthodox interior decoration. They stole Queen Zewditu's dresses and Queen Saba's shoes.

The French committed robberies as well. From Saint Raguel at Entoto, they stole Emperor Menelik II's bible. In 2018, France would return it in tatters. Thieves had ripped off its jewel-encrusted binding.

A retired lieutenant colonel documented thefts during the 1941 liberation of Ethiopia. Viceroy Badoglio robbed Ethiopia of 300 boxes of gold bars and ancient books. General Graziani stole 79 boxes of gold, silver and diamond artefacts. In April 1941, the UK gave safe passage to the war criminals. It guarded them through eastern Ethiopia and Somalia. The French did the same through Djibouti. Others escorted them across the Mediterranean. Mussolini welcomed them as heroes.

Before Haile Selassie's homecoming, the UK blocked the border at Eritrea. It enslaved Ethiopian refugees, forcing them to dismantle infrastructure. They destroyed a bakery, telecommunications and 80 kilometres of cable car equipment. The UK transported much Ethiopian infrastructure to Sudan and Kenya. Eritrea's brewery was too large to cart thousands of kilometres, so they made slaves throw it into the Red Sea.

In Addis Ababa, UK forces rounded up Armenians, Yemeni and Yugoslavs in the night. They coerced them into dismantling, breaking and looting infrastructure and businesses. Anybody resisting, especially if Yugoslav, was killed or enslaved.

The English dumped Italian construction vehicles in Debre Zait's seven lakes; broke bridges; and, with spitfire jets, chased giraffes, elephants, lions and tigers into Kenya. Patriots shot down three.

In April 1941, patriots were on their way to the city. UK forces armed captive Italians and ordered them to kill Ethiopian civilians at Triana Bar in Piazza. By the hands of others, the English murdered 150.

They took the soldiers to B'hata Mariyam Monastery. Years before, monks had told the English about needing to hide crowns and Stars of David from fascists. They refused to reveal the place: inside the grave of Emperor Menelik II. The English made the Italians shoot them all.

Next, they took them to dismantle the Berhanoena Selam

Press printing machine. Patriots caught up with all at Ras Mekonnen Bridge and killed them. UK forces then tried to bomb B'hata Mariyam Monastery.[6]

Haile Selassie returned. UK administrators of the UN said our southern borders needed securing. In Sidamo they erected a barbed-wire fence around our gold mines. These included Laga Dambi, also called Adola Gold Mine, and Saba Mine. They built a secret prison and enslaved traditional miners, making them mine for gold and imprisoning any who refused. At the end of shifts, soldiers forced miners to drink water with 'English salt'. This gave them diarrhoea in case they had swallowed gold.

The English did not deposit bullion into our Reserve Bank, smuggling gold out through Kenya. At Isolo in its north, patriots shot two smugglers. The UK claimed they destabilised border security, but Haile Selassie investigated. He removed the UK from Sidamo.[7]

After World War II, monks hid our cultural treasure. A cave held 10,000 Orthodox goatskin books with boxes of crowns and gold artefacts. The books were about medicine and contained herbal ratios for remedies. Others had diamond encrusted covers.

In January 1976, the Derg stole part of the treasure. Mengistu sold it to Germany and the Soviet Union communist party and purchased military hardware.

Wanting more, Mengistu's soldiers beat Abun Tewflos, who was a regional Orthodox pope. He refused to disclose the location of other treasuries. For 48 days he took no food or water. Abun Tewflos died in the palace prison in March 1976.[8]

Forty years later, TPLF employees would sell our heritage to foreigners. At the Lalibela rock-hewn monasteries an official asked about my companion. 'Is she looking for a gold coin? A copy of *Audenegiste?* We have the real one. I will give you good commission after she buys.'

US President Clinton found a stolen copy of the 800-year-old book. Its title translates as *The Secret of Life*. Literate in Ge'ez and knowledgeable of Hebrew, he identified it as genuine and returned it to Ethiopia. The text is a cypher containing our monastic healing wisdom.

Germans sneaked a copy, learned Ge'ez, and decoded some of it themselves. A pharmaceutical company used the knowledge: *Behyer* is Ge'ez for clean air plant. Germany later returned our book. It retained our formulae. Two were for aspirin and surgical anaesthesia.

Traitors amassed profits from stolen wealth. They opened foreign bank accounts. This bought them instant citizenship in countries such as Australia.

Ethiopia lost bright people. Italian fascists hunted down our intelligentsia and graduates.[9] Under Emperor Haile Selassie I, scholarship students completed their qualifications in Europe and the US and some stayed there.

A cousin of my father's was a nuclear chemist in America. He came home to visit his mother. CIA agents injected him to make him forget secrets, destroying his mind. He paced Piazza endlessly. My brother used to buy him lunch and coffee.

The administration of Emperor Haile Selassie I censored the weekly magazine *Kaman Anche* or *I Am Not Smaller*. He closed another named *Amro* because he did not want it to provoke the muscle heads of the West.

Lord Kebede Mikael had written for *Kaman Anche*, criticising English practice in Africa. The magazine poked fun at Western pride in physical size. Author Abay Gobegn referenced that in a political satire with a donkey dressed in a three-piece suit standing for election. *Amro* featured articles on politics by Dr Haddis Alemayehu, Lord Kebede Mikael, Paulos Gnogno, Abay Gobegn and Wegayu Nigatu. Dr Haddis wrote the column "Thin Lips"; the BBC did not realise that it was about English fascism.

The Derg closed a magazine called *Menen* (Manan) that covered internal affairs. It imprisoned and tortured Abay Gobegn and made him homeless. Abay had dared to write about the Red Terror. He died in his early fifties.

Ethiopian intellectuals wrote in the tradition of Q'ine. This had two layers of meaning.[10] It subtly conveyed controversial messages.

Using Q'ine, a journalist wrote about the murder of *Yehuda* boys. The popularity of his writing drew attention to him. The Derg arrested and tortured him.

He had a letter smuggled to his wife in Gojjam. 'I will never be able to walk again. No good as a man, I am in great pain. Please help with this. I ask one other thing: do not cry for me. Be brave, for you are now both father and mother to our children.'

His wife wrote back to him in Ge'ez and Hebrew. Gaolers would not be able to read those languages. She sent him a shirt. Its collar was laced with fast-working poison. Shackled and bound, her husband sucked on it and was released from agony. His loved ones fled to Sudan, then Israel gave the widow asylum. She would have spoken textbook Amharic, which some city dwellers found difficult.

Mengistu addressed a gathering in the Amhara region.

He asked, 'What do you fear?'

An elder raised his hand. 'The communist revolution.'

Henchmen took a step forward, but 100,000 locals stopped them. 'Arrest us too!'

The president posed his question again. Another elder said, 'Chairman Mengistu, I cannot afford to buy an ox, nor can I afford a mule. I can buy a donkey. Will it then drop big air (pass wind) like Derg officials?' The crowd laughed, but Mengistu and his officials did not. 'What did he say? I do not understand him.

Put him in prison until I know.' The elder spent eight years in gaol.

The European Eastern bloc took our gifted youth. Soviet Brezhnev gave education passes to some 300,000 young Ethiopians. Some studied in the Soviet Union, in Moscow or Odessa. Others went to industrial GDR, Budapest in Hungary, Prague in Czechoslovakia, Sofia in Bulgaria, Bucharest in Romania and Tirana in Albania.

They took traditional handmade garments and blue jeans, exchanging them for contraband. Some returned with a bedside lamp, camera and suitcase. My wife's brother left with seven pairs of Ethiopian leather shoes and five leather jackets. He bought a jeep. Highly ranked military did the same.

Students returning from the GDR had a torch, a shaver and shoes. Those who had studied in the Eastern bloc wore the same clothes in which they had left. They had queued by shifts to get a glass of milk.

Some brought home Russian wives. I met one who was an engineer. She monitored a pipeline south of Addis Ababa. Walking eight kilometres daily, she removed her work boots as she approached villages. Under the TPLF she would fight to stay in Ethiopia.

Ethiopians in the Eastern bloc said, 'How can this course be three, five or seven years long? At home it takes nine months or one year.' An Ethiopian fighter jet pilot's course took 27 months. After nine months students flew by themselves on military missions. They graduated able to fly MIG27 and MIG29.

Soviet helicopter pilot courses took three years. For months they studied HOW TO WEAR UNIFORM. Socialist political studies dragged out courses.

When my brother studied in Prague, Czechs gave Ethiopians 28-day courses on using cutlery. They said, 'We will do this alone, thanks,' and learned in 20 minutes. Then they crafted hygienic wooden spoons as gifts for those that underestimated Africans. Enrolled in social science, journalism and law, the students were not technical.

Military manufacturing companies in Moscow and Odessa sought out students who finished second year. 'Why not stay on?' In return for a low wage, they gained factory experience or inside knowledge of jet or nuclear submarine technology. Then they broke away, disappearing into the West from Hamburg. Secret police—Soviet KGB or GDR Stasi—traced and killed them in West Germany or in the UK. Everywhere were unknown enemies.

My friend Yonas studied marine engineering in Bulgaria. Classmates said, 'We can learn better in Ethiopia.' Yonas arrived prematurely in Addis Ababa with four others. The Derg arrested them at the airport. It imprisoned them in Mihakelawe.

A general laid down his service pistol. 'Release these sons or I resign. Which way is this country going? Innocent citizens die each minute at the border.

'Outsiders designed the war with our Eritrean countrymen. The government is waging it on their behalf at the cost of countless young lives on both sides. It is killing us.'

He had been made to fight Eritreans, who were as brothers. Their families lost breadwinners and probably died too. Foreigners supporting them did not die; Ethiopians and Eritreans did. By killing the young in prisons or at the front, we lost our wealth. They were not reproducible like factory goods. It took 20 years to rear one youth.

The general said, 'If any word I have said is wrong, kill me by my own gun. I am three times older than those you have locked up. In dying fighting for them, I am reborn.'

Two months later the Derg released the boys. It sent the general to Moscow.

In the 1970s, both the European Eastern bloc and West offered asylum to a major general who had commanded a force of 36,000. He chose the US because his daughter was there. It gave the major general a job collecting supermarket trolleys for 4.50 US dollars per hour.[11]

In foreign countries today, Ethiopian graduates drive taxis.[12]

---

1. Kebelay Gedey, Lalibela, 48
2. Kiunguyu, "Plundered Ethiopian Maqdala Treasure"
3. Bahru Zewde, A History, 56-7
4. Ababa Welde-Tensay, Asidenyaki, 7
5. Gashaw Ayferam Endaylalu, "Mustard Gas", 508
6. Ababa Welde-Tensay, Asidenyaki, 87-89
7. Ababa Welde-Tensay, Asidenyaki, 108
8. Ababa Welde-Tensay, Asidenyaki, 110-13
9. Pankhurst, Ethiopia, 547-48
10. Songs, 307
11. Hussein Ahmed, Rete and Honey, 181
12. Cohen, "Foreign Involvement", 9

Chapter 13
Calculator

In 1979, Mengistu closed high schools for two years, filling them with political prisoners. We were left with grades 1–8: elementary to junior secondary school. I'd graduated from university in 1977. Having completed school in eight years, I did bridging courses at Teg Bara Id, the polytechnic in Mexico Square. I studied engineering and military science. Due to arbitrary arrests, I had plenty of absences, but completed a work experience mosaic at Menelik Referral Hospital.

At Building College, I enrolled in Design and Construction Engineering. The college's name was Sihinensa Tibeb which meant building wisdom. Our course was 100 per cent Ethiopian. From helicopters, we read topography using aerial maps. We studied mineralogy to evaluate building sites. Then we selected materials of suitable strength and weight.

We used the same construction methods as for ancient Abyssinian pyramids and water reservoirs. Engineering students practised traditional bar bending and chiselling. Stonemasons used different techniques for limestone and basaltic stone. Slabs interlocked, each pair having a unique key that we calculated with algebra. It originated in Ethiopia.

Dr B'hata was Faculty Dean. It was he who built the hydro-electric power dam at Gilgel Gibe River. He had studied water supply systems in a monastery where water charged uphill without electricity. Orthodox monks pioneered construction and water technology. Their job title was 'working with water'. They never called themselves engineers. *Bwanbwaseratenya* meant working as a plumber. Only a retired plumber would be called that.

Academics came from abroad to hear his lectures. They were educators from universities in Japan, Iran, Egypt, Uganda and Nigeria, who wrote textbooks and research articles. Their fields included astronomy, geology and water development. No European attended.

Dr B'hata said the world as we know it would not last. Through selfishness, humans would hasten extinction. Which generation would witness the end? A fifth century scroll stated that one day it would be dust. Everything had its ending. That bible contained illustrations of dinosaurs and species then in decline: frogs the size of turtles and beetles with rainbow-coloured wings.

In the 1960s, a tortoise became ill after ingesting a plastic straw with grass. Dr B'hata encouraged students to protest at thoughtless consumption of plastic products. Ethiopia remained free of plastic bags until cigarette companies donated them.

He took youth under his wing. A 19-year-old vanished from college, conscripted to the front. Dr B'hata said, 'He can be of more help to the country if you let him go.' A colonel forced him out of the field office at gun point. 'None of us want to be here.'

The youth returned from war with one leg amputated. He sold coffee beans, charcoal and potatoes on the street. His girlfriend, a nurse from Eritrea, joined him. When he broke it off, she said, 'I will kill myself.' They married, had two children, and moved to Jimma in the south-west where he worked as an engineer.

Building College had 2,300 students and professors. Academics lobbied from inside and outside Ethiopia to keep the college. It survived under the Derg.

Alumni included medical scientist Dr Aklilu Lemma and Yidnekachew Tessema, who was Sports Commissioner and President of the African Football Confederation.

Dr Aklilu's research centre and rabbit farm were on campus. So was his bronze statue proclaiming his achievements. He had developed the cure for the parasitic disease *bilharzia*. In the 1960s he received the Nobel Peace Prize for this though the UK opposed it. Haile Selassie told them they could not use the remedy without acknowledging the scientist.

He developed a vaccination for foot-and-mouth disease that transferred between farms, killing cattle. The UK had introduced it to Ethiopia. Dr Aklilu told farmers to purify water with *indod* and *berbera* – purifying plant and bush bean. The UK used *indod* except in Kenya. White South Africans smuggled it to South Africa, Zambia and Zimbabwe. They profited and gained hubris.

The German government threatened to close the Volkswagen factory in Argentina if farmers used *indod*. It blocked it in Brazil. The Australian government did the same in Samoa and Fiji. *Indod* became the biggest black-market item in the world, an abuse of our science.

Two decades earlier, Dr Aklilu had combatted DDT. Ethiopia lacked the manpower to bury livestock killed by mustard gas. A yellow ant and white louse fed on them and blinded living livestock. Aba Paulos, our pope, cautioned, 'Do not throw animal corpses in the river. Do not let birds eat them.' Russia helped bury corpses using hydrated lime.

When the US and UK distributed DDT Haile Selassie stopped shipments. The UK complained in the UN about the waste. Dr Aklilu said, 'Machine guns are quiet, so you start a silent war in the name of peace. DDT is no compensation for fascist atrocities. The poison kills more of our animals and us. Did you hope to take the country?' English military chemical engineers said, 'Concerning ecology and animals, these people are more advanced.'

Yidnekachew Tessema pioneered bans on cigarette and

alcohol advertising in sport. Influential with the International Football Federation, he pursued African representation of FIFA, and advocated for increased participation by African countries in the World Cup. In Geneva and Paris, FIFA met Yidnekachew at the airport with a limousine. In Ethiopia, the Derg detained him at Bole International Airport for three hours.

College inspired. At our canteen, a European scooped *injera* and stew with his fingertips. In vernacular *yerada lij*, my friend Yonas said, 'That man of no colour has Ethiopian table manners.' The European responded in Amharic. 'You display a lack of culture.' He asked me if he was my friend and I nodded. 'No good for you.' Then he farewelled us with, 'Blessings.' Yonas said, 'That was Alula.' Suffragette Sylvia Pankhurst was his grandmother.

The youngest of 700 engineering students, my nickname was Calculator. In the 1970s, wristwatches with calculators were fashionable. One day, Dr B'hata let slip, 'Where is Calculator? We have not heard anything new at college.' At 15, I said, 'Life is not a ninety-minute soccer game.' Dr B'hata said, 'I am telling the other lecturers. If something happens to him, I will not be able to go on.'

Dr Haddis visited Dr B'hata. When I washed mud off my hands before greeting him, he covered my hands with his. 'Do not wash your hands before coming to see me.' He asked to see my exercise book, secreting 10 *birr* among its pages – for some a week's wage.

Education was free under the Derg, but I supported myself. In a Piazza shop *gash* (shields) adorned the ceiling as reminders of patriots. Owner Shumeta would say, 'Big Man, I have an envelope.' I interpreted the letter and wrote his response two rows per line. He gave me exercise books, graph paper, pencils, set squares, T squares and protractors.

The Addis Ababa business area Piazza or Piassa was really Arada. In 1936 the fascists bombed it and banned locals without passes. They changed its name. If locals said, 'Arada,' a black-shirt would cut off the phalange of a finger.

One night, on my way home to Arat Kilo, soldiers dragged me into the Ministry of Defence and beat me. I awoke on concrete. A major was asking, 'Why beat him? What has he done?' 'He was looking inside.' The stone wall was too high for that. 'He has Building College ID. Release him.' How many boots had landed on me? My drawings were mangled, set square smashed.

It was not worth travelling home some days because the family had food shortages. The Derg forbade buses and cars on Sundays. A friend took me home for dinner until, suddenly, he vanished. Conscripted? Purged for braininess? Realising that I helped in Workshop, lecturers arranged for me to stay at the college hostel. This reduced the time that I spent in transit with the risk of arrest.

City street ditches became full of husks and silks of corn, which blocked drains. A woman fell into one with her baby on her back. I grabbed her shawl and a passer-by pulled, but started to strangle the baby. Climbing into the ditch, I lifted the mother to ease pressure. She renamed her child after me.

In Arat Kilo, the Derg banned us from cleaning the village in September – so Western imperialist. The Organisation of African Unity complained of the stench, so the Derg reinstated it. The dwellers' association said, 'Help is required from one person per household or pay a ten-*birr* fine.' I offered to work and the new chairman accepted, but the old guardian said, 'Why not you Missus Tewode? Are you *Falasha* too good for this? Your son is too young to do decent work.'

'I am strong. Remember, I thrashed you.' The new chairman said, 'Let him work. If unsatisfactory, the family will pay the fine.'

With my polytechnic wrench and spanner, I tightened leaking water pipes, and serviced the poor people's water point and the association's generator. They gave me dinner and a contact number for emergencies in Addis Ababa. Women said they wished I was their son, brother or boyfriend. Girls sent letter poems that I hid from my siblings. Friends nicknamed me Solution Bringer.

Mengistu continued to infect the superstitious. '*Falasha* are not human.' Families closed their shutters against Mum and me when we passed by. At soccer, another Jewish boy and I would find ourselves alone on the field after joining in a game.

Safe among loved ones, I sketched fast with cooking-fire charcoal. Itiye Messelo said, 'He has a beautiful flower in his brain.'

Ethiopians who brought joy to others suffered. The Derg attacked musicians. An officer shot a singer who refused to perform for his daughter. Mengistu sent a whole orchestra, with brilliant singers, to entertain troops at the front. A bomb killed them.

A government minister demanded that a celebrated singer write 10 songs in praise of the Derg. 'I expect them in three days.' The musician completed two songs – with lyrics, composition, and band setting. The minister imprisoned him without his family's knowledge. He was with 500 men and 400 women.

After eight years, the commandant told the prison captain, 'Ten trucks are coming with young people, very important prisoners. We are going to teach them a lesson, all 800.'

'We are full. What about the others?'

'Ah, the old ones. Spray them tonight.' The commandant was ordering a mass execution. When he left, the captain opened the doors. 'Go now! You are to be put before the firing squad. Before they come back, run. Run as far as you can until your legs can no longer carry you.' Then he shot himself.

The musician ran. He did not know where he had been imprisoned. Naked, he found himself on the streets of a strange town. Monks took him to their monastery. From rush-filled ponds they flicked holy water. He returned to normal and asked to stay and serve. The monks took his pulse. 'No. You have more living to do.' He got accepted into Norway where he taught musical performance on traditional Ethiopian instruments.

Another musician did not go to a monastery. He was a singer-songwriter and pianist. One classical 45-minute composition doomed him. The Derg put him in Alem Bekagn prison and tortured him. Upon release he fled to the US. He had to work as a kitchen hand and petrol bowser attendant and lost some of his mind. The Ethiopian community sent him home, paying for his hotel in Addis Ababa.

At the Ethiopian millennium, I found him. We conversed while he slipped in and out of his true personality. Twelve years later, he posed in the street as though soaking up sunshine. It was July and raining. He swore at me. The next day, national radio played one of his old love songs.

In 1975 the Derg arrested Tesfaye Gessesse, who was director of our National Theatre. Tesfaye had written a play critical of its rule. From then on it enforced factory worker plays and peasant dramas. The government deducted ticket prices from workers' salaries, who took along blankets and slept. Better received was a bilingual performance of Shakespeare's *Macbeth*, translated by Lord Kebede Mikael. Halfway through, the auditorium filled with Derg Security. It arrested audience members, actors, crew and ticket sellers – too many to imprison.

The Derg took us to the Forest Training Camp oval. Cadre harangued us all night with Engels-Marxist-Leninist-Stalinism.

In 1987 the National Theatre Troupe of Ethiopia produced the touring show *Hizb le Hizb* or *People to People*. Ethio jazz exponent Mulatu Astatke directed it. It promoted our culture abroad.[1] Later, the Derg detained the lead dancer. She had probably taken part in some small protest.

Mengistu's wife had nothing to do with persecution. She was from Gojjam though he hated Orthodox. She visited the military hospital where we volunteered, like any mother walking about alone, unguarded. People loved her. They made up this joke.

One day, a retail assistant from Gurage served her at Addis Merkato. She was shopping for traditional clothing. Climbing a ladder to reach a garment, he passed wind.
    'Do not do that here,' she said.
    'Your husband closes our mouths,' he replied. 'And you close our arses.'
    She left a generous sum of money and departed.

In Arat Kilo, a retired colonel kept an eye on our soccer team. If we were rambunctious, he ordered us to his compound. We stood at attention, tormented by the aroma of his wife Itiye Konjit's cooking. An hour later we tasted some. The army tree looked askance at the cadre and Derg military. He had a German shepherd, his corporal. When his master died, the corporal kept returning to his grave, pawing at the stones.
    After soccer training, we walked home with shoes off, so as not to disturb the village mothers. They would be absorbed in evening spinning, embroidery and sorting of corn cobs for popcorn. If they heard us, they pulled us into their houses to give us diluted beer or wine with nuts. Their sons were imprisoned or sent to fight wars that nobody wanted.

Ethiopia's tiny worlds thrived due to peasants and monks. Monasteries have always kept bees. They constructed bamboo hives like baskets, with doorways and interior partitions that lifted out. These provided easy access for bees and removal of honeycomb plates without disrupting the hive. Honey could smelled 500 metres away like flowers and wine mulled with cinnamon.

Butterflies and bees were not to be disturbed. Holy men would arrest anyone doing so near a monastery. They made offenders clean the compound and fill compost drums with fallen leaves. Monks said, 'Humans cannot make honey.'

Ethiopia had more than 50 bee species. Bees that lived underground produced the best honey, delicious with lime. One had a black thorax and lemon wings. It made tiny amounts of honey though it was large: 1.5 centimetres long. Another species hung wasp-style under the eaves of huts or in tree-trunk crevices. Others nested in spires. People obtained the honey through bamboo tubes.

The hive of one species was spoiled if disrupted in the afternoon. Another type killed people with four or five stings. Others only killed in big groups. Farmers made a lotion containing tree sap for cows' eyes and ears.

At Building College, each student had a vegetable garden plot. Though small, they fed families. We landscaped and built dams with dykes and water treatment plants. I did the pointing for a masonry wall. Brown pigment mixed with plaster made it stand out. Friends called it Mesfin's wall.

My water technology thesis was on Aba Samual, the 21-square-kilometre dam west of Addis Ababa. It was below a mountain with Aba Samual Monastery atop.

The Derg made *chichi* to sell to Angola, Zambia, Tanzania, Mozambique and Algeria. It did not build water treatment plants. Cattle drank from rivers near munitions factories and became ill. Farmers took them to the curative waters of Aba Samual dam and lake. The system made its own tunnels and filtered itself.

Part of the lake contained cyclones. People who swam there were pulled down, surfacing when dead. Because our lake's shores had no snow and ice, Russians were attracted to the deep water and came in busloads. Generals with gold fillings, bottles of vodka and cigarettes jumped in, climbed out and jumped again, forgetting to remove their guns first.

Soldiers from Romania and Hungary killed themselves. Priests of Aba Samual Monastery leapt in after them, golden henna robes flying. They pulled the victims out of the lake. On sour mouths they performed Expired Air Resuscitation and Coronary Pulmonary Resuscitation. Gold fillings lay down like puppies.

Construction engineering students went on field trips. Red Star Action projects were under way. One was the hydroelectric power dam at Milke Wakane River in the Bale region. The GDR and Czechoslovakia funded it and Ethiopians built it. The dam would supply Uganda and Kenya with electrical power.

Our group shivered atop Bale Mountain. We were above the two-kilometre-wide river, volcanic crater lake, and a modern building. It had a concrete wall and search lights. I asked a soldier about it. 'Oh, that. It is a political ideology school.' It was a secret prison. GDR's Erich Honecker had funded the Bale hydroelectric power project as part of a deal. The GDR built torture chambers in the prison and trained the Derg there. Cadre learned to destroy evidence by chemically reducing victims into a kilogram of ash.

Bale people did not sell or trade. We asked them for water; they gave us milk. Everything was a gift. They spoke Oromigna, but I understood when they urged us to drink milk, yoghurt or sorghum soup. Students were all slight. People lined up to donate food: barley, a goat, and two huge sheep. My friends cried at their generosity.

Holding a lamb under one arm, elders felt our biceps. 'Ah, you are skinny. You do not have a mum? No dad? How many cows do you have? Let me keep you for a fortnight. You need more muscle here.' A naturally thin boy took to wearing three or four jackets when around those people.

On our first day at Bale, a young boy strong as ten city youths carried a wheel-size wooden platter of clarified butter. It was for our hair. We laughed because at home we only got to eat it. This was my country? These were my people? Life was cruel in the city. Those Oromo people were all kindness.

I took 12-year-old Samual there. He slept with five lambs for warmth and did not want to leave. I asked, 'What about *Maye?*' 'I have dozens here.' Daughters of Lucy and Saba.

In the 1970s, the communists removed the free market. Villagers could not sell one chicken. The Derg controlled sales through Irrsha Sebel Gabaya Dirijit, the farming product purchasing organisation. Cadre collected produce—livestock, beef, grain, fruit, poultry and eggs—yet failed to distribute the food. In Welega in the west, earth movers mounded corn cobs that burned for a month as people starved in the east.

The Derg had acted upon the Ethiopian Student Council slogan of 1965: LAND TO THE TILLER. Land rights were historically important.[2] However, Mengistu nationalised all land and abolished land tenancy.[3] Between 1978 and 1986, he grabbed traditionally owned land belonging to half a million people from the northern regions of Tigray and Welo alone. He tortured and murdered farmers who resisted.

He would fly above an area that looked green: acacia bush with no waterways. Forces dumped farmers in resettlement camps with no food, drinking water, seeds, tools or infrastructure. Snakes and malaria mosquitoes attacked. Infectious and chronic diseases abounded. One-and-a-quarter million peasants and farmers died. It was genocide.

Emperor Menelik II had set up Imbita Wibe Mikilakei, a malaria and locust defence program. Using horses, it sprayed leafy zones with non-industrial chemical compounds, preventing plagues. Under Emperor Haile Selassie I, it used an aeroplane that also serviced Sudan, Uganda, Kenya, Djibouti and Rwanda.

The Derg seized the aeroplane, painting it military grey green, and turned the office into a socialist political training centre. In 2020, Ethiopia and Somalia would deal with locust plagues. Cadre killed beneficial species though. A politician's son hanged himself with a silk scarf; so, in Harer and Gojjam, they sprayed acacia and a tree similar to the banana. They housed silk spiders and maggots.

In 1958, Dr Aklilu of Haile Selassie 1st University attended a conference in Cairo held by the United Nations Educational, Scientific and Cultural Organization: The Mutual Appreciation of Eastern and Western Cultural Values.

It ignored African non-literate contributions such as Ethiopia's Oromo *gada* system.[4] According to author Donald Levine, it made people adaptable.[5] Yet cadre had all the say. The TPLF would later force pastoralists into villages and make farmers buy harmful fertilisers.[6]

Factories producing yeast, wine and beer used traditional products. They sterilised beer and wine barrels with herbal disinfectant and soap leaf. When communists appointed untrained cadre supervisors, workers cleaned boilers with caustic acid from Italy. It arrived in metal barrels instead of plastic. Metal oxygenated caustic acid, which corroded metal. The acid then partially evaporated, becoming concentrated. Workers scooped caustic acid from barrels without protective gear. Eyelashes and hair fell out and they lost fingers. Derg torturers began to use it to maim prisoners.

Akaki Textile and Cotton Factory, 38 kilometres from the centre of Addis Ababa, was the largest in Africa. It had 23,000 permanent full-time workers and 10,000 permanent part-time workers. At harvest in December, when cotton flew through the air obscuring aeroplanes, it operated 24/7, employing up to 50,000. Egyptians and Pakistanis referred to it as the devil's cotton factory. It had many customers in the West and supported 22,000 producers.

Akaki had two institutes of agricultural science, agricultural economics, environmental science and factory production. 1,200 students graduated annually. The factory provided social services and collected garbage.

The Derg installed directors that had no technical or management skills. They brought in Soviet workers, ignorant of the semi-tropics. Cadre forced staff to produce 120 million Soviet military coats. Payment was painted-over old military hardware.

They paid workers with monthly rations: three litres of cooking oil, between 50 and 100 kilograms of *teff* grain, and three kilograms of sugar. All were worse off than during the 1972–73 famine. Dr B'hata said, 'This country was the century's breadbasket. Now it is a hunger factory.'

Employees became anti-government. The military sent my sister's husband Lieutenant Tsigay to investigate. At the threshold, a furious mob killed him with shovels and axes. His young family of six children was never compensated. Itete was pregnant with a seventh.

My brother-in-law Lieutenant Tsigay. Photographer unknown, 197–?

Cadre incorrectly operated the factory and caused Akaki Textile and Cotton Factory to burn down. High-level, innovative scientists killed themselves.

---

1. cybraddis, "People to People"
2. Bahru Zewde, A History, 223
3. Bahru Zewde, A History, 242-43
4. Library of Congress, "History"
5. Levine, Greater Ethiopia, 3471
6. Asebe Regassa Debelo, Yetebarek Hizekiel, and Korf, "'Civilizing' the Pastoral Frontier", 930 & 947

Chapter 14
Forgive Me

Mum gave underwear, socks and shoes to the military as they plucked her 17-year-old from home. 'With these he will be able to work better and be of more use to you.'

She did not plead. Neighbourhood mothers wailed. Mum said, 'Get out of here. Let him go. He is a man'. She did not want me jinxed by tears. With a revolver pressed to my temple I maintained silence. Self-control would help. I was cross with Mum though.

Soldiers had stormed our house at midnight. By 1977, the Derg surprised youth in bed. We avoided college gymnasiums, a source of fit conscripts.

Ethiopia faced incursions from Egypt and Sudan. She fought rebels in Eritrea. That was part of Mengistu's Red Star Action.[1] Addis Ababa had become one big military hospital full of wounded soldiers.

Youth volunteered in wards. My Building College workgroup washed corridor floors and windows, tended the garden and cleaned stretchers full of blood. We had to be quiet. The soldiers were traumatised.

A 30-year-old gripped my shirt collar. 'Shoot me, I am no use like this.'

Orderlies came and injected him. He had a poisoned lead bullet in the thigh. To stop its spread, doctors had paralysed him from the hips down. Others were passport photos with half their body blown away.

Ethiopian National Military Service reduced the life span of Ethiopians more than anything. The very young were dying in war zones. A teacher said, 'You will not attend your parents' funerals. They will attend yours.'

Mum tracked down officers whom Dad had taught. They told her I was at Burayu in an Air Force training base. Its name was Tadik Tor Sifer. This meant wear your gun belt for war. It was the biggest military camp on earth, training militia by the hundreds of thousands. There were four sections: Airborne, Air Force, Air Defence and Ground Force. I was with Airborne.

Mum and a brother came 10 kilometres by bus and 11 on foot. She said, 'If you survive, help the desperate people. Your father died doing that. I never saw a man cry like Lord Tilahun. He knelt, held your father's hand and gave him his Colt revolver. "Help me to help all these dying people or kill me."

'Your father lifted him to his feet. "I have thirteen children. Are you begging me to betray them and my wife?" The lord said, "My Badge, that number is too small. You have to save hundreds of thousands."

'He threw his patriot's medal onto the floor. "I will never wear this again." He had worn it for 34 years. For the first time since the fascist occupation, I started putting my gun under my pillow. Your father saved hundreds of thousands of people's lives.'

Mum gave me his inscribed Omega wristwatch. 'I kept it hidden. If you die, have your friends bury you with it.' Derg generals did not have that brand. She also gave me a bean-sized gold coin and a red and yellow book called *Golgota*. Carrying the 43 millimetre miniature saved owners from bad people, evil spirits and depression.

The training base at Burayu had once been called Siga Meda or meat ground. Green and wet, it had been a pasture for orphan bull calves that grew enormous. Under the Derg, it reverted to its old name. The communists sent conscripted farmers to the front after three months of military training. A father and two young sons would arrive at Siga Meda together. The whole family was as good as dead.

At the training base, I did mechanical engineering. To suit African conditions, I modified military equipment. We had lime and sticky clay mud. Eastern bloc tanks and jeeps were made for European snow. They jammed in heat and cracked. The machines had let down Somalis in 1975-77 leading to soldiers' capture or death.

Only 65 per cent of conscripts survived the initial training period. I escaped death but not the military. It microchipped conscripts. This compounded nerve damage from Derg torture.

I made 69 parachute jumps and received my Airborne wing. Then I trained recruits as well as other staff officers. Twice, I received scholarships to Haifa in Israel to study commando and airborne military science, plus aeronautical engineering. I gained knowledge of wind-knot speed, gravity and helicopter, jet and normal aeroplane dynamics. This complemented airborne science.

I was also a dispatcher for parachute jumps. Conscripts jumped out of Illusion helicopters or Antonov aircraft. Each of those elephants' backsides carried 400 soldiers. We had 65-kilogram packs that held a gun, bombs, ammunition, first aid kit, safety parachute and dry food. Us boys weighed less.

Russian parachute kits were half a century old. One day our

Soviet squad leaders roared at us to board the plane. I finished checking my kit. It was all right, but others were faulty. Boys fell to their deaths, bodies not found. At heights above 8,000 metres, Airborne recruits' parachutes lacked pressure and failed to open.

Often only 13 or 14, boys needed the most knowledgeable dispatchers to tell them when to jump. However, Russian dispatchers did not know African conditions. It was impossible to teach them because they were aggressive. None comprehended the factors involved in jumping safely. We needed the right combination of height, gravity, individual body-weight plus gear, air speed and cloud cover. The Soviets also did not communicate with pilots.

Under-skilled dispatchers forced kids to make jumps 5,000–7,000 metres above ground. They booted them out. 'Jump, jump now!' Little hurricanes caught parachutes or boys pulled the cord too soon even though they counted the seconds properly. Gravity being weak, they stayed up there slowly rising and floating.

Dispatchers made us jump while the plane was manoeuvring, but I said, 'No, wait. You will hit the propellers or wing. And you must avoid the exhaust.' The Soviets did not try to understand our Amharic. Older commandos made a sport of spitting from the plane. It was minus 40 degrees Celsius. If anyone opened his mouth it would turn green. The boy would be dead in 30 minutes. Countless died this way. Russians said, 'Our soldiers are number one in the world.' They were top murderers.

I confronted a Russian colonel about the deaths caused by unqualified dispatchers. He court-martialled me. A Russian general said, 'This is a dangerous *Yehuda*. Shoot him in front of recruits.' Ethiopian General Demissie Bultu saved my life. He said, 'You would need to shoot me too.'

A Soviet major tried to make me jump with a broken parachute. I asked, 'Can we swap parachutes?' Baring his gold-filled front teeth, he said, ' *Yehuda*, do not confront me. I blame Hitler and that pussy Mussolini for not doing their jobs properly. Why did they not kill your mother?' Pulling aside a small table, he challenged me to an arm wrestle. I weighed 62 kilograms; he was 86 kilograms. I said, 'If you fight, I will fuck you here in your Antonov and kill you.'

Military police stripped both of us of our guns. The major put his beefy, sweaty forearm to mine. A colonel said to a pilot, 'If he kills this puny Jew, in Moscow they will make him colonel and in Leningrad they will celebrate.'

I challenged the bully three times, beating him at each go. Then I released my Airborne buckle and dropped my pants. 'I am not fucking you with this beautiful penis.'

'Stop,' said the colonel.

I said, 'I am fastening my trousers ready to throw this stinky pig off the aircraft.'

The colonel said, 'The game is over. Get back to your crew.' We arrived at Haile Selassie Airport, Asmara.

Two days later, I was court-martialled in Kagnew Station. They had a strong case against me: insulting comrades and Ethiopian-friendly Soviets. My imperialist disposition was a danger to the communist military. They would investigate my hidden knowledge.

The Airborne commander Colonel Gerume intervened. Removing his cap, he placed his high-rank officer's baton on top and said, 'Let me join this young man. Prosecute me as strongly as you do him.'

General Demissie and another Ethiopian general joined in. The latter said, 'I do not think you have one heart. Let us send you to a military hospital to check you out.' He added, 'I have never seen a young soldier so big hearted. From this court, I dismiss myself. If you kill this soldier, each one of you will die twice.' General Demissie freed me.

Afterward, the Soviets dubbed me The Pretty Evil for I was tall, thin and curly- haired. They told other Airborne, 'Keep well away from this human devil. He will poison you.' Ethiopian General Abera Abebe said, 'If anyone calls him that, we will court-martial you. You Soviets are sore losers.' Later, propellers cut two of my parachute ropes and I landed hard on my left hand. The injury has troubled me always.

We learned hand-to-hand combat. Russian trainers liked to slam boys. We got Ethiopian officers to teach us how to fall safely and protect ourselves.

An Arat Kilo neighbour carried her son to the lavatory. Before conscription he was a second-year mechanical engineering student. His life was ruined by a trainer who broke his back.

Military teachers were bullies from the GDR, Yugoslavia, Hungary and Russia. They did calls at dawn. If we lingered for longer than 30 seconds they yelled, 'Action!' and startled us with gunfire. We dressed and made our beds in seven minutes.

On the battlefield we would have to follow any order or be shot in front of the others. After jogs, we sat in a circle for psychological refreshment.

'If you are ordered to shoot the man sitting beside you, what are you going to do?'

'Shoot.'

'At the front you are free of religion. Do not think of God or family.'

Photos of mine were inside my helmet. They made me think that I must save myself and win battles. Despite our treatment every minute of the day, I was not a machine.

Trainers said, 'Your boots are designed to explode if you urinate. At the front save your pee for when all is lost, and the enemy is close. When you die, so will the five enemy soldiers who will have surrounded you. You will have saved yourself from arrest and terrible torture.'

There was a saying. 'Do not be too smart. It could cost you your life.'

I watched our commander dismantle, clean and reassemble a gun once and then did it. My bed was made too well. Voices of childhood ill-wishers returned: 'The blade will be sharpened so much that it will cut through the sheath and then cut you. Beware.'

The best survival skill was silence. In the military, each word or show of excitement or sadness betrayed you. Never say, 'I know.'

I gained high marks and was sworn in as a soldier. Biting the blade of a knife, I took the Ethiopian military oath to never betray my country, children, the elderly and humankind. I swore that I would never take advantage of the gun in my hands.

The military transferred me to the Derg military training base at the old airport. It was founded by Emperor Menelik II. Keeping it secret from the UK, Emperor Haile Selassie I made it into a military training centre for Air Force and Air Defence. The 22-square-kilometre site housed the Cuban Embassy.

I trained for the Ethiopian Airborne Special Force. Emperor Haile Selassie I had started it. Israelis called it Rangers. Russians tried to change the name to Red Fire Commandos. For over a year, we had intensive training 16 hours per day. Ethiopian rangers, Israeli Airborne commandos and Russians taught us.

Mum and our little sister came 21 kilometres by bus from Giyorgis in the city centre, then more on foot. They carried a lidded basket with food. My sister was thrilled to see me in uniform and Mum was proud that I was defending our country. She gave me a jacket into which she had sewn 50 *birr* wrapped in plastic.

One day our group was practising firing missiles at a range of 3,000 kilometres. Precise calculations were essential to avoid hitting water systems, schools and hospitals. The supervisor could not do this without a calculator. In real life his missile would have hit a hospital. I told him this in front of the other students.

He strode towards me. 'Say, "I'm stupid."'

'I am not.'

He called the military police. I handed in my rifle, first turning the butt toward them. They sent me before the Academic Court. Military trainers from Israel and Ethiopia said the instructor had made an error. They released me because I had not defied a battle order, but warned, 'You cannot show him up in front of the others.' To the instructor they said, 'You are stupid. He is not.'

To complete our training, we went to Eritrea. We were stationed at a fruit farm atop a mountain in Keren. From there we could be deployed anywhere. Training for all weathers, day and night, we descended from mountains and cliffs and into gorges – by parachute, rope or free-fall. This prepared us for missions impossible and prison breaks.

We earned the Airborne badge on our sleeve. It had the Star of David with a tiger in the centre and the *Mo Anbesa*. On our caps there was a black lion. Later, Erich Honecker sent GDR rangers. They replaced our badge with a red flag.

Dedessa Camp in Welega had 120,000 recruits from all over Ethiopia and beyond. At 5 a.m. youths dribbled on. They were oblivious to our wake-up calls, so we used the gunfire alarm on them.

The military then sent us all over Eritrea: Afabet, Tesseney, Agordat, Keren, Nagfa and Massawa Kagnew Station at Asmara. Each day we had suicide missions. For the riskiest, the military used educated Airborne youth. Survival rates were lower than 35 per cent.

We parachuted into the desert and broke sieges. If enemy had surrounded a mountain held by 3,000, we went in. During night jumps, we could not know if we were above the Red Sea, a dormant or smoking volcano, or cliffs. Enemy could be close to where we landed. We could not roll up our parachute, so carried two.

Airborne accompanied convoys. 12 Special Force members would be assigned to protect 35 munitions or food trucks. They were travelling between the Port of Assab and Asmara. It was impossible to see the end.

Eat well today, for you die any time. The words rimmed our Airborne silver dishes, tiger mascot in the centre. *Do not finish me. You might not get water for three days.* This circled our mugs, the open mouth of a lion forming handles.

We walked up and down cliffs, advancing ten steps per metre in sliding sand dunes.

'October 4th... So what? Weather? Payment?'

An Airborne soldier had napalm burns to 50 per cent of his body. We radioed, 'Airborne in trouble.' Post Command said, 'We are not sending a helicopter for one person.' I said, 'He is an Ethiopian soldier paying in blood and flesh.' The military took him by jeep eight kilometres to the next station for proper first aid and glucose. He died 27 minutes after arriving.

Derg made us line up for two hours for Lenin bravery awards. We discarded them, praying for quick deaths.

A bouncing 20 metre missile from Syria chopped away a quarter of a mountainside. In a few seconds, 100 men became 65 or 70. We loaded bodies like sacks onto Antonov planes to be dropped down cliffs and into gorges. No time for burial.

The soldier you shared a cigarette with 30 minutes earlier had half his body mortared off. Another burned with chemicals impossible to extinguish. He walked towards you, eyes melting, teeth exposed. The helicopter would take three days. He would be slow-dying like a cat. If there was a hand, you left your gun beside it. Or you fired at your friend and ran from the next bomb.

We emptied corpses' pockets: pay, wedding ring, watch, cross. In the Red Cross tent, we tagged belongings for Ground Force in Addis Ababa. It would take them to wives or parents. If the camp was attacked, we rescued the pile.

Not distinguishing us from the Eritrean liberation force Shabiya, Ethiopians might bomb us. Bunker digging missiles buried soldiers 20 metres deep. We filled water canteens and dried food packs. Then we blew up bulk water and food supplies and big guns, and ran.

11 metre missiles uprooted 10 metre trees, hurling them a kilometre. Birds, eggs and lizards perished. MIG25 fighters passed overhead in seconds, blasts sounding afterward. Eritrean soldiers returned to homes containing no life, a loved one's hand hundreds of metres away. Next morning, pus poured from eardrums.

When guns were silent, the young forgot. 'Do you have a girlfriend?'

'Why are you quiet, man? Thinking of mum? 'Do you have sisters, brothers?'

We caught an Arab, injecting him to weaken him. Only Airborne did that. He had napalm plus six coconut bombs, one machine gun and three military knives with poisoned blades. Those could not be used to slaughter game. If you ate the meat you died. Stabbed body parts had to be amputated.

A friend saw Shabiya rebels attack Eritrean civilians in a chicken and banana market. It used napalm. Syrian TV recorded it as being carried out by Ethiopians.

Syrian and Iraqi napalm attacked us. Waving, bouncing fire like a volcanic eruption held tens of thousands of small balls. They blinded and lodged everywhere in the body. Gas stopped thinking, worse than being drunk. Victims could not even remember to roll.

Each morning I kissed the Omega wristwatch. I carried the *Golgota* miniature book and remained whole. Until one day a napalm attack surprised us.

In Addis Ababa, a boy had been conscripted on his way home from school. He had six months training and went to the war front. He barely knew not to touch freshly dug soil or a flower, nor pick up a cigarette from the ground. They were landmine traps, enhanced with napalm.

The boy's back was on fire. I ran, lowered him to the ground and covered his burns with sand to extinguish the flames. His backpack contained inflammable supplies. I removed that and threw it far.

While I was calling the helicopter, blood seeped down my leg. I had sprung away from the fire, yet exploding napalm balls had hit me. 0.25-centimetre fragments lodged in my thigh, under an armpit, and over my heart. Russian field doctors did not remove them. Later, Mum used fat and antibiotic herbs, but they remain in me to this day.

Medicos saved the boy's life, though he would walk with a stiff back. His mother changed his name to Mesfin.

At Afabet near Keren, we had a Russian squad leader. His mouth was full of gold fillings. He had bad breath, a bottle of vodka and no sense of humour. Stinky Breath ordered us to our deaths: 'Cross that field.'

The area would be mined with two-tonne bombs intended for tanks, as well as 200-gram 'pen' bombs, which blasted humans. Not one body part could be collected.

I argued military science: 'We did not set this minefield. We do not have the data to cross safely.'

Stinky Breath turned purple in the face. '*Nyet, nyet!* I will have you put in prison for a week and court-martialled for insurrection.' He called the Ethiopian major. I told him about our forced-suicide mission. The major called the Ethiopian general, who came and kissed my forehead for having saved the squadron.

If Soviets killed people—subordinate or civilian—their punishment would be going to the war zone, nothing more. However, we boys could not surrender. White handkerchiefs meant the firing squad.

One of our squadron, Yared, stopped with his foot over a landmine. I called to him, 'Do not lift your foot!' It would have raised the bomb's pin. Yared froze, exposed to the enemy. We slithered towards him on our chests and scooped soil from around the mine. The pin lowered. Yared back-flipped.

We all rolled and crawled far away because landmines explode in a mushroom shape. Then we shot the mine. For a while Yared could not bear the word 'bomb'.

At the next village, Eritrean mothers came out. They brought water and food. We could have killed their sons, but they treated us like their own.

When boys surrendered, we took their guns and then gave them water. One of us would share smoked beef. Somebody else would give a cigarette. We stayed around them for surrender was mortifying. Patriots had never raised their hands for traitors. If we could get our captives to smile, they would make it.

One week, Airborne was stationed at Massawa on the Red Sea coast. It had been quiet. Troops were doing laundry or playing volleyball. I rested in the heat reading a magazine, Uzi and AK-47 on either side. Then our helicopter exploded, firing missiles that would land anywhere. It was a Shabiya suicide mission. Shooting lasted 20 minutes.

In his office, the colonel was on the floor firing his pistol. A bazooka had almost severed his leg above the knee. Shaking, a corporal said, 'End his pain. Shoot him.' The colonel quietly covered his face. 'No,' I said. 'He will survive. His upper body is fine.'

The colonel removed his cap and took out his knife. With one stroke he cut through the rest of his leg. He said, 'Bring powder,' referring to first aid. I radioed the navy to transport him to Asmara Hospital.

Those who survive military service never know peace. Twenty years later I would be in Geneva for a UN meeting. Journalists barraged me. 'Have you seen children die in front of you?' 'How did you survive?' 'How many prisoners did you take for the socialist army?' 'How many people have you killed?' Impossible to reply; I felt like an empty shell. Not one asked, 'How did this happen?', or 'Why?', or 'How many died?'

Lucy's People

The luckiest conscripts returned home with deformities. They were missing an eye or two, or an arm, or one or both legs. The next most fortunate came home in a box. The unlucky never returned home – families only received a message.

Senior communist military killed many. Being maimed in battle in the wrong way was a crime. During conscription, the military recorded dates of birth and whether a boy was left- or right-handed. If a left-hander lost his right during battle, Derg officers claimed that he had shot off his own hand to get out of military service.

Any youth who developed a stutter as a result of trauma was also in danger, as the Derg thought the condition could and would be faked. After hand-to-hand combat, a soldier was a faker unless he had lost both legs, half a face or both eyes. Those with slight injuries our leaders charged.

'He injured himself so as to be discharged from the army.' They assembled troops of so-called fakers.

'Today we have 110 who have been faking it. They come with doctors' and nurses' letters.'

There would be three rows of machine gunners, 12 in each. Those in front crouched, men behind them knelt, and the back row stood. Youths on crutches or limping, perhaps with bullets lodged in their backs, would be lined up.

A nurse would remove the first doomed youth's black blindfold. A three-star officer read out his name and place of birth. And with that, his trial was over. Gunners carried out the sentence in front of all. Most of those boys were too young to shave.

Wounded Ethiopian generals also had harsh treatment compared to others. One served for ten years all over Eritrea, was wounded twice, and admitted to Massawa naval hospital. He was discharged rapidly and sent to the front. No soldier had sufficient recovery time in hospital before returning to battle.[2]

Boys were often shot while attaching new ammunition magazines to their weapons. I taped together ammunition magazines so as not to interrupt gun fire. Troops copied this and it saved lives. The general called me 'son'.

Each AK-47 magazine had 360 bullets. With an oil-based permanent marker I wrote on all of them, 'Forgive me.' If a bullet wounded a soldier and was removed, he would get it in a jar. He would read the message from another youth who also did not want to fight.

A Russian general pulled his Makarov to menace me. I stood at attention with chest puffed out.

'Are you Jesus Christ?'

'No. I am not, sir.'

'Why are you acting like Jesus Christ?'

'I am not, sir.'

'Then why are you writing, "Sorry" on bullets? Are you a priest or a soldier?'

'A soldier, sir.'

'Act like one.'

'Yessir.'

'Can't hear you.'

'Yes, sir!'

They humiliated you to take your best part from you.

Military police beat me. The Russians put me underground in a black hole for seven days and nobody talked to me. One cup of porridge twice a day was all I got. Then I cleaned the camp for ten days.

After re-education came counselling. 'Do not feel sorry for killing. Never think smart.'

Five high-level generals, a psychologist and a doctor court-martialled me.

The psychologist said, 'He is advanced.'

A general said, 'He will make the others cowardly. A bad influence.'

It was GDR and Soviet in style, crazier than any English military court. Three judges determined that I had to go so as not to pollute other youth who might think for themselves.

'You will be dropped from a helicopter into crossfire in a war zone.'

The commander tied my hands tightly behind my back. This was for show as I left the court. The general who called me 'son' had intervened. 'Touch that boy and I will shoot every Russian here.' He had me unbound.

The military re-deployed me to Hadar in the lower Awash River Valley. I dropped from a helicopter into the desert with little food and no water. This was Lucy's birthplace. In 1982 the whole area was devoid of rivers and waterways.

The military training camp Keloma was top-secret. The largest in Africa, it was the size of Djibouti. Fenced in, its perimeter was mined and planted with napalm tripping devices. The area had Border Security Forces and guerrilla fighters. We might have to shoot, but also beware of hitting one of our own soldiers.

I was in a small group. Training was both a demotion and way of terrorising us. The Derg was creating human killing machines by preparing special forces in this desolate environment. The West would later pay the TPLF to dismantle the camp.

Being dropped off in the afternoon helped. At night, the survival rate was 5 per cent: the whole area was land-mined. Men could be blown up while relieving themselves.

'Do not touch freshly dug soil, pick up a cigarette from the ground or scoop up what looks like fresh fruit. Boom!'

During the parachute fall, my group had kept together. We could not have survived alone if separated from the others. Used to war front service, we got through three days without food and water. In the heat we suffered extreme thirst.

We ate oily ants, tasty snake with skin that peeled off like a pullover, scorpions—avoiding their poisonous carapaces and tiny livers—and rats when we could catch them. Lizards had feet that looked like human hands and felt like that in the throat. Boys vomited them up rather than swallow them. The meat was too lean, but they were our main food when we could not catch snakes.

Ethiopians were accustomed to fasting. Children born into my religion participated in short fasts from when they first could speak. A physician examined us beforehand to rule out any illness. We went hours without food and drink. There were also religious restrictions: no meat, egg or dairy products for 42 days during the lead-up to Easter. Orthodox Christian fasted for 55 days. All religions had their own way.

Our ability to endure hunger undid invaders. Smoke from cooking fires brought killers. Early in the sixteenth century, Grañ Ahmed's jihad lasted decades. Ethiopians ate *shola*. The fruit required no cooking. A single tree sustained hundreds of people daily. When Turks came back with the English in the 1860s, they destroyed any tree.

During fasts, we did not gossip or swear at people or livestock. We did not prune plants, pick up valuables from the ground, borrow money or attend court. Restraint helped us remain mentally present during the desert ordeal.

We did further survival training. From a cut branch we hung an empty bottle. In the morning it was full of distilled water.

The Soviet Union supplied canned food that caused kidney problems. Boys said, 'I am urinating gravel.' The army tested the food and found it to be high in chemicals.

On Ethiopian travelling soldier food, we had no swollen feet and ankles, nor sore, red eyes. We ate roasted corn, with vinegar and garlic as preservative. Our dried food was smoked beef with lemon and chilli and high-quality fat. It gave us stamina during 20-kilometre marches with packs. Chilli and salt treated wounds.

Nearby was Africa's largest post-command base: Kagnew Station at Asmara. In 1974, the Derg took it over from the US. It had a 12,000-bed hospital and nuclear bomb shelters for people and wildlife including spiders.

Training over, my regiment waited at a base. Officers gave us 20 minutes' notice. 'Pack your stuff and get in the helicopter.' Our regiment was headed for helicopter pilot training in Moscow or Siberia. But the military kept me back to continue my military science education.

---

1. Kasaye Chemeda, Yeto Meda, 124
2. Kasaye Chemeda, Yeto Meda, 185

Chapter 15
Enough

The military sent me to Debre Zait in the Rift Valley. At the Air Force base, I began training as an anti-hijacker. This involved being prepared to kill a terrorist trying to take over a plane. They could be anybody. Anti-hijackers might even fight with their bare hands.

Teachers took apart various types of weapons, and I reassembled them. After three weeks I entered the advanced course. At the end, I was promoted to lieutenant. I wore a red Airborne Force cap on the right side, tiger and wing at forehead, and red star on my left shoulder.

I worked in the weapons workshop. It had an ocean of armaments, many imported from the European Eastern bloc. My job was to select weapons suitable for use by us anti-hijackers. I adapted them by altering barrel lengths and angles. If anti-hijackers had to fire a gun inside an aircraft, the plane needed to be left intact. I calculated the capacity of guns, including range. Component sizes determined this. Without this skill an anti-hijacker could fire no weapon.

I trained officers in assessing firearms. Many were older with higher ranks. Some did not have mathematical skill. Unable to calculate firearm capacities, they did not progress through courses. My mathematic ability, youth and seniority brought enemies in my regiment. One afternoon, colleagues left early, overdoing their farewell. The workshop perimeter was mined, prematurely armed. I cut the power line and slipped away.

A superior castigated me for this. If I had been blown up, the workshop would also have been obliterated. He did not investigate the men's action. They pretended to have been unaware that I was left behind in the workshop.

That same year, I was about to get into a military vehicle when a soldier saluted too formally and opened the front door for me. None of the other passengers moved to get in. Even the driver remained standing outside and looked ready to run.

I said, 'I will get in when the driver does.' One soldier's thumb was on the button of a small device, a detonator. I pulled my gun on him and called the military police. The group had placed a coconut grenade under the front passenger seat where higher ranked officers sit. They had pulled its ring lock.

The general who had saved me during the court martial in Eritrea was meant to be in charge, but he was on leave at a monastery. He was being treated for injuries after having fallen out of a helicopter. Fully recovered, he took up his appointment as commander of the regiment at Debre Zait.

Within a year I would have become Operations Leader and Weapons Expert. However, attempts on my life would have continued. Citing mental strain, the general had military doctors admit me to the Ministry of Defence Hospital in Addis Ababa. Human interaction consisted of basic orders. 'Sit down. Stand up!' After a few weeks, doctors discharged me, and I returned to Airborne service.

The general became desperate at the slaughter of very young conscripts on both sides. Twenty years later he killed himself in Eritrea after wrapping himself in the Ethiopian flag.

When Airborne boarded Antonov aircraft for missions, a song of forgiveness by Tilahun played.[1] One day it moved our dispatcher Abibew so much that he bit into his field jacket coconut grenade. Within an hour we were in the line of fire. Fewer than one in 10 would survive body intact.

Monastic physicians accompanied squadrons. Traditionally they went with armies to war. By law there had to be one monastic physician per 25 soldiers. In 1980 this was not possible. Our armed forces were numerous, and monasteries had been destroyed and holy ones killed.

The physicians used bamboo surgical instruments. Since Saba's reign around 1000 BC, humans and animals received advanced medical treatment with bamboo instruments. These included injections and intravenous supplements to boost immunity.

Before a severed limb would be discarded, physicians would say, 'Do not throw it away!' They stitched it back on, toes or fingers twitching before they had quite done. Using poultice leaf, they sucked out bullets, wounded soldiers' faces relaxing and brightening. They returned intestines to their proper place.

Some compromised Airborne safety. Younger ones prayed outside or did astronomical observations. Soldiers stopped them. 'Go back to the bunker.'

They protested: 'That star will come out at 2.30 a.m. It is only seen once every two years.'

Without firing guns, Airborne warded off attacks by wild animals. If we gave into the star counter, enemy would detect us and calculate our location. The mountain that we held would be blasted out of existence for one little star.

It was impossible to tell the rank of physicians. Who was nurse and who was head surgeon? They said, 'With love you have the power to heal in your hands. Never think that you are better than someone else.'

In remote Ethiopian areas, humans and animals got injured. Thanks to herbal medicine, they did not suffer amputations and gangrene. One herb grew best at a latitude of 10 degrees north at the back of a Gojjam monastery or underneath it. It had adhesive bactericidal sap that maintained skin cells so that wounds did not need stitches. It healed gashes inflicted in battle.

Monastic physicians had pioneered non-surgical bullet removal. Lay field nurses gained skills from working with them. Combining animal fat, healing plant roots and leaves, they saved many lives at battlefronts.

In the late nineteenth century, Emperor Menelik II's field nurses used the technique. The traditional healer Azaylech Qibirinu went to the Battle of Adwa 1896. Large lead bullets lodged anywhere in a limb or body part. There was no imaging to locate them. Azaylech combined animal fat with herbal antibiotics and poultice leaf. She coated whole body parts with this and bound them. Bullets pressed themselves out. It saved tens of thousands.

The Derg took my classmate Tagegn, dressed in school uniform, from the street. He trained at Asmara for six months, 1,000 kilometres from Addis Ababa. At the front he received a bullet wound in his leg.

His mother and mine wrested him from Soviet doctors. They sent him to Debre Libanos Monastery, its Rift Valley sky a lid of calm above blunt cliffs. Monks removed the bullet non-surgically.

Sent back to the front, Tagegn was hit in the torso by a bullet that spun into his back. I took him back to Debre Libanos. Monks said to leave it. He stayed there for three months.

Later, he became disturbed by the sight of worse-off youth, many of them amputees. Moving to the West he became unstable and died.

The 1984 census reported 40,000 soldier amputees, most under 25. Disabled persons received 85 *birr* per month. This barely funded a poor diet. There was no compensation for war injuries.

Wounded soldiers without monastic physicians were treated callously. Russian field doctors refused to remove fragments of exploded shrapnel or bullets. If these lodged in an ankle, hand or finger they amputated at the knee or elbow: quicker.

Conscripted farmers—and militia not part of the regular army—received no pension if they suffered amputations. They gave thanks if they received a flesh wound because they would be able to work in the fields. Many wounded farmers awoke from anaesthetics asking, 'Where are my legs?' They then used their revolver in blessed suicide.

In Arat Kilo, our neighbour Biruk was 15 when he did not appear at soccer training. Three months later he returned from war minus an arm and leg. He sang drunken soccer match songs in the street after starting on garlic liqueur at 7 a.m. Four or five brave city police would bash him. When he was 19, he hanged himself in his family's outdoor kitchen. Biruk was not counted as a casualty of war.

Another soccer team-mate returned from Eritrea with an empty eye socket and a missing arm. He cheered at our matches. Grit would blow into his socket and I would remove it. A boy with stumps for legs clapped loudly when we scored goals. Doctors had given him useless artificial limbs. He removed them and hurled them away. War veterans were not allowed to criticise the military.

Mothers wore black for the rest of their lives. The Ethiopian People's Revolutionary Party pretended to support them. It encouraged women to protest against the waste of young lives but did not warn them of the danger. Women gathered in Addis Ababa for a peaceful demonstration: Crying Day of Mothers. A few were armed with wooden spoons.

A friend's mother was a professional mourner at funerals. She led the women in song. The Derg gunned her down first because she was out front. Then they murdered the other women in front of village children.

My final mission impossible was at Algena in Eritrea. Usually 45 degrees Celsius, it was always above 40. It had not rained in 23 years. Displaced Eritrean children died of thirst in that desert. Airborne special forces dropped supplies from helicopters, then jumped down with military-canvas containers of water.

Now we were to break a siege. Twelve thousand Ethiopian soldiers from Nebelebal or 'Flame' Battalion were stranded at Algena. Ground Force generals had sent them to the wrong place and betrayed them to Shabiya, the Eritrean Liberation Front and the TPLF. They sold the details of the battalion's destination and arrival time.

The generals had done the same to three other battalions, and rebel groups wiped them out. Each day, they accepted bribes and informed on our forces: 'One thousand are here at...' 'They carry the following types of weapons...' Mengistu had accelerated the unqualified generals' promotions.

The battalion had been trapped in the desert with no food and water for three weeks. Their lieutenant colonels had repeatedly called for help. None came. Enemy encircled our soldiers and closed in. Both sides almost intermingled. Air Force could not drop a bomb to enable the battalion to break away.

The military was dropping 300 Airborne special forces into the middle. Our mission was to open an escape corridor for the battalion. How could 300 save thousands? Only 35 Airborne were highly skilled.

We jumped at 11.21 p.m. Beforehand, we made the ends of our guns spark like a candle offering. At first light the ground was too hot to walk on even in shoes. It took one minute to cross three metres. We were fighting the land and sun.

Trapped Ground Force soldiers were either very young or over 50. Most had trained for only six months, with inadequate shooting practice. I had been in the lockup for refusing to train recruits with only 30 practice bullets allocated to each.

These stranded boys would have been unprepared for the front. They approached me for water and food. One said, 'Sir, when you go home, please tell the rest of my Year 9 class that I will come back when I am discharged.'

Some walked towards the enemy hands-up. A shower of bullets cut them down. The nervy quickly finished their limited ammunition. Older soldiers with guerrilla fighting and hand-to-hand combat skills had shot themselves in front of their soldiers. They had served for 45 years. Their line officers did the same. Of 12,000 deployed, fewer than 10,000 were left.

For nine days we waited with the parched and starved at Algena. No supplies came. Old soldiers wanted to shoot the weak, but Airborne distributed them among the 300. We divided the battalion into three sections, ready to lead soldiers out. I sang and this boosted morale. More joined my group. We did not kill a single Ethiopian soldier.

Rations protruded from the pocket of a dead boy: Hungarian biscuits. Corpses clutched something – a photo of an older couple, or a letter, or a neck chain. The Year 9 boy had been shot in the head. Perhaps only 5,000 Ground Force were still alive.

On the rebels' side were corpses of Syrians and Iraqis who had come to kill us.

One afternoon the sky opened like a tap. By 8 p.m. we were waist-high in water, and rebels had to run from the flood. Exchange of fire ceased. We could cross the sand. The Air Force flew four MIG29 jets in a sky dance as a diversion. We signalled Ground Force.

'Break and run! Follow us.'

Airborne opened a gate through retreating rebels. Soldiers ran through the break in the circle two or three at a time. Our smoke bombs confused the enemy. When the gas changed from black to yellow it could not be inhaled. Those awaiting their turn held their breath. They needed to pass through within 30 seconds. Our superior was there for more than 45, getting weak soldiers out.

Five thousand trapped Ground Force escaped. We headed for a small mountain. From there we kept the enemy down until we could radio the Air Force. Four jets bombed the rebels for six hours. The midnight sky was lit up the whole time like midday.

After the jets stopped flying, we waited two hours before walking. Until then, we were at risk from our own side. Sparta para-commandos came later, but Airborne had done the work.

The Airborne signal operator cleared the way to Asmara. For three days we walked. Now we had 4,000 Ground Force. Of the 300 Airborne who had jumped, 32 were left. 300 men had rescued 4,000.

We met a broad-shouldered army god, built like a tree. General Demissie was Commander of the Second Revolutionary Army in Asmara. Saluting me, he asked for our radio operator, whom we had under heavy guard. He submitted transcripts of top-secret reports. General Demissie's handshake was firm. It made you look into his eyes. He called me 'son'. During a UN Peacekeeper round in North Korea he had served with my father.

He loaded our group of five Airborne into his jeep. At headquarters a major interviewed us and gave us our first swig of Melotti beer, an Eritrean household name. Then our superior lurched onto my shoulder, bleeding from the nostrils. General Demissie called an ambulance to take him to Asmara Hospital.

He examined us. Through him I felt the touch of my late father. Like my eye father, he slept in a military tent. With us he ate smoked beef and drank water – no champagne spa with peers. He gave half a flask of honey wine to soldiers. All silence, he clutched his own. It broke.

Our Airborne superior died after five days. Toxic gas from the smoke bomb had affected his brain. The general gave us a three-day holiday in Massawa at the Haile Selassie Palace.

General Demissie recommended us for promotion. He nominated us as war heroes to be awarded the Star of Bravery medal by the Ministry of Defence. He paid us all three months' advance salary. We were to report to the Air Force base in Debre Zait before going home.

At Asmara Airport, General Demissie asked the eldest in our group his age.

'Twenty-six.'

'I have been at war for thirty-three years. Do you want to pass on misery to your children? What do you harvest from war?'

He stepped closer. 'Mesfine, I checked your file before you came to Alfabet. Do not die here to be fed to the sand. Explain your academic achievements.'

I looked down. 'Look at me.' Tears rolled down his cheek and off his chin. 'If you stay, your friends will die. It will affect you for the rest of your life.'

The four of us were to go straight home and lay low for three months. 'Do not report to base. After three months you will be counted as dead. Please disappear.'

He released us from military service, from facing death and witnessing horror daily.

During my unofficial leave in Addis Ababa, a member of Airborne Special Force came with a telegram. Mum asked, 'What has happened to my son?' I was safe inside the house. Our group of four had each been awarded a posthumous bravery medal. Meeting for the last time, we bit knife blades together and swore to keep the secret of our disappearance from the military.

After the Derg fell, I told Mum about General Demissie's initiative. In stillness she listened. Whenever I paused, her audible intake of breath said, 'Go on. I hear you.' Afterward, her hands shook.

A survivor at 19. I had written on my jeans, 'Let me walk. These legs are mine. I was born free. Do not chain me.' Dr B'hata, 1979.

The Derg then imprisoned me. After my release, Security picked me up while I was walking in the street. They took me to the Air Force base.

A 17-year-old said, 'I don't want to fight for Mengistu and the communists.' His odour betrayed his lack of motivation to control his bladder and bowels. They shot him.

The communists pulled the mentally ill from the streets to serve on the front lines. Mengistu did not regard them as unfit. 'There is no mental illness in socialism and communism.' Even if his Red Terror and Red Star Action had brought about their conditions.

Only monasteries could help. One man ate dirt and banged his face against anything. His father had disappeared in Eritrea. Monks healed him, and he regained his habitual grace and returned to work.

The Derg leader alleged that priests and monks were using gimmicks to attract more followers. He said, 'Let us close monasteries.'

During this fresh conscription, the communists held youths on the tarmac for three days and nights unsheltered, unfed and without water. They were going to fly us directly to combat in Eritrean Asmara. I recognised an officer from my military service and asked him to phone my sister's husband. The colonel strode onto the tarmac and extricated me. I fell asleep in the jeep on the way home.

Gash Tesfahun sickened at the horror: Somali wars, two Red Terrors, and constant war with Eritrea. He collected me in his military jeep. We stopped by the river.

Both of his sons had fled the Red Terror to serve at the Eritrean front. The younger achieved the rank of major and the US wanted him. He disappeared. His older brother Lieutenant Colonel Minkir was with Airborne.

In May 1990 he too would vanish, taking off with 16 others from Asmara in a Soviet-made Ethiopian helicopter. Gash Tesfahun would never learn his fate.

I read later that Major General Hussein led that escape. The helicopter was meant for domestic warfare and had no navigation equipment. They flew for five hours. Over the Red Sea, the major general ordered the men to destroy their ID and war documents. They discarded it all into the water but held onto military gear.

Above land, the fuel gauge showed empty. Major General Hussein told the pilot to put down. It was 5 a.m. with no traffic. They landed on a tarmac road. Were they in Yemen?

A truck stopped. The driver asked, 'Are you really human? Can I touch the helicopter?'

'Can you tell us what country we are in?'

'Saudi Arabia – Jizan. Where did you come from?' 'East Africa.'

'How did you cross from there?'

'Can you put us in touch with a military base?'

Senior Saudi military came with a bus. Courteous, they did not disarm the Ethiopians. For three days they gave them food, accommodation and helpers. They took them to get civilian clothes. To the major general these were uncomfortable. The lifelong soldier had given 12 years of continuous war service in Eritrea and northern Ethiopia. He did not know anything except military uniform.

The Saudi military invited them to go the city, where they sought asylum. Only then did they hand over their weapons. 'These are not our personal property. They need to go back to Ethiopia, along with the helicopter.' Officials agreed. They registered every item, including small knives and handguns.

Saudis had the latest US surveillance equipment. It had not detected the helicopter when it crossed the border. The West wanted the craft as well as the Ethiopians: 'You cannot keep these war criminals. They are dangerous to Saudi Arabia and might start a coup.' The Saudis said, 'These people are conventional military, not mercenaries.'

Some soldiers took their own lives rather than risk detention by the West. They had been in the military for 17 years and were finished with war.

The Saudis retained the Ethiopians, guarded them closely for their protection, and treated them humanely. For three or more years the men played chess and cards. The restless then returned to Ethiopia where the TPLF imprisoned them in the worst places.[2]

In 1989 there was a ceasefire with Eritrea. Senior Ethiopian military were fed up with 20 years of family warfare. Borders made by the UK and Italy had split up families. People had to fight on the wrong side. One general said, 'I murdered both of my sons.'

In Asmara, General Demissie said, 'Enough. I will not witness all young Ethiopians and Eritreans being wiped off the face of the earth. I was born a soldier, but war is not the solution.'

Twenty-six generals refused to continue fighting. Mengistu was on his way home after meeting with Honecker in the GDR. However, the Ethiopian dissenters did not attack his aeroplane because innocent crew would have died.

And so Mengistu murdered them all. Among the first was General Demissie, saviour of boys.[3] Television showed his severed head attached to the front bumper of a Soviet *kraz* jeep. His body was attached to the tow bar and driven all around Asmara. After vomiting, I hid in my bedroom for two days, alive thanks to that angel.

Air Force chief of staff General Amha shot himself in the Ministry of Defence office in Addis Ababa, wrapped in the Ethiopian flag. A major during the 1975 Somali invasion, General Amha had bombed the port of Berbera and disabled a Turkish ship with an old F5 jet.

In the palace prison, the Derg murdered another veteran of that war, General Fanta.

African leaders who supported Ethiopia intervened. 'We cannot watch these children dying.' Emperor Haile Selassie I had helped their predecessors. They initiated UN peace talks in Algeria which were successful. Both sides agreed that Eritrea would have self-government. Opposing rebel groups from Ethiopia and Eritrea were in accord.

The West undid this. It insisted on talks in London. Foreigners told Eritrea that communism was finished. Keep fighting and strive for separation. Shabiya split into two factions and the ceasefire was over. Two million Eritreans fled, many settling in Scandinavia. The West told the TPLF to take Ethiopia.

The unemployed joined Shabiya, and its leaders had limited

military expertise. However, rebel groups had skilled anti-Ethiopian foreign advisors. Egypt, Sudan, Syria, Iran, Iraq, Saudi Arabia, Bahrain, Qatar, Oman and the United Arab Emirates budgeted their support of rebels. They provided offices, land, logistics, military science training, medical expertise and weapons including napalm bombs.

The West knew about this unconventional warfare. Iraqi and Iranian conflicts and Yugoslav wars used napalm. Brezhnev and Reagan signed a deal not to produce it. Later, it was banned by more than one hundred nations.

Eritrea and Ethiopia had been one, brothers at peace for thousands of years. After Adwa 1896, Italy, France and the UK designed their separation. Sixty years later, war began.

In 1991 alone, 70,000 Ethiopians and Eritreans would die in renewed fighting.[4] Of 350,000 Ethiopians returning from the front, one-third were badly injured or disabled.

Assab Port would go to Eritrea. Ethiopia became landlocked. In 1994, TPLF and Shabiya would destroy Africa's only refinery at Assab. They would paralyse the Red Sea boat building industry, once ours. Eritrea, followed by the TPLF, would imprison our bright naval officers for two decades.[5]

The Derg had committed atrocities against Tigrayan people of the north. It suspected them of supporting insurgents, including TPLF. The TPLF then bombed Tigrayans—their own people—and blamed the Derg. This tricked foreigners. They backed the TPLF, and it increased in strength. The West and Middle East would support the TPLF as it dismantled Ethiopia.

A non-government organisation could work against its host government.[6] Some supplied guns, medicine and food to rebels. In the 1980s, two Australians went to Ethiopia. Officially they worked for a humanitarian organisation, but the couple ran guns for the TPLF. They bought them from Egypt and Turkey.

When Eritrea separated from Ethiopia, the TPLF made them consulates in Australia. For 20 years, they did business with Ethiopia paying for a premium rental. There they sold contraband gold, handmade traditional clothing and six varieties of coffee. In 2005 the Melbourne diaspora community protested at the gift to mercenaries. Australian Immigration punished them by blocking applications to bring children and spouses.

An Eritrean friend said, 'My brother was conscripted. The military made him work in a mine for less than 1 US dollar per hour.' The Australian mining company was paying workers' wages to the government. Eritrean diaspora appealed to the company to pay workers directly. It refused.

In 1997, the Eritrean leader refused to host a US base and Middle East military presence. The West imposed sanctions on food, fuel and medicine. This led youth to flee Eritrea to drown in the Mediterranean. Arabs harvested the body parts of those that took a different route. By 2018, four hundred thousand Eritrean youth had died.

Sanctions remained even after the Ethiopian prime minister was awarded the 2019 Nobel Peace Prize for helping end border conflict with Eritrea.

---

1. Addis Regassa, "Mote Enkwan Cheken"
2. Hussein Ahmed, Rete and Honey, 159
3. Bahru Zewde, A History, 266
4. Ababa Welde-Tensay, Asidenyaki, 109
5. Alemayehu, "World's Last People"
6. Mueni ma Wuiu, "Colonial and Postcolonial", 1326

Chapter 16
Khalid

My Design and Construction Engineering course had concluded in 1977 with practical assignments. The class built the Sebeta Meta Abo Birra factory, south of the city. I was team leader. Our group constructed the water treatment plant and dyke from scratch.

I had a travel allowance to go from there to Welliso 112 kilometres from Addis Ababa. It had a population of 70,000. My task was to maintain a well that the English had built in the 1940s. They had not installed gravel filtration, and so it was useless.

During World War II, fascists razed 2,000 Ethiopian religious centres, such as churches and monasteries. Those included traditional medical treatment centres. Rural women suffered. If something went wrong during childbirth, there were no local centres to help them. There were no passable roads to reach maternity hospitals elsewhere.

Wellisso locals told me about a group of young women in a mud hut. They were separate from the rest of the community. During protracted childbirth, the girls had been severely injured.

Urine and faeces ran out of their birth canals through holes called fistula.[1]

My boss at Sebeta gave me permission to help them. Driver Alemayehu and I put the women in a van and took them to the Addis Ababa Fistula Hospital for treatment.

Twenty years later I revisited Welliso. Locals said that once a year for three years cured women asked about me. On their way to a local monastery they asked, 'Is he dead or alive? Do we light a candle for him?'

Building College had also sent me on work experience to Hararghe in the east. I worked as a construction engineer on a food project for which there was an allowance. With that I bought a contraband Seiko 5 watch.

During our final exams at Building College, students held a strike against the government. Derg forces moved onto the campus, arresting all youth including cleaners and canteen workers. They did not distinguish serious students from strike organisers.

The Derg took us to a remote army base to torture us. Ringleaders were to go before a firing squad. One of them was named Mesfin, but he was absent from college that day. The militia put me with the condemned group.

The firing squad captain was aware of the swap. He sidled up to me. 'I know you have been wrongfully arrested and that you are not the Mesfin we seek.'

I kept silent.

The captain said, 'If you give me the Seiko 5, I will free you on the quiet.'

Minus my wristwatch, I disappeared at the first signal from him and sought refuge with local Oromo. Did they know Tulu's people? They never betrayed my existence to any outsider. Silence is not dumb.

Two Americans, a brother and sister, lived with them. At ages six and four, they had become lost in forest outside the city. Peasants rescued them, and farmers took them in. They eventually adopted them, dunking them in milk and anointing them with butter. The children lost their English language, made fuel from cow dung, and learned farming. Both married within the community.

When the brother was nearly 21, he visited a community member in hospital in Addis Ababa. Police asked whether he had a sister like him. He replied, 'Yes,' thinking of his adoptive parents' biological child. He and his sister identified as Oromo and their people had never told them they were different.

The police reunited them with their birth parents. The girl visited them in the US, but both chose to stay with the Oromo.

Three months after my escape, I returned to the city. After my military service, Building College lecturers urged me to apply for a UN Development Programme scholarship to study at Cairo University in Egypt. Mum sold an heirloom to fund the application fee of 50 US dollars.

The application form was a book. I had to battle with representatives at the embassy for my application to be accepted. Through power of veto in the UN, the UK prime minister blocked applications from Ethiopians. In 1984, I was the only scholarship recipient from the whole of Building College. There were numerous outstanding applicants.

Twenty-eight graduate engineers from all over Ethiopia won places to study at University of Cairo or Gamal Abdul Nasser. I enrolled in a Bachelor of Civil Engineering, Water Development.

Mesfin Tadesse & ianet Bastyan

Final year of Building College: Sebeta Meta Abo Brewery Construction Project team. Left to right: Adera, Me, Fikadu, Tadesse, Aworq, Kasahun, ?, Birhanu. Hinsihina Tibeb, 1977.

Lucy's People

I learned Arabic and took the Sunni name Khalid. In second year, an Egyptian classmate realised I was Ethiopian. *'Adon,'* he said. This meant slave in Arabic. He raised his voice. 'You murdered Christ.' 'Why don't you read history?' I said, 'You all would not exist without us. We built Egypt's water reservoirs.'

My friend asked why sought after texts on water development engineering were written by Ethiopians. In antiquity, our stonemasons built pyramids with water canals that cut through them.[2]

The university received UN funding for Ethiopian students, yet staff called us sons of devils. This hatred was 3,000 years old. An Austrian visited our land that extended to the Gulf of Aden. To Europeans this was Eden or heaven. He stayed at Lake Tana, source of the Blue Nile – in Ge'ez, Ghion River. Saba had him learn to read and write in a monastery. However, he killed an elephant and she deported him. The man moved to Egypt where he badmouthed the queen.[3]

University library staff controlled access to study materials. Waddling low to the ground, officers attended only to privileged students. I went before the student council ten times for copying passages from books. 'They are required reading and the UN pays for our places.'

One woman crushed me into the corridor wall. The next time, I backed up asking, 'Are you wearing a mattress on your back?' In the library stacks, she reached to a top shelf and passed wind. When she turned around, I pretended not to have noticed. Days went by and nobody joked about her. The following week she provided me with articles that she had withheld. She became kind and invited me to stay at her place, but I remained on campus. The others teased me about her.

Her boss liked to be called sir, and hated Emperor Tewodros II. 'Worse than Hitler. He built churches with swastikas at Lalibela.' He had the wrong Ethiopian king and was out by six centuries. It was King Lalibela who built the rock-hewn monasteries during the 13th century. Tewodros II lived during the 19th century.

The swastikas were *minga*. They were in the windows of Bete Mariyam monastery at Lalibela. *Minga* is an ancient Orthodox symbol of life that is energising.[4] In the 20th century, the German Third Reich took it as their symbol. While killing European Jews, Nazis wore uniforms featuring an ancient Jewish motif.

Another symbol was our three-pointed star. It symbolised Selassie or the holy trinity. Built in 1885, the Adwa 1896 monument in Arat Kilo featured it. The star would become the logo for a brand of luxury vehicle.

I sought a book about Emperor Tewodros II by Egyptian historian Professor Gamal Nour. Censors had changed its title to *The Fight Between Evil Eye Black Jews and the Children of Mahomed*. Off the shelf for 25 years, it described a pair of angel wings on our emperor's shield. In battle he wielded it as though divine forces were diverting bullets fired at him. The author criticised the cruelty of grabbing alcohol, meat and youthful girls from Egypt and India before going to war in Ethiopia. President Nasser imprisoned him for 21 years.

I topped First Year university. Students from 21 countries were enrolled in the course. The Assistant Dean of our engineering faculty made me take a second final exam with different questions. I sat it in his office with three invigilators. Water technology, Ethiopia and accomplishment were a suspicious combination. He said, 'This is the first time an Ethiopian has been dux.' It was a lie. We were thousands of years ahead. Before 1000 BC, Ethiopian engineers widened Lake Tana. We had trench-digging technology even then.

In 1000 BC or earlier, King Salamon (Solomon) of Israel wrote to Queen Makeda of Saba (Sheba). He said she created heavenly buildings and moving buildings on the sea: ships. Her Lake Tana people had woven garments, healing bread, clean water and stonemasonry. Salamon heard of her wisdom and skill through merchants and the birds. He begged her to visit him. Israel would not exploit her or her people.[5]

Saba sailed from Lake Tana to Jerusalem via Aden in Yemen. Her fleet carried advisors, meteorologists, astronomers and physicians, as well as 500 aids, 800 soldiers, 3,000 horses and 1,500 camels. She gave Salamon 3,000 gold bars from her mines at Adola in present-day Sidamo and Kaffa.[6]

Our engineer queen built a gyprock roof over Salamon's palace. Then she covered it with gold. It would last forever. Today it is El Aqs Mosque, featuring her people's mosaic work. This is in the blood of *Falasha*. Mum came from Qur Amba in Gojjam, Saba's homeland. With no training, I would earn my living by mosaics.

Babylonians described Saba as tall, thin, black and beautiful. Persians said that, when she smiled, she was like a shining black diamond. Salamon called her the Black Angel. They conceived Menelik I. Then Saba departed Jerusalem leaving behind 11,000: boat builders, stonemasons, mosaic craftsmen, gun-powder makers, and nuclear physicists.

At our Cairo campus, kitchen workers ordered us about. Ethiopian scholarship recipients unloaded pasta deliveries. Twice a year the minister of education from Norway visited its two scholarship students. That country valued its youth. One was a virtuoso pianist. The campus had a three-tiered piano on which she played classical pieces. I interrupted with improvised songs in Arabic or bursts of keyboard nonsense.

In class, the Egyptian student said, 'Arabic and Ge'ez both came from Sabaean.'

'Hebrew and Amharic too,' I said. 'Arabic and Hebrew go from right to left.' 'And Amharic and Ge'ez left to right.'

He said, 'I can read old Arabic books.'

'Same with Ge'ez and Amharic.' Our writing systems stabilised before Europe's.

He opened an English textbook. Roman alphabet 't' and Amharic *ta* were identical. W, U, H and O were copies of Ethiopian characters for different sounds.[7]

Our innovations benefited others. In 1868, General Napier captured 8,000 stonemasons from Abba near the Blue Nile River. En route to England, 5,000 of them stopped eating, threw themselves overboard or picked fights to the death with soldiers. The ship's captain refused to ever return to Ethiopia. 'The Abyssinians are a wonderful people, and it is a very hard thing to fight them.'

The surviving captives from Abba built St Thomas of Canterbury Church. Locals learnt new skills. A twentieth century Swedish pop group would adopt their name.

The Egyptian classmate raised his voice again. 'You get fifty US dollars a month. How do you spend it on the weekend?' I showed him the latest receipt for the 45 US dollars sent home. 'This will keep ten, maybe twenty, people alive.'

'That leaves you five dollars a month. How do you survive?' I had seen him getting into expensive cars at the end of the week. He could have no idea about us.

'We use our brains.' He became quiet. Egyptian middlemen stole our scholarship entitlements. For two years we did without stationery and pocket money. We washed our socks each night and did not go out for coffee. I sent most of my living allowance to Mum. Hard times continued, and she was without a husband. I tried to send extra.

On Saturdays, another Ethiopian student and I visited sites at Zamalek, Luxor or Alexandria. We spread a t-shirt on the ground and mimed playing the harmonica or saxophone. Tourists dropped coins onto it. My friend was shy, but I launched into

Arabic. Flocks of five or six tourists pulled us into the middle of their groups. We posed with them for photographs. They gave each of us 50 US dollars plus money for the 40-kilometre train ride home. Foreigners were thrilled to meet descendants of those who had built the pyramids.

Enslaved Ethiopians supplied water to Alexandria and Cairo, which helped ancient Egypt flourish in the desert. On the remains of edifices there were Sabaean characters such as the one pronounced like the English word toe. My people developed pyramids, had already built them at home from the time before Queen Saba. Useless to say that they were indeed the technology of our ancestors and that we were Ethiopian.

For tourists, Egypt was the epitome of ancient culture. One said, 'I can die happy. I have visited Egypt, the source of civilisation.'

In Egypt during the 1980s, historically rich areas were full of foreigners. These were the grounds of anthropologists, archaeologists, historians and zoologists. Academic elite blended with wastrels, such as a young Scot who failed his zoology course five times.

Criminals exploited African heritage. For centuries, they had smuggled antiques from Luxor. Nowadays they were White South African, Belgian, Swiss and Dutch. They sniffed around the workshops of anthropologists, archaeologists and zoologists. Then they made fools out of tourists, some mad with wealth.

A middle-aged English man boasted, 'This piece of brick came from a tunnel at Luxor. I sold my car to get it.'

Westerners bought hair from Jesus Christ. Tonnes of it were out there all around the world. Hawkers advertised other body relics. 'We have the skin of the donkey on which Jesus Christ rode... Cleopatra's left eyebrow. Get it here.' How would owning a relic make a person better? Would it change the world? Stop wars? Feed the starving?

One afternoon at Zamalek, my friend bought a bag of samosas for 1 US dollar. Cooked by enormous black-clad women, the pastries were meaty and rich in honey. A single one fuddled the brain. My friend would sell them back at campus.

A man spoke to me in Arabic. 'Would you like to earn 200 US dollars?' He gave me a five-star hotel address in Cairo, and a packet. 'Deliver this today and collect three thousand US dollars from two American tourists. Take that to your campus. We will meet you at the bus station.'

I hid the packet inside my shirt. Was it a bomb? No, too light for that. Then the man told me what it was.

In Cairo, I excused myself from samosa distribution. At the hotel, the couple feigned interest in me, the young international student. They were Catholics. I did not tell them my religion or nationality.

Small talk over, the woman ripped open the packet. 'Is this really Jesus's rib-bone?' she said. 'From which side?'

'The right,' I said.

'Can you get more relics?'

'An eyelash, and a finger bone.' 'Which one?'

I held up my index finger. They smiled. How many hundreds of thousands of Christ's fingers were owned by rich Westerners?

'Tell us where we can find you.'

I wrote down my address while they filled a plastic bag with gifts – an XXXL t-shirt and size 46 shoes that had walked to the pyramids and back.

On campus, I deducted my commission from their payment. Before I could offload the charitable donation, the Zamalek men appeared.

'Did you get our money?'

'Yes.'

'What's in the bag?'

'Ten pounds worth of goods for sa—' 'Five.'

'Eight.'

'Seven—'

'Done.'

I merged with a crowd of students.

'Wha-at? This is made for the Statue of Liberty.'

'These are travel bags.'

The letter from the Christian tourists had no salutation – only some choice words, followed by a message. 'That rib bone is not from a human.'

Near the end of our water development course, the Egyptian student said, 'Stay. Work here. We have a big house and you can live with us.' I thanked him but had to get back to family.

In 1986, a volcano erupted in the Afar region of Ethiopia's east. There were no casualties, yet the BBC reported that 10 million had been killed. Ethiopia's population was 40 million. One in four were purported to have died. Those abroad were frantic until they confirmed that loved ones were unharmed.

Later, the BBC would announce that Mengistu had died. Students ran joyously into the streets. The Derg caught them and killed them.

Of 28 scholarship recipients, three returned to Ethiopia. The others left before graduation, disappearing into the European Eastern bloc. Now a civil engineer, I worked in Ethiopia.

---

1. Hamlin and Little, Hospital, 249
2. Kebra Negast, 107
3. Ababa Welde-Tensay, Asidenyaki, 225
4. Kebelay Gedey, Lalibela, 48
5. Kebra Negast, 103-6
6. Ababa Welde-Tensay, Asidenyaki, 174
7. Scriptsource, "Ethiopic (Ge'ez)

Chapter 17

Western Influenced

I worked for both the Ministry of Construction and Ministry of Water, bouncing between them. My main boss was an engineer named Kassa. He built the 4.2 metre bronze Vladimir Lenin statue at the African Economic Commission. In the early sixties he was site engineer for the construction of Tikur Anbesa Hospital. Its name meant black lion.

Three thousand years ago, Orthodox astronomers predicted that the Rift Valley would rend during a solar eclipse in the 1980s. This happened. A gorge opened at Burre-Lekamt between Gojjam and Welega in Ethiopia's north-west. An earthworks and engineering group built a 300 metre suspension bridge across the gap. It used unique Ethiopian engineering technology. Gash Kassa sent me there.

One side of the gorge had medical and herbal experts; on the other were geniuses of cheese making. They gave me yoghurt to drink. After each draught they wiped milky residue from my small moustache.

I then supplied drinking water to the Gurage town of Welqite in Jimma. Between 68,000 and 74,000 locals had a single well at the Ethiopia Hotel. They travelled tens of kilometres, often by donkey.

Welqite heard that an engineer was coming. People expected a bald head on a belly atop a donkey. He would be accompanied by women, two for honey wine and smoked meat, one holding a parasol, and another for lap comfort. They got a skinny youth in a t-shirt and mud- spattered blue jeans.

Pure mountain water came from 20 aquifers close to one another. The supply was so abundant that we had to avoid collapsing the aquifer system. As we drilled, we drove in a two metre diameter pipe. From within that we drilled holes at the level of each aquifer. We pumped it out at the same time. If water showered, surrounding ground plants sprouted.

Tapping of aquifers attracted silty mud. To filter the water, I had volcanic gravel brought by truck. We did not crush and use the basaltic stones in the nearby river. Those contained concentrated minerals unsuitable for drinking water. For the sake of people's teeth, we added no chlorine to the supply. Gravity carried pure, bubbling water to the town.

I then refreshed the well at Ethiopia Hotel. Its source was so plentiful that it filled the hotel's swimming pool. Bubbling water tickled the armpits of swimmers.

Back in Addis Ababa I did a water development job at a government site in Piazza. The cadre had me arrested for no reason. They released me to work on their dedication to Derg glory. This was the Tigalachin Hawelt Victory Statue and Monument at the front of Black Lion Hospital. I built the fountain, waterfall, reservoir and bullet resistant concrete wall.

Communists emptied banks of imperial coins, bronze and silver. They had the bronze melted down in North Korea to make a statue of Mengistu for the monument. Somebody sabotaged it.

In front of my Victory Monument build. Zeleq Tadesse, 1987.

My first professional job had been building water supplies for the army at the desert war front. I was in charge of 800. None had been paid for weeks. Most were labourers, drivers and mechanics on low wages with hungry families in the city. Five men went on strike for a fortnight.

The Derg sent ten soldiers. The captain made an announcement: 'Everybody in the camp is to present at the flagpole tomorrow morning.'

At dawn, workers assembled. A soldier called out the names of the five strikers. The men all stepped forward. With no warning, let alone blindfolding, the Derg machine-gunned them. The captain said, 'Any more of this anti-revolutionary behaviour will be paid for in the same way!'

Workers dug makeshift graves and buried the victims.

Attacked by rebels, we abandoned the site and walked through desert until the military stopped to give us a lift. I sat female workers in truck cabins. We recuperated in a village. In Addis Ababa my boss cried over the murdered workers. He gave me a break.

I worked on Gifirse Dam on Ambo-Gouder Road. It was 15 kilometres long with a U-shaped wall. Fifty years previously, fascists had used Spitfires to dump poison into the water. This killed livestock and children. Locals loaded donkeys and horses with a plant similar to *girawa* – soap leaf. With that they purified it.

My job was to build the treatment plant, a generator and electricity supply substation. Each day, party officials stole time from the project, demanding explanations.

'What's that dot on the plan?' 'A manhole.'

'What is that?' 'A pipe.'

Water expert bosses could not stop them. Cadre came with five corporals. A colleague went to prison for a month after forgetting to remove his cross.

There were flash floods. A worker drowned in chest-high water that encroached on the muddy shores. Lifting one foot out made the other sink deeper. One afternoon, the river swelled without rain. Abandoning our work vehicle, we leapt over juniper buttress roots and dodged eucalyptus.

River water gushed. To filter it, I built a series of stepped-down dykes and graded-pressure release pipes. We added one gram of chlorine to 10 cubic metres of water. That destroyed water-borne disease organisms. Gifirse Dam supplied Addis Ababa with water through flint-coated pipes. Extra pipes left in the bush for decades never harboured a single weed. Future generations would enjoy the hygienic water supply.

Cadre interruptions delayed work so that the substation did not get a lightning fence. People dwell close to it. Living creatures need to be 500 metres or more from radiated accumulated power. It shortens lifespans.

Five workers were to receive an award for hard work. I was among them. The cadre blocked my nomination, for I was not a model communist employee. They never promoted those who did not join the party. I could not hope for a salary increase. In 1988 my salary was 620 *birr* per month – equivalent to 310 US dollars.

After Gifirse, I worked on a larger dam at Wabe Shebelle River in Ethiopia's west. It was so remote that we went through dense bush to get there. Oromo locals welcomed me with a goat, which I kept as a pet.

Up to December each year, the dam was silty porridge. I would be covered in red mud yet could not afford daily laundering. Blue denim jeans only required weekly laundering, so I wore those. Cadre reported that I was Western influenced. Despite my specialisation in water development engineering, the Derg took me off that project. It sent me to the Rift Valley, in the southern region of Oromo.

Until mid-1989, I worked at the Muger Cement Factory on the Brrite River. Muger was 107 kilometres south of Addis Ababa. The Brrite deposited minerals for 800 kilometres from the Rift Valley to central Shewa. The factory bagged clay and pure Portland cement mix. I built the water treatment plant, dam and dyke.

Muger's water treatment plant had a capacity of 200 million cubic litres. There were three weirs and a 1.2 kilometre chamber high enough to stand in. Two hundred people worked for me: stonemasons, bar benders and plumbers.

More than half were Cuban. Excellent masons, they built tunnels as water conduits. They were cheerful and not racist. Light-skinned workers readily reported to dark-skinned bosses. Some Ethiopians automatically reported to light-skinned workers.

My supervisor was the project engineer. He had worked at Niagara Falls in Canada. Gash Belete respected nature and traditional landowners. This made the work satisfying. Muger was virgin bush, with wild fruit trees and goats. Farms had quarterly yields. Bees, butterflies, grasshoppers, birds and mammals abounded.

Brrite is Oromigna for my money and very clean water. It flowed from the mountains over volcanic gravel and stones that filtered it. When rains came, gypsum and hydrated lime made the river fizz and smoke. No water-borne disease could survive. People only drank the water after bubbles evaporated when left in an uncovered bucket for half a day.

In one area silver fish nibbled swimmers. They died when the current took them to water with high mineral levels. One species survived in that spot. It had umbrella-shaped gills.

When the Brrite flowed into the Nile, Omo and Awash Rivers, those fish became a feast for hippopotamuses, amphibious pythons and crocodiles with very hard skin that grew up to six metres. The biggest crocodile farm and skin factory in eastern and central Africa was on the Omo River at Arba Minch. Skins were in demand for bags, shoes, belts, jackets and suitcases. The Brrite had to remain clean.

Muger Cement Factory was the largest in Africa and fourth largest in the world. During the wet season it produced 500,000 bags of cement over three shifts. To protect the environment from this large-scale operation, I recommended increasing the height of the mineral processing silo chimney. Gash Belete lengthened it from 43 to 55 metres. An extra carbon filter reduced air pollution by 35 per cent.

A by-product was red mud: 51,000 truckloads per year. I shaped the dam to accommodate changes in seasonal flow. It caught sedimentary silt deposits during June-August rains that turned the water red-brown. The dam's design prevented water levels from dropping too low, protecting river fish. After August, the factory scooped red mud for sale as fertiliser to Pakistan, Yemen and Saudi Arabia. It was also used on state farms in Ethiopia.

We gave some to local plantations for restoration. Muger Cement Factory looked as though it were in the middle of a forest. Bird and animal life flourished. It was then a city surrounded by nature.

Locals taught me Oromigna. I asked elders why they did not collect horse manure from the river at certain times.

'The manure shelters butterfly nymphs,' they said. 'At the end of their life cycle, honeybees use the dust of dead butterflies to help grow new wings'.

I told Gash Belete, who instructed mine workers to remove the manure only before rains. Honey production flourished at Muger.

One day, Gash Belete called me into his office. He offered me a seat. What was wrong?

'Mesfine, I need you to do a job. Ten officials are coming to review the project. Can you prepare progress data? Include a technical explanation and a wall chart. The engineering office will be ready for you.'

The Ministries of Industry, Mining, Socialism, Military Resources, Housing Corporation and Highways were sending their people. Our boss was showing his contempt for cadre by having his youngest engineer address them.

'Gash Belete, how am I going to do this? They are big.'

'I am not asking you to carry them. Come as you are. Do not change out of your work gear or remove cement, mud or paint from your clothes and shoes.'

He added one or two words to my report and said, 'Just do your job.'

The cadre arrived in bulletproof V8 cars and a helicopter.

The presentation went well. Then came question time. They had not listened. One minister asked, 'When will the project be completed?' The minister of mining asked, 'How much will the socialist government benefit from this?' I had presented a chart of costs, environmental considerations and mineral production.

Perhaps they were distracted by my dress, which was not in the socialist cadre style. I was a mining worker, knee-deep in mud and cement. Nor had I flattered the government, its ministers, the president and the unity of socialist states.

The Derg televised the presentation nationally. While explaining the data, I had kept one hand in my pocket. Years later the cameraman from that day greeted me in Piazza and invited me to lunch.

'My pay was not increased that year because I recorded you with hand in pocket. It was worth it. I enjoyed it.'

The Derg took my lifelong habit of putting my hand in my pocket as a sign of disrespect.

Muger was a partnership with the German Democratic

Republic (GDR). Its cheaply drafted construction plans confused party members. Before the cadre could call a meeting about them, I would escape. At the water supply construction site, I learned to drive heavy machinery.

The design construction minister summoned me. From a pile of complaint letters, he chose five. 'At a meeting he put his hand in his pocket.' The minister smiled and sent me back to work.

The cadre organiser for Muger-Ambo-Gouder had been a file clerk. Project Engineer Belete was hands on, surveying and planning for projects including Lake Tana. One day, the organiser wanted a meeting with Belete about Marxism-Leninism.

He burst onto the worksite. 'Call Engineer Belete.' Belete never docked anybody's pay. That day, he said, 'For calling me engineer you lose three days' wages.'

The cadre went to Minister Kassa, asking, 'What are we going to do about him?'

The minister said, 'Do not touch him. He is my senior engineer, ranked third in the whole of Africa. In 52 countries there are only six like him.

'Do Ethiopians all have water? Do they have full bellies at night? Without Belete your cement factory will not be.'

'He cut three days' pay.'

'Why?'

'I called him engineer.'

Kassa docked two more days and pulled 50 *birr* from his pocket. 'For your honesty. Now get out of my face.'

Thirty years on, everybody would be Engineer So-and- So. Ask one, 'Can you fix a pipe leak?'

'That is plumbers' work.'

'Replace that cracked tile... Repair this broken column? Could you re-paint that wall... The flaking ceiling?'

'Way below me.'

'How can you be self-sufficient?'

Today in Addis Ababa, the blind cannot negotiate footpaths. Those are like bomb sites. People in wheelchairs become stranded outside supermarkets with no access. Pedestrians are killed on zebra crossings. Even traffic police do not stop for mothers crossing with children and babies. Government department toilets have no water. In one, a plastic hose snakes around the staircase to the ninth floor. Lifts rarely work.

When I finished at Muger, the Oromo community gave me a milking cow. Unable to take her to the city, I asked them to care for her. They posted her milk takings to us: eight, 10 or 15 *birr*. With that, Mum bought items unavailable at Muger: cooking oil, and salt blocks for cows to lick during milking.

My next stop was the Gouder Tank and Missile Factory. Gash Belete told cadre, 'I cannot stop you from taking my engineers. But do not push them to have a communist party card for reasons of religion.'

Lucy's People

Muger Cement Factory workers. From left: electrician, site keeper, me & soil tester. Photographer unknown, 198–?

The Derg forced engineers to build weapons factories. Sometimes we worked unpaid for our mother country. Giving us no chance to grab a change of clothes, soldiers would load engineers onto an aircraft.

One day, they flew us to the Port of Assab on the Red Sea. We disembarked in 38 degrees Celsius heat and got to work fixing the port's Italian dyke. It was not built to cope with military ships the size of cities – they displaced so much water that it overflowed onto the wharf.

Me and a young colleague named Yonas checked the dyke. Fooling about, Yonas got too close to the edge and fell in. His face reappeared several metres away, gulping extremely salty water. 'Mesfine!' I raised the alarm. 'My friend has fallen in. He cannot swim!' Doubling back, I could not see him. The emergency service recovered his dead body 600 metres away.

Yonas was an only child. When he was one, his father had served at the war front near Eritrea and was shot in the groin. Russian field doctors cut off his penis. His pension was so small that his wife made lace to support them.

I made a headstone for their son's grave with grey Ambo marble, chiselled his name and dates onto it, and applied his lacquered photograph. His father did not survive one year.

Early in my career, the ministry had sent me to a factory build. After the mid-1980s famine, Japanese Volunteer Services funded the Fafa project. The factory would produce nutritional supplements and foods for children, including the instant porridge Celerac.

Construction was stalled with only the shell of the building erected. There were no electrical or water services, pest proofing, air filtration or containment barriers. The production line, machinery, packaging, storage and palletising systems were not ready. It was close to the scheduled completion date.

Materials such as concrete, nails and timber often went missing, though the site was fenced. The unqualified site supervisor was corrupt. I employed guards who stopped the thefts.

We then had an excess of construction material. Cadre told me to discard it, but I used the leftovers to help site workers. Their pay was poor, around 12 *birr* per day. Those with three children at home came to work with a slice of bread for lunch. I sold the materials, and the workers' committee divided the proceeds. After good sales we bought them an ox to slaughter, home brew and honey wine.

One day a wealthy builder came to purchase materials. 'Where's Engineer Mesfin?'

I pointed to the site office. The man was angry at my apparent insolence. 'Take me to him.'

I led the way. He looked around for a belly in suit and tie. 'So, call Engineer Mesfin.'

I moved to behind the desk. The man broke out in a sweat. I sold him the building materials.

The site supervisor put strangers on the payroll. There was a list of masons, plumbers and carpenters who never turned up to work. He demanded that I sign for the wages. 'My father is Minister of Trade.' I refused.

The next day two policemen with guns came. 'Watch out. We will kill you.' They handed me a letter from the minister telling me to stick to my job.

I fled hundreds of kilometres, unable to explain my action to the project manager, my friend. She would have been put at immense risk. Fafa became a working factory though it took too long.

Ethiopia produced brilliant building technicians, engineers and surveyors. So where are they today? Few of my former colleagues are left. Some fled to menial work abroad. Many died under the Derg and TPLF.

The Derg's workers had to behave like dedicated socialists while a few bosses had zero communist ideals. One high-level minister studied politics in Yugoslavia under Emperor Haile Selassie I. With the revolution, he became Mengistu's political assistant.

In 1984 he sold 175,000 *Falasha* to Israel in Operation Moses. The Derg received napalm bombs, cluster bombs, air-surface missiles, intercontinental ballistic missiles and Apache helicopters. The political assistant became wealthy.

The operation split up families. Ethiopian Airlines transported them from Addis Ababa and the Sudan to Tel Aviv. Israel had grabbed children from marketplaces while their mothers were left behind. Fathers were long-gone, having fled the operation.

The same man airlifted another 80,000 in an operation called The Journey of the Twelfth Tribe of Israel. Ethiopians called the twelfth tribe *Bete Israeli* – House of Israel. This was another name for *Falasha*. In the second airlift, Israel took only the healthy, strong and young. Relatives could not reunite for decades.

My friend Maru was one of those. He spent eight years in Israel away from his mother and 17 siblings. After a visit home, Maru was conscripted to part-time defence work. He had already done national service. At a Gaza Strip protest, he needed to move Palestinian children off the road. They were in danger. Maru lowered his weapon so as not to scare them. A sniper shot and killed him.

The political assistant had himself airlifted with the *Bete Israeli*. In Israel he did no military service. Then he went to the US. Decades later he would return to a warm welcome in Ethiopia. Former members of the diaspora were with him. Some would have been tortured by his former colleagues.

The Derg used the armaments against Ethiopians, who resisted removal from traditional lands. It also used them in the 17-year war with Eritrea in which Ethiopians lost family and friends on both sides. My family had relatives in Eritrea. They estimated that 10 per cent of its population was wiped out. More than half who died were children.

On our last evening at home, Hewan and our sisters prepared gourmet chicken stew. Our oldest sister made *injera* flatbread. I added piquant twigs of book-leaf eucalyptus to the storage basket. That was my favourite of the trees given to Emperor Menelik II by Australia in the late nineteenth century.

Samual had gotten out of killing the rooster. He said that he had sex on the Sabbath, and so was cursed for seven weeks. Nobody could ask him to slaughter a chicken, goat or sheep. My sisters made him eat off a paper plate. When he finished, they carried it by the brim to the rubbish bin. But everybody still smiled at him.

The aroma of Mum's chicken bread enticed us to the kitchen.

Chapter 18
Second Home

When I worked in the south, Mum wove a basket and sent me chicken stew. It kept perfectly for two weeks. Co-workers called her Tewode the Sweet. The recipe included boiled eggs steeped in the sauce.

During my teens, I was a guest of Inkulal Bete, Menelik's egg store. Schoolmates and I had sheltered there during thunderstorms. The Derg made it into a political prison, where they shot many civilians.

Security had arrested me in the street with another student named Gomus. The Red Terror communists felt threatened by any youth who worked hard and was bright. Soldiers disliked my Building College ID.

'You are too young to attend college.' They called the college to check.

'Yes, he is our youngest student to date.'

'Ah, if he reaches too high a level at a young age, he could be dangerous.'

The Derg imprisoned us in a cell called Siberia. It was a death sentence. Security had scheduled Bren machine guns for use on its occupants that night. They would fire rounds of 10,000 bullets like spitfire.

I said, 'We will hear a rushing waterfall.'

'No survivors. *Mirishin*,' Gomus said, citing the Derg slogan CHOOSE TO KILL.

Though beardless, we were tall. The officer in charge of logistics chose us to help a truck driver take supplies to the main prison south of the city, Kerchele.

As we unloaded the truck, the driver said, 'If you go back to the Egg Store, you will be shot tonight. Stay here, even though it is for life. Better than dying so young.'

Kerchele was the old wound of fascism, the first prison ever built in Ethiopia. Its name was Italian and meant 'locked'. We had no equivalent term. Closest was *serbet* – Mary's anguish at the foot of Christ's cross.

Ethiopia once rehabilitated wrongdoers, counselling them during something akin to house arrest. As a last resort, those who could never re-enter society went to work at the Shakiso or Adola gold mines. A death sentence was reserved only for treason. Torture was uncommon. Our crime rate was low.

In 1936, Mussolini's fascists built a hell the size of a small town on a Jewish site. It was home to a hospital, school and a church named Mikael Bete Kristyan. The occupiers locked away men, women, children, priests and Europeans who had fled: Yugoslavs, Armenians, Albanians and Greeks.

In 1941, the British moved their Sudanese, Kenyan, Tanzanian and Somali prisoners to Kerchele. Patriot Belay Zeleq protested. 'Our country is not to be used to help make colonialists feel safer.'

Defence Minister Abeba said, 'When we fought the fascists it was not to help another breed grow. Your prisoners are not to be tortured and starved on Ethiopian soil.'

Ethiopians walked from all over to dismantle Kerchele with bare hands and shovels. Three thousand horsemen surrounded it and set fire to it. The English left with prisoners in canvas-covered Bedford military trucks.

The Organisation of African Unity claimed space around the prison and church ruins. Addis Ababa became Adu Genet. It meant new heaven for she welcomed everyone.

The communists re-opened Kerchele, built more prisons, and made torture chambers never seen by our people before. This was to make them abandon their traditional lands. Scholarship recipients went to the German Democratic Republic for training in building prisons, guarding and torture. European communists continued the work of fascists and Nazis.

Gomus and I had arrived in the centre of Kerchele at Alem Bekagn. The name meant world over with. It was for those sentenced to life. A prison within a prison, Alem Bekagn was a circle of concrete like a water reservoir.

It had one entrance and no exit. Nobody survived two winters there, let alone life. Prisoners died of pneumonia because it was open to the elements, with a grid and no roof. Rain or sun beat down upon them.

Escape was impossible. In each corner there was a seven-metre-high Mama control tower with five guards and multi-directional machine guns.

There were no windows, lights or sleeping mats. One thousand prisoners slept with legs in a V, slotted in with each other in a variation of top-to-toe. A tall person could not stand upright. Gaolers gave prisoners half a glass of water once a day. To make them thirstier, they played the sound of running water.

There was no lavatory. Before 6 a.m. soldiers herded prisoners to a trench. They used it at gunpoint in front of everybody. Nothing shielded women from view. There had once been a five metre deep hole in the floor. People dived into it to die. Now, there was a single half-barrel over which urine slopped.

The guard house was above the centre. Guards worked eight-hour shifts with no break. They relieved themselves where they stood, one hand on their machine guns, through a hole in the flooring. The area below was unusable.

A 75-year-old priest chanted prayers at midnight and at 5 a.m. Prisoners could observe any of five or six religions or be non-believers, yet all had to listen. Soothing for me, but unbearable for those returned from torture. Tormentors wore dark blue uniforms and crochet masks, working in the dark. The priest was protective, thug-wits torturing prisoners in front of him.

To prevent sleep by day, gaolers blasted noise into cells up to 48 hours straight. For mental health, elders made rosters for sleeping, push-ups and walking. The educated gave historical accounts and recitations of poetry or whole texts. Some had also memorised banned works.

We held formal debates. One topic was "Leonardo da Vinci's Mona Lisa is More Beautiful than a Hundred Lale Guma". She was the beauty lauded in a song by Tilahun.

The scholarly priest greeted all contributions with contempt. 'I cannot believe you are educated.'

'Indeed, we have not dedicated ourselves like you to decades of monastery education.'

One day a monster barged in: Kerchele's second in charge. Barely literate, single-stripe Corporal Damtaw was prone to such excesses that colleagues later murdered him. During house raids he silenced dogs with bullets. Without a warrant, he searched the house of survivors of the fascist invasion. He burned a portrait of the late emperor and a copy of his book *My Life with the Progress of Ethiopia*, and shot the owners in Piazza. They were philanthropists and had adopted orphans.

Barren from the effects of mustard gas, the wife started an elementary school for children who had lost parents in war. She worked in its kitchen, dedicated to the best nutrition. Alumni included professors and the champion marathon runner Mamo Wolde. At Haile Selassie's invitation, Mamo joined the military as a boy scout. As sergeant he won a 42.5 kilometre marathon in Rome, showing up the fascists. He protested against the Derg's inhumanity, so it imprisoned him and he became ill and died.

Damtaw picked on the priest. Pointing his handgun, he said, 'Sing.' We shuddered. Such commands were a prelude to murder. Slightly bowed, eyes down, the priest chanted in Amharic.

> This you brought, Gebriel
> This you brought, Mikael
> You created a wild animal –
> Come and take it away.

He was challenging God and the angels Gabriel and Michael over their creation of Damtaw. The man was a model *yerada lij*. The corporal could not understand him. Unschooled in etiquette, he focused on the priest's body language. 'Stand straight. Look at me!'

The priest did not alter his posture, humble and courageous. It spoke for him: 'Do you think I am afraid of death? You are asking me to entertain you?'

A youth burst out laughing. The corporal held his pistol to his head. 'What's so funny?'

We shrank back, squeezing our bodies to minimise the target area for spurting blood.

'Sir, I never heard such a beautiful song, and expected you to laugh too in appreciation. It is the best song there could be about you.'

Damtaw clapped. His applause of the insult made the youth laugh again, but he lived. Flattered, the torturer departed. In Ge'ez, the priest chanted a prayer of thanks.

Older prisoners protected Gomus and me. They provided cardboard for sleeping, shielded us from the sun and saved rations to feed us.

After our arrival at Alem Bekagn, they had asked, 'Sons, tell us how you ended up here.' We told them about the move from Siberia. 'Do not tell the guards or they will shoot you.'

They made plans to get us out. At the monthly head count the Derg would discover two extras. We pretended to be disabled. Elders rehearsed us.

'Where did you come from?'

'Don't remember.'

'How did you get here?'

'Don't know. I came back from having holy water and found myself in the street.'

This worked. Guards removed us for observation by the prison chief. We let him think that we had been in a monastery for treatment of depression.

He asked guards, 'Do they know how to get home? Put them in the lockup for one week to see how normal they are.'

The food was reasonable. We had a mattress, table tennis set and volleyball net. A television screen showed Lenin, Stalin and Red Square over and over.

The chief released us, and we hid with my aunt. When it was safe, she phoned our families from a public booth. They complained. 'Five weeks of worry!'

'If I told you straight away, Security would have noticed you acting strangely. Officers would have asked around and found out your son was missing from prison. Then tortured you to find his whereabouts before killing us all.'

The TPLF would later build a replacement for Kerchele – Kilinto. For political prisoners, they built a cold alpine prison. With foreign aid, they opened secret underground prisons such as those run by the CIA.[1] The 2018 government would locate and close them, freeing the forgotten before imprisoning others.

Lucy's People

I prefer silence regarding my incarcerations. However, a fellow survivor of Mihakelawe prison and I commiserated. For the sake of those who did not survive, I will not keep quiet. Let me tell you about my second homes.

Central was under the auspices of Derg Central Intelligence. Mihakelawe was a hell made especially for youth. It had GDR set-up and design. Prisoners suffered extreme, systematic maltreatment by professional torturers trained in the GDR and Romania.

When I was a young teenager, the Derg locked me away in Central. Torturers abused me so severely that I weighed 27 kilograms. They chained me upside-down and beat me on the soles of the feet. Then they left me for dead in the prison yard. A guard noticed my eyes move and dripped water into my mouth. For weeks I could only walk on my bottom.

Intellectuals, including lecturers at Addis Ababa University, suffered worse. Most ended up crippled. Many lost their minds and killed themselves in prison or later.

Soon after the foot sole torture I developed a high fever. The Derg took me to the military hospital with other very sick victims. The triage nurse refused to admit me. 'He is not sick. Send him back. We only take the sickest.'

Unable to walk, I leaned against the wheel of the military truck. I would soon die. Back at Central there was virtually no food and water, no lavatory, no bed and no medical help. I used my spiritual strength to leave my tormented body behind in the open air and sunshine.

A doctor came along. 'What are you doing here?' I said the nurse had sent me away. He replied, 'Ah, we know who she is,' and put his hand on my neck, drawing it back swiftly from the heat. Admitting me to hospital, he set up a glucose drip. He kept me as long as possible before my return to Central.

Severe abuse continued. Torturers filled barrels with cold water. In those they dissolved Omo laundry powder boosted with bleach. They upended youths, immersed them, and held them down until they stopped moving. Balloon-sized soap bubbles floated out of survivors' ears.

Shoving us into a cell one day, a soldier bashed me with his rifle butt. The wound bled for two days and left a two centimetre scar on my head. Another coward slammed his rifle butt into my mouth, attempting to shatter my teeth. Guards tied my hands to the tow bar of a vehicle and then drove away fast.

The Derg tormented us mentally. Cadre threatened us with execution without notice. Their favourite game was putting us before firing squads on one of the city's five mountains. We were without blindfolds. Rifles aimed at us. Soldiers fired shots above our heads.

In a chamber immediately above our cell they tortured our friends. We could hear everything throughout the night.

They tortured us in front of the others. A 30-year-old prisoner named Isayas had sat with me as I regained consciousness from being tortured the first time. Accused of anti-Derg activity, he was missing five or six fingernails. Torturers pulled one each week. He kept quiet and refused to confess to accusations untrue and ridiculous.

One day the cell door opened. We cowered in the corners. In the greenish hue I made out the tall form of Isayas. Four guards held him while another opened a briefcase containing instruments. In his place, how many would have died from heart attacks? Isayas had had enough. He grabbed the pincers from the head torturer, snipping off the first phalange of his own index finger.

'Here, is this what you want? Take it!' Blood spurted all over the floor.

The torturers said, 'Gentlemen, let's go.' In silence they packed their instruments.

They left the cell, locking it six times. 'Chk-chk-chk- chk-chk-chk.' No clean-up, first aid, or wound dressing.

In that hell with no sunlight or sanitation—where prisoners

existed on starvation rations and half a glass of water once a day —Isayas survived. Within a week his wound had healed over without treatment or pain relief. It left the smallest of scars. I never found out if he lived but recall his defiance. He was a real man.

Mihakelawe was a whole system of Soviet-era deprivation, torture, and psychological torment. Tetracycline smuggled into the prison could not heal repeatedly opened foot sole and back wounds. Survival rates were extremely low.

Professional torturer Seyoum was the worst offender. Trained in the GDR, he was employed by Central Investigation Headquarters. For at least a decade he made life hell for countless youth. Seyoum tormented us physically as individuals and mentally as a group.

I was imprisoned in Mihakelawe before the wounds down the side of my chest from battlefront service healed over. This made me a target for torturers, who forced prisoners to inflict pain on others. Seyoum tied my hands behind my back. He wedged newspaper doused in kerosene into my armpit. Pointing his gun at another youth's head, he ordered him to light the newspaper. Flesh burned over my heart. Today I have large scars there. Fabric is uncomfortable.

One night, Seyoum hurled his latest victim into our cell. It was Markos, a fourth-year university student. Torturers had reduced his foot soles to liquid. Bone thin, he had swelled up all over. Liquid continued to run from his wounds, yet the Derg never took him to hospital.

Unable to speak, our friend indicated his trouser area with his eyes. Seyoum had embedded a barbed hook in his genitals. He had weighted it with a full water bottle while torturing him in additional ways. The hook would not come out. Torturers like Seyuom often repeated this fascist method two or three times. It mutilated the victim and permanently deranged any who survived.

All night we tried to help Markos. We gave him drops of water. It ran off his lips. He could only move his eyes. We held him and prayed for his quick death, but it was happening too slowly.

Twenty-four hours later the cell door opened again. Seyoum's enormous feet appeared at our friend's eye level. Markos raised his head to confront him, moved his lips to speak, and died. Seyoum laughed in delight. Mengistu's monster had put him in the cell to mentally torment us.

The following night he returned. 'Would you like a blanket?'
'Ye-e-s.'
'Use him as a blanket. Ha-ha-ha.'

He left Markos's body in the tiny, crowded cell for three days. Wherever we looked we could see his tormented face. The smell was appalling.

Survivors spared his mother the worst details of his death. She had supported her son all her best years by selling *injera* on the street.

Loved ones could not possibly know where youth were disappeared to. And so how could they appeal on our behalf? They had no idea where to bring blankets, water, food, medicine and wound treatments.

Sometimes they received confusing information. During the second phase of the Red Terror, one sister walked four kilometres to the morgue to collect my body. She waited all night on the cold hospital floor. I walked out alive.

On another day, her younger sister ran barefoot, hair wild, to Number Six Central Prison. I was there and the Derg had just shot many teenagers.

'My brother, my brother!'

The officer slapped her hard. 'You will be lucky to bury him. We might feed his body to the hyenas.'

Whenever I vanished, my toddler niece asked, 'How will *Gashe* eat lunch? Will they untie his hands?'

By now a colonel, Damtaw recycled himself at Mihakelawe. He poisoned bean paste on bread and gave it to all the prisoners. We survived.

I am one of four brothers who suffered. Boys as young as six emerged from prison missing fingers. Whole families were traumatised.

Detainees had no recourse to justice at any stage. To protect themselves against future prosecution, tormentors tortured prisoners into forgetting their names. They immersed us in icy water at dawn, sharp gravel underfoot. This affected my ability to recall people's names, including those I liked. Otherwise, I remembered whatever I heard or read.

People in positions of influence were blind to human rights abuse. Senior Orthodox Christian clergy held gold and diamond crosses that meant nothing. Derg torturers have never been brought to justice. I know of no victim or relative who has ever been compensated.[2]

The West gave Derg abusers swift resettlement. Seyoum gained a new life in Germany, rewarded with freedom. Decades later, he took his own life. He never faced any court or justice. What if those tortured youths had been white?

Under the TPLF, some Derg Security officers served short prison terms. Afterwards, they emigrated to the West, unusually rich – the Derg rewarded systematic abusers. Survivors saw their incarcerators and torturers in the streets. At community events they might be obliged to greet them, shaking hands that had spilled their blood.

We prisoners of the communists retained our humanity. Security told a man that he was about to be executed. He turned to me and gave me his small pillow. The only thing that cannot be taken away from you is dignity, even when others violate it.

We held hands in a circle to identify who was being taken for torture. We prayed for him. Let him not be returned worse than dead, to die slowly, useless hope still intact and brain damaged without knowledge of who and where he was. I prayed on my knees. When would I not return?

The sixth imprisonment was in a cell scarcely four by four metres. 53 of us were there on the first day, and more came each day. We never panicked. Ridden with lice, we kept our integrity. Once a day a plastic sheet arrived piled with food. We took turns to have one bite each, counting. At first, we slept top-to-toe. When there was no room for that, we stood and sat in shifts. We held our heads high.

My family fought to free me. I am alive thanks to a fellow prisoner. Due for release, he memorised the phone number that I told him. He rang my sister's husband Colonel Wibishat. 'Mesfin is in Central. He is to go before the firing squad.' The colonel appeared in full military dress, rescuing me. And he saved me from being killed in prison on two other occasions as well. Another time, another sister's husband, a government worker, obtained my release from Mihakelawe. He put his job on the line.

Colonel Wibishat saved thousands of boys' lives by ordering their release from prison, some only 12. Later, the TPLF never considered this. The colonel needed simple surgery because Soviet field doctors had left shrapnel in his chest. It pressed on his lungs and they filled with fluid. The new government denied him proper treatment in the military hospital. Colonel Wibishat took one long month to die, suffocating on a mattress in a public hospital corridor.

After my time in Central, my family was supportive. Nieces hid their packets of Omo laundry powder. I would forever be traumatised by the sight. Itete took me to a monastery, where a physician warned me off synthetic shoes and soles. Heat exacerbated my foot nerve pain. Mum made special linings for my boots and a niece knitted me soft booties. A military specialist said, 'Your nerves will begin to die when you are 50.'

Released from Mihakelawe, I weighed 40-50 kilograms, though I was close to my adult height. Ethiopian people finish growing later than Europeans. I wore a size 27 belt, smaller than most girls. It took six months to build myself up for matches with Saint Giyorgis soccer team.

Once again playing attack, I sped across the field. My low body weight spared my soles. Still, I was unable to play two successive games without injury to them. The boy who played wing attack had suffered the same torture. About to score a goal, crowd roaring, he would collapse in agony from a nerve dying in his foot.

Years later, I bumped into Ethiopians from those soccer days. Some of them felt my face to be sure they were not dreaming. Men did not expect to reach 20 let alone 50.

In 2016 I attended a celebrated musician's gig. In the bar, he exclaimed, 'What! You are alive?' 30 years previously he had worn my Giyorgis soccer team shirt number. He asked, 'Do you still have that great energy for life?'

Our soccer coach had once spoken of my bright future and how nature had created me well. The Derg took that.

In my mid-thirties, an elephant stood on my chest. A hospital nurse and doctor remained with me for five hours. I breathed, though more than half of my heart had seized. Parachute jumps, Seyoum and non-stop work was causing two massive heart attacks.

The cardiologist said, 'Cigarette?' I had something to celebrate. 'You are the only person to walk unaided from this unit.'

God said, 'Live'.

My aunt said, 'Eat green beans and raw onions. Same ingredients as in aspirin.'

Today, I am affected physically and mentally by incarcerations and torture. Nightmares never leave me alone, and I awake in pain at any moment. My foot soles burn. Longing to immerse them in cold water, I refrain. The pain returns twice as strong, shoes will not go on, and a day's work is lost. After prolonged labour, my joints twist and swell. Yet I complete several men's work in a day.

Throughout my youth, Ethiopia was the land of suffering. Then on Addis Ababa's Central Police Station, the TPLF installed an English-language slogan. It declared that it cared for the people. Many differed.[3]

Kidane Mihret is the sacred being of Orthodox. Regardless of their religion, all Ethiopians revere her. Her name means forgiveness for the world. We call upon her during hunger, thirst, sickness, war, natural disaster and drought. Even if nothing can be done, she alleviates the suffering of Saba and Lucy's people.

People of Afar have her image on cow bells. Animists and people in the southern region of the Awash River Basin follow her. They say, 'Kidane Mihret will save us from this heatwave.'

My love for Kidane Mihret sustained me through the Red Terror. Half-frozen and starving, I met her in waking dreams. Sometimes Mum and my part-time mother Itiye Messelo were with her.

---

1. Sophia Tesfamariam, "Ethiopia: A Classic Case", para. 16
2. Firew Kebede Tiba, "Trial", 181
3. tangodaa. "Drastic and Gross Human Right Violation"

Chapter 19
Hagere Mariyam

Miserat, Hewan and I left for the south during the third week of May 1991. Mum gave us a bottle of her handmade perfume – a gift for the mother of Miserat's husband.

The driver of the old Fiat bus said, 'Students have crossed into Kenya. They caught the bus and played music all the way.'

'Were they from Bilate Military Training Centre?' This was a five-hour walk from the southern border town of Moyale.

'Yes. Brand new conscripts pulled straight out of universities. About 15,000 of them.' They cradled AK-47s like dolls. Now Derg soldiers, they could not return home.

Rift Valley oxen pulled wooden ploughs along rectangles of dark earth. A farmer played the bamboo flute, strolling behind cows and brown sheep.

At Lake Abijata (Abiyata) the lunch menu was all fish. The sky darkened like inside a tent. 'Pelicans are flying over,' said the waiter. Abijata had two million birds.

Then at Dila, the gateway to Konso in the Oromo region of Sidamo, nobody mentioned the government and rebels. They said things like, 'How is your cow?'

'Terrific, thanks. Last week she had twins.'

'My barley is so heavy that the stalks are bending.'

Animals were relaxed. In the city, they started if a person picked up an object.

Dinner for three cost less than two *birr*. Locals insisted that we stay overnight. They knew Miserat's husband.

Southern men were all muscle with gentle manners. However, they had stood up to Mengistu. An 88-year-old asked him, 'Why are you killing our children and grandchildren?'

The Derg leader said, 'They are no good for communism.'
'Why give our best things to Russia?'

'They are our comrades.'

'You are an ugly and dirty beast, disaster bringing motherfucker, and son of evil born after midnight.'

All waited for the bullet. It did not come. Mengistu had murdered a 105-year-old monk, but now he said, 'This old man is another Yuwagobesh Mirsha.' He referred to Mama Teliqwa.

The next bus driver stopped at Yirgachefe. Its name meant my cool, green fields with shallow waters and pampas grass. He said, 'Pick bush bananas and mangos. Watch out for snakes.' Locals gathered medicinal bush coffee. A farmer pointed out a 300-year-old tree. He was an Animist of the Konso tribe. There were also Sidamo Semites of the Guji tribe.

All spoke Amharic, supplementing it with body language, pictures and expressions. They stuck their infants, toddlers or chickens to my chest. Babies gurgled jokes at me. The whole bus laughed when I removed the skin from a mango before devouring it. Rift Valley people leave it on, eating it for the health- giving oil. I felt confident. Lucy's Rift Valley land restored some bodily organ removed by disaster bringers.

We continued to Addis Alem or 'new world'. King Kaleb founded it around 1400 BC. He built our first underground monastery which sixteenth-century Turks did not find. Queen Saba read Kaleb's archives in which he described Addis Alem, and visited. It had several species of tigers and lions, five species of elephants, pigs, and rhinoceroses. She took its ivory, frankincense, roses and *jaffa* oranges to King Salamon in Israel.

At Addis Alem, a local invited us to stay with her family rather than at the hotel. Help for Miserat would be at hand if she went into labour. We walked to her farming village. Men carried Miserat on a litter. It took us 45 minutes; locals would have done it in 30.

Ochre-painted youth bowed low. They softly stamped a foot in thanks to mother earth while greeting us with, '*Selam*.' A girl covered her nose. Her people never caught colds and flu. Consequently, there were no pharmacies from which to buy toiletries and they disliked our soap and scent.

Wild horses grazed underneath trees. They directed their noses towards us, mahogany and blonde manes on end. The farmer said, 'They tolerate us, but can smell city folk.' They were brumbies, their name originally Oromo.

Birra ambi meant clean horse. People settled in the alps and won wars in Oromo and Amhara with them. They were the bush horses of the Australian Kosciusko National Park and Snowy Mountains. The English used them in the Boer Wars and in World Wars I and II.

At the farm, an elder greeted us with the confidence of one who has enjoyed a long life. A boy brought a goat. I leapt over it in traditional blessing, though would rather have kept it alive.

Children groomed two big horses with barley stalk brushes and our host fed them avocado. That breed pulled ploughs and was never saddled. The horses followed their owners to a marble trough for their next course of boiled barley and salt blocks. Then they ate freshly picked carrots, green tops still on, and laugh-neighed their thanks. Donkeys too.

The compound housed five families. Each smooth, round, light-grey house had a bamboo spire for a beehive. A spear planted in front of one signified DO NOT DISTURB. The lady inside was with her boyfriend. Konso women married when they chose or not at all.

At sunset, elders formed a circle around a spear. They thanked the sun for the day, for her warmth, and the light in which all things grew. Cows loved her. Nobody could own, package or sell the sun. In the morning people would look for her again.

The host's family lit a log fire. Hewan sneezed. The husband pulled an oxygen supply from the wall for her. We ate at a carved table inlaid with mosaic glass and white quartz and bluestone. A youth topped up my honey wine flask.

The tomato salad was from the previous year's crop. The farmer said, 'We store our surplus. Barley and maize keep 70 years. We have five types of tomato, and cold press the juice between planks to avoid fermentation. The high iron and antioxidant content are excellent for children under five.'

Her children wore bracelets or anklets in 24- and 28-carat gold. To speak to somebody opposite they walked around the table and conversed almost in a whisper. Nobody talked above the others.

The doorway made a tinkling sound. The smallest child picked up a lizard and took it outside. It had set off an alarm made from seeds and bark built into the threshold. Our host said, 'We have no vermin because nothing enters without being heard.' Miserat said, 'See the leaf worn behind her ear? It keeps away mice. No poisons.'

The washing area backed onto a garden adjoining the lavatory with three kinds of pedestals: secure highchair for toddlers, ordinary seat for older children and adults, and carved wooden chair for the elderly. A temporary display cage housed a coiled snake. The whole amenity was therapeutic.

In a hut all to ourselves, I had no nightmares. Hewan and I awoke in the same position in which we had lain down. She said, 'We should not disturb our hosts. It is still dark.'

In the main house, farmers had been waiting with breakfast for an hour. They had let out their cattle to lick dew from the grass. The host asked me to open the window. There were no shutters or hinges. A rectangle of insect screening betrayed a vent window, sealed magnetically. I tugged gently on a string and it opened outwards, letting in the scent of roses.

She asked me to bring honey for breakfast. Her daughter handed me a wooden scoop and pointed upward. A door was set in the ceiling centre. From inside the house, I harvested honey.

Our host brought horses to tour the farm. A donkey pointed her ears in a way that indicated rain. Hewan and I put on gumboots. Most workers remained barefoot.

Mango, banana and four species of peach grew wild. Streams irrigated the farm. Intensively cultivated, it produced *teff* grain, wheat and barley. Farmers varied production from year to year, restoring the earth.

A dyking system captured tepid rain. It flowed in decreasing circles into storage. The water was so clear that we could see the bottom four metres down. The farmer added bush bean. That killed small insects and bacteria. He purified the water with purifying plant. Every three years he added sacks of volcanic filter gravel. The community was free of water-borne diseases.

For 3,000 years the Konso and Guji had farmed in the Hagere Mariyam area. They never accepted Derg cadre. Farming life continued as before. The TPLF could threaten Ethiopia's food supply chain, but southern farmers would feed millions.

In 1978, farmers of the Omo River Region to the west had rejected Derg rules for selling produce. Mengistu sent General Fanta to bomb them. He told pilots to fly high so as not to frighten cattle, and then leave. Eleven years later, Mengistu murdered him during the ceasefire with Eritrea.

The Konso farmer said, 'We have no government offices,

politicians, electricity supplies or medical clinics. Not necessary here.'

Hewan said, 'In Addis Ababa the average life expectancy is twenty-nine years. Random executions, conscription and military service get us young.'

Miserat said, 'In Hagere Mariyam it is eighty-five for men and ninety-two for women.'

'Your lives are good. Houses are comfortable and cool,' I said, 'No prisons.'

A crimson-and-green bird perched on a vine. Another whistled. Our bird responded with a variation. In the seventh century, such birds had inspired Saint Yared to create the pentatonic scale for sacred chants. The bird flew off to join the other at a small pyramid wall, the area reservoir. They sipped condensation. The farmer said, 'It must be full. I will check the float.'

Tiers of stonemasonry supported a vertical garden. Squares of moss grew in the pointing, which was pure river sand. The retaining wall was constructed without heavy machinery. Konso and Guji used hammers, shovels and chisels made from hard wood. Large horses and oxen helped with assembly.

At the compound, dogs and chickens greeted visitors from across the river. News of our arrival had spread. They brought stew and goats, sheep and chickens. After kissing our hosts seven times, they drank coffee on the community hall veranda. Villagers kept a clay coffee pot there. Through a narrow spout they added drops of melted clarified butter. Elders took it with salt.

The farmer said, 'Put that fire in your mouth.' He was inviting me to smoke.

The visitors bathed us and applied butter to the girls' hair. It was as though we city kids were their own sons and daughters. Fresh air filled our brains.

I boasted of Addis Ababa technology. Barefoot masters smiled a little. Then they showed me their water technology. Without booster pumps, Konso made water flow up a mountain through bamboo pipes. They had drilled out the solid nodes. Elders refused to be called scientists, engineers or architects, yet they were all those things. Konso and Guji youth did study in the city. Once qualified, they returned home, discarding Western clothing and shoes.

I had come south with Dad's Omega wristwatch. An elder glanced at it. 'What time is it?' Before I could respond, his companion told him the time to the minute. Neither wore watches. No wonder the inventor of Global Positioning System technology was born in Ethiopia.

The elder asked, 'Can we get you land?' My heart lifted, but Hewan kept silent. Miserat needed to reach home. He gave me a beautiful cow with a necklace of gemstones. Konso and Guji only made gifts of living things: a plant, cow or goat.

They celebrated birthdays, but the person having the birthday did the giving to one other. They told them, 'We will meet again in five years. You will tell me how many cows you have now. We will drink honey wine and laugh together until we fall off our chairs.'

To the elder I said, '*Gashe*, I will meet you here in five years' time and tell you how much milk the cow has given and the number of calves she has made.'

Our hosts brought saddled horses. The farmer talked to the lead horse. The mare's necklace signified her status. Thrilled to have been picked, she moved her ears back and forth, showing her understanding of the journey. When she came to a river, she would look out for quicksand or mud. If it was impassable, she would paw at the ground. Men would measure the depth of the crossing with sticks and find another place. Lead mares also doubled back to urge on stragglers.

Hewan's mare knelt down camel-style. With a pull on the reigns, she stood. The horse lifted her front legs, right, left, right, left, and set off.

The men carrying Miserat's litter trod delicately in their sandals.

My wife pushed me to leave, but my feet stuck to the earth. I cried. A woman said, 'Let him be. He needs those tears.'

On the way to Addis Alem, our host picked up black basaltic stones. They stored heat. Others collected dead wood and fallen leaves. The sun was strong and oily frankincense trees were endemic. Catastrophic fires could occur, but never did because of the people's land care. Elders chose when to prune trees. On the same day each December, farmers did controlled burns. To protect livestock, they herded the animals into circular structures the size of a shopping centre, with mud-covered walls.

At Addis Alem, we arranged for the cow to go to Miserat and Gashaw's mother's farm. Our Konso hosts gave us ten baskets of oranges and peaches. They packed eggs in straw and placed everything on the roof of the bus for the journey south to Hagere Mariyam. Not one egg broke.

A fellow passenger had well-developed neck muscles. Miserat asked him, 'How was the competition?' He was a glass blower. A farmer had a new gun with mosaic work on the butt. My zest for life and will to help others were restored.

Hewan asked, 'What is that?' On a mountainside, a nine-storey monastery angled across the access road. Builders had tunnelled through the hills. Miserat said, 'Soldiers tried to occupy a nearby monastery, but had to leave. Snakes and wild animals attacked.' As a regional pope said, 'Ethiopia is the land of angels.'

The bus pulled over. Hewan said, 'Who wants hot coffee with salt and clarified butter?' She scooped it into halved nut shells. Men came with mango and chilli spice.

Miserat said, 'On Saturdays, locals prepare food for travellers. Pass by and make sure you are hungry. If you refuse any woman's offer, she will ask God what she has done wrong.'

At the Hagere Mariyam farm, dogs, hens and a peacock ran toward us as though people had never hurt any member of their species. Gashaw's mother Hiwot said, '*Maye, maye.*' She took Hewan and Miserat to rest, then picked herbs for goat soup. This would ease Miserat's labour – too soon for Hewan. We picked turmeric and ginger from the ground. Medicine was everywhere.

Gashaw was Agricultural Economist for the Sidamo region. He was a graduate of Jimma Agricultural Institute. We discussed water development opportunities. He said, 'Our community would appreciate your work. How wonderful if our children grew up together.'

Miserat said, 'Do not let him stay for too long. He will never want to leave.' She re-arranged her shawl. 'How safe is it for ex-military? What will I tell the family if anything happens?'

This was rehearsed. Hewan had put her up to it. She wanted to get away from the countryside. I would help at the farm for ten days then we would cross the border into Kenya. Love of my country invited pain.[1]

---

1. Ejigayehu Sibabaw, "All Her Music"

Chapter 20
Market Day

In May 1991, Mengistu fled to Zimbabwe. This prevented the death of a million. TPLF forces reached Addis Ababa. They bombed depots without warning residents. The young, elderly and sick died from toxic smoke inhalation.

Gashaw said, 'Rebels set fire to Shegole Meda food and ammunition depot. Still burning. They sacked ten thousand permanent workers. No redundancies.' Some had worked there for 50 years.

The TPLF set fire to Tayit Fabrika. Emperor Menelik II had built the Mexico Square ammunition and gun factory. They burned the tobacco factory. For a week, Tayit Bete—the ammunition depot in Arat Kilo—had been firing like popcorn.

The European Union had set up a foreign bank account for the TPLF with a large deposit. In return, rebels destroyed our armaments and export industries. They ruined infrastructure from Tigray to Shewa. The TPLF burned municipality archives including all my personal records. There would be carcinogenic pollution from all the fires.

We telephoned Arat Kilo. Mum said, 'It looks like a war zone. Tanks are in front of Menelik II Palace and the African Economic

Commission. Rebels drive them through lanes and streets like small cars. In the railway station too.

'They defecate in the streets; it stinks. And drape dirty clothes from Qedamawi Haile Selassie.' This was the hand built municipality office visible from Menelik Square.

'Are you all right?'

'Smoke everywhere. Your brother hung up wet sacks for the animals. We use the jerry cans you filled.'

Rebels intended to raze the city, but three million citizens put on a show of support. They climbed to the outside of fences, strewed green rushes in front of rebels, and clapped as they drove in. Tanks hit fences; people did not show anger.

Mum said, 'Not one bank or shop has been looted. Ethiopians have waited 17 years for the Derg to go. We will put up with a new mother-of-idiots for a while.'

TPLF stopped *yerada lijoch* on the street. They hung PICKPOCKET signs around their necks and shot them.

Rebels disabled a refinery. Then they closed down Fafa Factory that I constructed, without employing a technician. The transformer caught fire. Toddlers were now without food supplements. Non-government organisations would import genetically modified food. Its high levels of manganese impaired mental development, especially mathematical ability.

By June 1991, five million Ethiopians would need emergency assistance. Both rebels and communists had destroyed farms and much infrastructure. Our population was more than decimated.

- Red Terror security forces murdered 500,000. Mengistu's forced agricultural resettlements caused 500,000 deaths.
- Two million civilians and soldiers died in the war with Eritrean separatists. This included hundreds of thousands of Eritrean children.

- The Derg exacerbated existing famines. It responded poorly to famines which killed between 275,000 and 367,000 people.
- Derg Security committed abuses that included torture and imprisonment in inhumane conditions. How many suffered in this way cannot be known. The Derg made victims' corpses disappear.
- Mengistu's leadership was indirectly responsible for the war with Somalia of 1975-77. That killed 300,000 soldiers, and 200,000 civilians near Ethiopia's eastern border. The Somali coalition invaded because Mengistu had murdered our military leaders.
- Communism drove Ethiopians to become refugees in inhospitable countries. More than 1.2 million civilians fled to Sudan and Somalia. Most died there. The Sudanese government profited from burials.

Mengistu never atoned for this. Ethiopia would try him in a domestic court, finding him guilty in absentia of genocide.[1] Canada and the UK protected him for having left voluntarily. He would live on in Zimbabwe on 12,000 Canadian dollars per month.

For decades the West would wage an indirect war upon Ethiopians through the TPLF. It killed wisdom. Unqualified generals dominated the military. They ignored profit-driven massacres.[2] Amhara girls were injected without informed consent and became infertile. Afterwards, the TPLF leader's wife became even wealthier.[3] Corruption increased and officials stole billions.[4]

In 2012 journalist Abebe would call out, 'We need freedom more than food. Freedom, freedom, freedom.'[5]

I would visit Piazza during the 2020 COVID-19 pandemic. Four adolescents squatted among parked cars. They ate from one takeaway bag – leftovers from the dishes of restaurant patrons. Others sniffed benzene.

At Hiwot's farm I built a mud hut with a vent for smoked meat. At coffee ceremonies, she served a variety: smoked chicken, goat, lamb and beef. Each helped with a particular ailment. I added a room for Miserat and Gashaw's baby. A retaining wall discouraged snakes – we called those belly-walkers. It would also keep the child cool during days of 40 degrees Celsius.

One day Gashaw said, 'A farm here produces butter sold throughout the south.' We drove deep into the country. Workers were burning a wood similar to olive. Its smoke reached kilometres, protecting livestock and plants from insects. We left the vehicle at the gate.

The farm had 20,000 cows and the farmer knew them all individually. The Derg had tried to make peasants mark their cattle with red and yellow paint. If necessary, they mixed wheat flour with water, then massaged it onto contented heads. They did not mix up herds in market trucks. 'I know my cattle; they know me.'

At the dairy, cows gave milk on a carousel. Two youths played a waltz for them on bejewelled cattle-horn flutes. For their music they received a foaming cup of milk. Other Ethiopian farmers tied musical instruments to cows' hooves, soothing them as they walked.

Hagere Mariyam cows were often named Generous One. Farmers did not over-milk them. Some did no milking on Fridays because cows' hair could fall into the milk. On the Sabbath they placed green grass or flowers on cows' horns. A senior mother cow in Guji and Konso might wear a diamond necklet.

Farmers classified cows, sheep and goats as horned. Horses and donkeys were long-necked and so were fed differently. Cows never ate chemically laden food. Pregnant cows ate barley with clay soil and corn cobs. This prevented high blood pressure. Fifty-kilogram calves or twins could cause that. Calves have horny hooves and strong skulls. Farmers massaged cows in labour with butter. They did not breed lean or very young cows. Animals grazed together, so women chewed a contraceptive leaf then fed it to them.

Ethiopians did not slaughter mother animals. 'That cow made five bulls. Let her live and wander about enjoying herself.' When the people of Hagere Mariyam killed an ox for meat they would play music all day beforehand. He died happy.

Farmers communicated with herd leaders, which followed instructions. Peasants around the Blue Nile said to senior cows, 'Go to the river.' When bulls pushed, they asked leaders to make a line. If the current was gentle, they told them to drink or put their front legs in the water. Cattle swayed their heads, lowing.

Gashaw asked about the food depot. An elder looked into my eyes. 'Come.'

Stone stairs cut into the earth. Intricately locked double doors could withstand a bomb blast. The underground chamber stored every type of grain. It could feed 500,000. Exits led to tunnels linking dwellings. Stonemasonry would have met Queen Saba's standards of 1,000 BC. In the south, her gold mines were designed to reduce risk. Caves had breathing pipes, winches and retaining walls.

Saba moved 1,100 kilometres from Lake Tanu to Aksum. She took 5,000 people and five statues of kings, the tallest 38 metres. Near Aksum she built the 85-kilometre Adolis Tunnel that is passable today by large jeep or camel. She added 20 kilometres of aerated chambers for food, water and veterinary clinics where livestock was checked: teeth and noses for viral infection, and under tails for salt and fat levels.

Back at Hiwot's, the peacock displayed and came to the window for a handful of freshly picked spinach. Tomato vines were laden. People said, 'Do not spill food here. Even if it is cooked, it will grow a tree tomorrow.'

Hewan asked, 'What does not grow here?'

Miserat said, 'Profit for profit's sake, socialism in a socialised community, and needless hunger.'

Marxist-Leninism was put to shame. It was market day at Addis Alem. Fragrant lemons and *jaffa* oranges drew us in. Men could barely lift the branches. Hewan picked up fruit. Oil oozed through its peel onto her skin. Peaches were beginning to ripen. A basketful sold for less than one *birr*. We bought a hand of piquant bananas. Those came out of you smelling clean.

A young woman in traditional Konso goat hide strip led donkeys to food and water. Wandering freely, they never got lost. They had borne large loads. Farmers wanted them to return home unburdened.

Near the market entrance, a mathematics teacher waited. 'I only pay rent here. No need to buy a single egg.' A Telecom worker from Addis Ababa and an electricity supply contractor from the Awash River Basin said, 'The sun will melt the butter.' I asked, 'What butter?' Miserat said, 'Wait until closing time.'

Butter on sale in Addis Alem came from Yirgachefe and cost less than olive oil. Its wrapping was the papery inner layer of a banana leaf. A boy wearing a bluestone bracelet sold a mound of it. He piled up the cash takings for farmers gone off to drink honey wine. Miserat said, 'It is not made using a separator. Farmers leave it underground on the south side of the house. Nature separates it.'

Buses drew up. Peasants boarded them, pouring oranges down the aisles. Farmers with cotton wraps crossed over their shoulders offered unsold produce: avocados, red onions, garlic, potatoes, sugar cane, wheat, *khat* chewing sticks, mangoes, pawpaw the size of pillows, eggs, bananas, oranges, hops, healing herbs, charcoal – and butter. 'Please bless my farm and take my produce home.'

City folk thanked them and left carrying what they could. Barely paid, farmers went to the pub. To Hagere Mariyam's Guji and Konso, food production was sacred. Those people treated it as a privilege. The only items that they did not give away were honey, *teff* grain, barley, frankincense, turmeric and ginger. Their production was painstaking.

Locals did not deal much with money. It threatened their way of life. Gashaw had not been able to change a 100-birr note. People said, 'Can you eat that? We trust our food store, not some piece of paper.'

They measured wealth by climate, rain, fertility of the land, health, numbers of livestock owned by everybody, neighbours' wellbeing and the quantity of stored dried grains. Happiness was a dance with others.

Farmers had left pawpaw by the roadway. The fruit rolled onto the road in slippery puddles. Some had also left eggs.

---

1. Firew Kebede Tiba, "Trial", 171
2. Moresh Wegenie, A Study
3. Change.org, "Stop"
4. CGTN Africa, "Senior Government Officials"
5. ESAT News, "Meles Zenawi"

Chapter 21

Departure

Gashaw and I spent two days together during which we joined mourners. A youth had died leaping a ravine.

Under a canvas shelter everybody cried. Young people wrote about him on sheets of bark. From dawn to dusk his relatives served sweetcorn, beans and coffee. To calm the youth's friends, they withheld richer food and alcohol. A child under three or an elderly adult would have been mourned less intensely.

At the dairy farm an elderly cow had died. The farmer had given her aged care close to the house. He filled hollowed tree trunk halves with water, barley and dry food. When he buried her, he placed her horns on a grass hut roof. He had many pairs. They earned his rank as community elder, able to pass judgments.

Visitors played trumpets to broadcast their respect for the deceased cow and her owner. Children distracted dogs from barking by giving them bread dipped in yoghurt. Neighbours brought a two-week-old hand fed calf to replace the cow.

We made a circle under a large tree. Visitors asked how the cow died. She had gone peacefully, so a farmer played the bamboo flute. They discussed how to care for sick cows. Then we ate together – roasted sweetcorn, milk with honey and home brew from clay pots.

Gashaw said the farmer suffered cattle theft. Foreigners smuggled Guji and Konso bulls out of Africa via Kenya. In the nineteenth century, England's General Napier stole 3,000 cattle then demanded 10,000 more. Sent to the US, our cows established its cattle industry.

He then took me to the Ministry of Farming and Agriculture. A convoy of trucks was loaded with cattle. Each day between 35 and 50 trucks came from Kenya. It was part of a government transaction. Some cattle went to Japan. It was more than 3,000 kilometres to the port of Mombasa. The cost of British Petroleum (BP) fuel was high, but profits offset this. Our organic beef meat sold for more than 200 US dollars per kilogram.

Drivers called to each other in Oromo and Swahili. They were Kenyan Kikuyu and Somali or Kenyan Borana (Borena.).

Gashaw said, 'Their daily return trips are at least a thousand kilometres.'

'That would take a lot of fuel.'

'They are locked into an agreement to buy only from BP. If they purchase another company's petrol, they must pay a high duty.'

Near home, a newborn lamb struggled to her feet shivering with cold. I wrapped her in my jacket. Pacifying the mother, I held her to my chest until she warmed. The ewe circled me bleating her thanks. Locals brought generous gifts: a sheep, goat and especially thick cotton wrap. They spat on me, signifying, 'You belong to us.' Gashaw said, 'Do not wipe it away or they will cry.'

Another 10,000 students had headed south. Panhard tanks and other Derg military hardware crowded the border town of Moyale. Derg Border Security had controlled it. Soldiers never stopped and questioned border crossers. They shot them. BBC and European broadcasters would not be able to interview dead bodies. Priests crossed by air.

With bosses gone, Derg Security neither attacked nor protected civilians. Kenyan police extorted bribes and backed criminals. Bandits killed for a bag, wristwatch or gold chain.

Gashaw's office was at Moyale, 80 kilometres from the farm. 'I have organised a network of border crossing guides. We'll spend a night in Moyale.

'You will need to blend in. Do not wear good jackets. Police arrest city folk and students. A kangaroo court will sentence you to ninety days. You will then present at a higher court with petty thieves and illegal fishermen.'

I gave our cow to Hiwot. Would she meet with the farmer to drink honey wine in five years? Fluent in Swahili, Guji, Oromigna and Amharic, Hiwot offered to come. 'I will help you at Moyale.' Then she stayed home in case Miserat's baby came.

With Hiwot and Miserat, we cried our goodbyes. The soil spoke to me, 'I love you. Here, I give my smell.'

Jackets and shoes were beside the Moyale road. Where were the owners? Bus drivers stopped in the middle of nowhere. 'We are increasing the price. We had to pay for fuel on the black market.'

Moyale was half Ethiopian and Kenyan. Ethiopian Moyale was full of shoppers: Kenyan government workers, police, teachers, Red Cross workers, and Border Security police. Somalis bought clothes and soap. Hewan and I kept our heads down a few blocks from Gashaw's office.

In the morning he took us to the five border smugglers. They would guide us 12 kilometres to Oda Reception Camp. Kenyan Border Security had retreated there. It set up temporary military barracks next to the office of the United Nations High Commissioner for Refugees.

Gashaw paid the crossing deposit. Hewan spoke with a Derg soldier. Head bowed he was a monk in army dress. He was loaded with equipment: machine gun in a bag, two Russian-made Makarov automatic hand pistols in hip and knee holsters and five coconut grenades across his torso.

She asked me for money. I gave him 10 *birr*. He said, 'What about you? This is too much. Don't you have less... Half?'

Hewan said, 'Everybody here has weapons. What if there is a crazy person?'

Derg ex-military had the never-make-you-disappointed guns that do not jam. They carried between 3,000 and 5,000 rounds of ammunition. Our Borana guides had spears and machetes. They would have been defenceless against our boys.

Different groups did not tangle and nobody seemed crazy. Derg soldiers with the rank of major or higher had been detained by the rebels. Those at the border were among the half-million sacked without compensation. Though destitute they were not interested in a fight.

We applied tree sap lotion against bees. Locals had been harvesting honey. The scent lingered. Our border smugglers were on their own land. Borana could smell whether an elephant had crossed. They knew if lions were around. The guides picked up a snake's tongue-whistling. They pointed to the waving of leaves, through which the 'chest flier' slithered. Hewan begged me to carry her.

Guides from Oda crossed our path. We asked, 'Is there a patrol or bandits?' Ours would have kept us at a nearby village if there had been.

Our route passed through their village. We rested at its centre, under a sycamore tree – an *odaa* beneath which leaders made laws. Women brought ginger tea.

Hewan said, 'They speak Ethiopian languages.'

Masai and Borana lived in both Kenya and Ethiopia. They came and went until the English split them up. The Berlin

Conference of 1894–95 made rules for colonisers. They disregarded the boundaries of owners.[1]

I said, 'The UK took Ethiopian Oromo and Borana lands. Emperor Menelik II got them back.'

Gashaw said, 'The anniversary is a public holiday in Nigeria, Rwanda and Malawi. In Algeria it is African Independence Day.'

Hewan asked, 'Is it celebrated in Kenya?'

'They are not aware.'

We left the Borana village. Gashaw hugged us. 'You will come home soon.' I could not look back.

'I have left my beautiful country.'

A bee flew ahead. Heat and dust bothered Hewan. Guides took our bags so that I could carry her. We had walked for four hours.

The leader stopped a kilometre from two tents. Beyond were a thousand Saba and Lucy's people. He said, 'Oda Reception Camp.' Hewan and I signed and dated our declaration of arrival for him to give Gashaw. We were refugees.

---

1. Mueni ma Wuiu, "Colonial and Postcolonial", 1315

Postscript

Samual would serve as a lieutenant in bomb disposal as an Ethiopian UN Peacekeeper. In South Sudan he picked up a dog. It had been cut in half by crossfire and was still alive.

The humane act enraged a Nigerian general and doomed our brother. Samual died weighing 41 kilograms. The TPLF had conscripted him when he was 75 kilograms. It did not feed its conscripts or pass on their pay.

I never saw our mother Tewode again. One day aircraft passed overhead. Fearing attack, Mum ran to the children. She fell and broke her hip. That night in hospital she died. Hundreds of youths attended her patriot's burial at Selassie Cathedral. Patriots crossed spears and held back weeping girls. I visited home two years later. Mum's handmade scent lingered on her chair. Then the TPLF bulldozed our house and sold the land for a crooked office.

The TPLF government imprisoned, tortured and harassed my journalist brother. He had written the truth about its corruption and inhumanity.

Hewan and I remained together for over 20 years.

Addendum

In Addis Ababa in 2020, a thin man with distorted limbs walked slowly in the street. I offered help. The torture survivor said, 'I do not need your money.'

The next day a two-legged cheetah snatched my neck chain before sprinting across four lanes. The rare memento of my late father was a bravery award from the Korean War. Emperor Haile Selassie I placed it around his neck. The chain held a black lion Airborne medallion. The thief dropped it, and a local rescued it. A true *yerada lij* – smart and self-sufficient supporter of the helpless.

It was 28-carat gold from Laga Dambi, Queen Saba's mine also known as Adola. For 3,000 years Ethiopians had mined there. From 1974 to 1991 Soviets depleted the rare gold reserves.

In 1997 under the TPLF, Sheik Mohammed Hussein Ali Al-Amoudi took it over. It became MIDROC Gold Mine and dumped toxic waste into the river. Locals who protested went to prison. Deleterious mine operations continued.[1]

I told our spiritual father about the theft. He is *Abun* at Debre Libanos Monastery. The Abun said, 'I have another tale about a chain for you.'

Addendum

1. Asebe Regassa Debelo, "Development by Dispossession?"

The Gold Chain

Visitors come from all over the world to Debre Libanos Monastery. On any normal day I deal with several foreign individuals and tour groups. Two years ago, I gave a White South African man a tour of our monastery and museum. He had a kind-looking face, was courteous and appreciated my tour. However, he was obsessed with geography and valuables.

To begin, I pointed out the surrounding New York cliffs with their high, blunt tops. This was the start of the Rift Valley and Line of Capricorn. Its latitude of nine degrees north supported abundant plant life. Ethiopians called it the Belt of the Earth.

I drew his attention to a nearby cliff top. Italian occupiers threw 3,000 people from there: priests, monks, female monks, and children. Many were very young, murdered for having been circumcised. Visitors cry upon hearing this, yet the tourist was unmoved. He concerned himself only with the natural surroundings of Debre Libanos.

Next, I showed him the museum's antiques: goatskin books, covers encrusted with precious gemstones. An Orthodox bible pre-dated the Christian era. The visitor exclaimed most over the

The Gold Chain

ornamentation on a crown. It was made of many different types of metal not mined nowadays. Valuable metal objects including Orthodox crosses excite Europeans. This man turned back to the crown three times.

Tour over, he wrote in the visitor's book. Catching my eye, he dropped a high denomination note into the donation box. 'I have been all over the world, yet never so impressed. I am going to see the Belt of the Earth.'

I then gave a group tour to Dutch and Italian visitors. One paid me a typical compliment. 'Father, you are a very good Catholic.' Smiling, I returned to my office. Somebody was asking for the Abun. It was the visitor from the morning's tour. He had returned with his Ethiopian driver who stood looking down.

'Father, I have lost everything.'

'How? You were here only a couple of hours ago.'

'I photographed the Belt of the Earth. Thieves took my camera, phone and wallet.'

My left shoulder was heavy. This indicated the presence of demons. 'Did you report it to the police?'

'I alerted them. But how will they catch them? Father, they stole all my cash and cards. I have nothing to pay this driver and owe five thousand *birr* for the round trip from Addis Ababa. I have my hotel bill to pay. This is a disaster.

'Until I sort things out with the bank, can you help me?' He asked to borrow an enormous sum from the monastery.

I kept quiet; he persisted. 'How can this happen in a holy place, the birthplace of the Belt of the Earth? I'm left only with this neck chain.' He offered to leave his passport with me as security, which I refused. Duty-bound to help, I handed over cash from monastery funds.

The man said, 'I am surprised at your generosity. Elsewhere nobody would help me. They would not give me a huge loan. I want to leave you my gold chain.'

'We do not hold people's possessions.'

The Gold Chain

'It will make me return here.'

'You can put the money into our bank account.'

'No, here it is. You have been so humane and generous towards me.'

'We do not need to hold anything from you. This is the monastery bank account number. You will not need to come back in order to repay us.'

The tourist smiled. 'I have to visit this holy place again. It will benefit me. I will get my chain then.' He departed with our cash, promising to repay it into our bank account.

One week passed. No bank deposit came. Two weeks, then three weeks went by. We received nothing.

After a month, the White South African had not returned. We could only deposit the chain into monastery assets. First, we sent it to Addis Ababa for valuation. The jeweller's report said that the chain was not gold. It was worthless.

The owner had had an air of wealth about him, whereas our monastery was not well off. He had made a drama of foisting his passport and chain onto us. His scheme had been about revenge upon Orthodox.

Crooked outsiders trying old and new methods will learn how we are still very generous. We are alert to their stories. People try that kind of thing all the time. They always have.

Intermittently, foreigners have waged full-scale war upon us. Bringing their finest killing machines, they have taken our land's healthy food. More recently, some have made a show of repaying us. Under the auspices of non-government organisations, they dumped food upon us that killed slowly by creating Western diseases. Today, small people such as the White South African man try to insult our great Orthodox institution.

These are not our first tests. In 1937, Mussolini's fascists destroyed our monastery and threw us live from cliffs. Fifty years later, any who spoke this truth disappeared. When our monks wrote about it somebody killed them.

The Gold Chain

Do not be surprised at the loss of your father's bravery award from our late emperor. It is not only your family's asset. It belongs to the whole innocent world. Greed spreads faster than coronavirus.
Our Abun
(Translated by Mesfin Tadesse)

Glossary

Aba – spiritual father
Abat Dad; father
Abun Orit Orthodox pope; regional monastery abbot
Abyssinian Ethiopian (archaic); from the land of the fathers
anir species of wildcat
Ato Sax Mister Sax, inventor of saxophone
behyer clean air plant (Ge'ez)
berbere spice mix
Bete Israeli House of Israel; twelfth tribe of Israel; Falasha
birr unit of Ethiopian currency; silver
chichi Soviet automatic rifle invented in China
dama board game similar to chess
Derg committee (Ge'ez); government 1974–91
Dinknesh you are marvellous and unique (woman's name)
Falasha Ethiopian Jew from the tribe of Jesus Christ
Fidal Ethiopian script; syllabary; letter
gash bulletproof buffalo-hide shield
Gashe my elder; my older brother / uncle / cousin /father
gebita table game
gelada species of Ethiopian baboon

Glossary

girar species of large, indigenous tree
gureza colobus monkey
injera flatbread made with *teff* flour
Itete my elder sister; my aunt
Itiye my respected aunt
jaffa species of orange endemic to Ethiopia
Kidane Mihret forgiveness for the world; Orit Orthodox spiritual being
krar Ethiopian lyre
Maye birth of creation (endearment); Mum
Mo Anbesa Lion of Judah
mozer – do not kill: defend yourself; rifle
Orit Orthodox Ethiopian Jew; Ethiopian Judaism
Pappas Orit Orthodox regional or national pope; bishop
Ras chief
selam peace; hello; goodbye (Ge'ez, Hebrew & Amharic)
shola large indigenous fruit tree; its fruit
teff crop grain (indigenous Ethiopian species)
tenadum health of humankind herb
TPLF Tigray People's Liberation Front; government 1991–2018
warka large indigenous tree; big shade
Yehuda Ethiopian Jew
yeradal lij smart and self-sufficient supporter of the helpless; Addis Ababa vernacular

Events

1868 Magdala Campaign; Emperor Tewodros II death

1889 Emperor Menelik II coronation

1896 Battle of Adwa victory

1913 Emperor Menelik II death

1916 Empress Zewditu I coronation; Ras Tefari appointed Regent Plenipotentiary

1930 Ras Tefari coronation; he is now Emperor Haile Selassie I

1935–41 Second Italo-Abyssinian War

1936 May 02 Emperor Haile Selassie I leaves Ethiopia

1936 June 30 Emperor Haile Selassie I address to League of Nations on Mussolini's chemical weapons

1936 July 30 Execution of Abun Petros (Ethiopian pope) by General Graziani

1936 Mesfin's grandfather Priest Alemayehu executed in Asmara, Eritrea

1937 February 19 Massacre by General Graziani of civilians in Addis Ababa

1939–45 World War II

Events

1941-44 British presence in Ethiopia (Occupied Enemy Territory until January 1942); in Ogaden to 1955

1941 May 05 Emperor Haile Selassie I returns

1947 Harer Military Academy founded by Emperor Haile Selassie I; Colonel Tadesse became Dean

1950-53 Mesfin's father's service with Ethiopian UN Peacekeepers in Korea and in US as military trainer

1959 / 1960 Mesfin's birth

1960 December 13 Failed coup by Council of Revolution

1963 Colonel Tadesse and family move to Jimma

1964 They move to Addis Ababa; inaugural meeting of Organization of African Unity held in Addis Ababa

1965-1974? Mesfin completes primary and secondary school in Addis Ababa

1970 Somali invasion

1974-1977 Mesfin completes Polytechnic course, followed by Building and Construction Design

1973-74 Tigray and Welo (northern) famine

1974 September 12 Emperor Haile Selassie I de-throned

1974-May 1991 Communist Derg rule

1974 November 23- Lieutenant General Aman, Mesfin's father, General Kebede, Prime Minister Dr Aklilu Habte-Wolde and 62 others murdered by Derg; Mesfin's mother imprisoned

1975 August 27 Haile Selassie murdered, while under house arrest

1975-77 Somali War

1976 Mesfin's mother released from prison; petrol dollar war begins in Eritrea

1977 Red Terror start; Itiye Messelo and Gash Birhanu's sons murdered by Derg; Teacher Yewobnesh murdered by Derg

1977? Mesfin conscripted to the military

1977-78 Ethiopian-Somali War over the Ogaden

1983-85 Widespread famine, worse in Welo and Tigray in the north

1984 Somali invasion

Events

1985 Mesfin leaves the military

1985-86 Completes Cairo University course in civil engineering (water development)

1986-91 Work on engineering projects in Ethiopia

1989 May Failed military coup against Derg / refusal to fight by Ethiopian military leaders

1990 Mesfin and Hewan marry

1991 May (1st week) Construction halted at Gouder; Mesfin goes home to Addis Ababa

1991 May (3rd week) Mesfin and Hewan go south to Hagere Mariyam

1991 May 28 Derg downfall; Mengistu Haile Mariam flees to Zimbabwe

1991 mid-June Mesfin and Hewan leave for Kenya

People

Family
    Mother: Tewode *(Maye)*
    Father: Colonel Tadesse
    Maternal grandmother: Mama Teliqwa (Yuwagobesh)
    Maternal grandfather: Priest Alemayehu
    Wife: Hewan
    Youngest brother: Samual
    Oldest sister: Itete
    Itete's husband: Lieutenant Tsigay
    Itete's 2nd husband: Colonel Wibishat
    Youngest sister: Miserat
    Miserat's husband: Gashaw
    Mothers' patriot brothers: Andwalem & Beqalu
    Mothers' patriot cousins: Belay Zeleq, Tesfahun, Wendson
    Other relatives: patriot Girazmach Alemayehu, patriot Tibebu, artist Gebre Kristos Desta

Childhood Friends
    Girma (2) – both murdered during Red Terror, Henok, Melaku

People

Arat Kilo Neighbours
Itiye Lomi, Itiye Messelo & her husband Gash Birhanu

Enemies
Communist Derg 1974-91: Cadre (employees loyal to the party)
Derg leader: Mengistu Haile Mariam
Derg opponents: Ethiopian People's Revolutionary Party, Shabiya – Ethiopian & Eritrean, Tigray People's Liberation Front
Italian military 1935-41: General Graziani (fascist commander)

Leaders
Patriots (1935-41 resistance): Lord Tilahun Desta (philanthropist), Haddis Alemayehu (writer), Leul (Prince) Ras Imru Haile Selassie, Ras (Chief) Abeba, Lord Gara, Lord Geressu
Military colleagues & superiors of Mesfin's father: General Gezaw (Ground Force second in command), General Jegama (military negotiator), General Kebede (Defence second in command), Lieutenant General Aman Andom (Mesfin's eye father; Chairman of Ethiopian Provisional Military Government), Major General Demissie Bultu (1989 coup leader)
Orit Orthodox popes: Abun Petros, Abun Tewflos, Abun Tekle Haykmanot
Educators: Lord Kebede Mikael (Minister & textbook author), Dr B'hata (Construction Faculty Dean at Building College), Teacher Yewobnesh (Jubilee in Palace School)
Prime Minister 1961-74: Dr Aklilu Habte-Wolde
Engineering bosses: Gash Alemayehu (Gouder), Gash Belete (Muger), Construction Minister Kassa, Construction Administration Head Tessema
Emperors: Tewodros II 1818-68, Menelik II 1844-1913, Empress Taytu 1851-1918 (Queen Consort to Menelik II), Haile Selassie I 1892-1975

Acknowledgments

Thank you, Hama Tuma, for permission to quote from your beautiful poem "Just a Nobody" in our epigraph. It features in *Songs We Learn from Trees: An Anthology of Ethiopian Amharic Poetry*. Carcanet Press editor Chris Beckett and translator Alemu Tebeje let us borrow Hama's lines. The whole book, in English language, is intriguing.

We are grateful to our Abun at Debre Libanos Monastery. He told us his story "The Gold Chain", with permission to share it. It is he who said, 'Ethiopia is the land of angels.' This sage sings like one.

Addis Ababa locals read the first edition of *Lucy's People* in 2020. One *yerada lij* messaged us his responses, with photos. Many thanks Addise.

Australian Sam Cooney edited our manuscript. His belief in Mesfin's story, insight and grace were indispensable. Tess McCabe designed the second edition, dealing with us 12,000 kilometres away.

When Australian stranded us 2020-21, the late Gashe Lemma gave us shelter. Ethiopia took us under wing. The West slammed her. Yet her religious leaders sang operatic prayers for coronavirus sufferers worldwide.

Brothers Danny and Habtamu, and the late Shwasegid, stood by us.

About the Authors

MESFIN TADESSE

Mesfin is an Ethiopian construction and civil engineer; nicknamed Solution Bringer, he directs water uphill. Descended from proud patriots, he is related to Emperor Haile Selassie I and warrior Belay Zelek. He will defend your rights in Ge'ez, Hebrew, Amharic, Arabic and English.

About the Authors

After graduating from Building College in Addis Ababa, he was conscripted. Ranked lieutenant with Airborne, he visited 121 countries as Air Marshall or anti-hijacker. He then won a UNDP scholarship to study water development in Cairo. He constructed UNHCR water supplies in Kenya, the birthday cake stadium in Wellington, New Zealand earthquake zone, and Sydney 2000 Olympic stadium.

Mesfin built in 20 countries, respecting locals. In Fiji he refused to clear iTaukei *makuti* to make way for an airport. Volunteering as a bushfire fighter in Victoria, Australia, he saved wallabies. In Western Australia, he is a registered master builder. He is inspired by Abyssinian Engineer Queen Saba (Sheba).

Lucy's People is his first book. Next: *Under the Pump: Water for Refugees*

IANET BASTYAN

Sixth-generation Australian ianet fell in love with Ethiopia 10 minutes after arriving there in 2016. The granddaughter of soldier-farmers appreciated people's honesty and resilience. A trained dancer, ianet identified steps that had crossed the Mediterranean, contributing to European stage dance. One

About the Authors

complete dance from Northern Shewa was replicated in Spain with castanets, its source unacknowledged.

She had lived in Papua New Guinea where her father taught agriculture. Aussies called local adults 'boys', and segregated children. Parents were furious when all kids—local and ex-pat—rode to school in the tray of the same utility truck, tumbling over each other in delight. ianet became a teacher and librarian, preferring settings with a fair go for all cultures.

Back in Ethiopia in 2020, she and Mesfin attended school assemblies and a workshop at three secondary campuses. One had been a prince's residence. Ethiopia's writing system Fidal is now her second script.

Visit us online at https://ianetbastyan.com

Yerada Lij
AUSTRALIA

You are welcome to post a review at amazon.com.

Bibliography

Ababa Welde-Tensay. *Asidenyaki Asigeraminya Asazagn Awinetenya Yehagerachin Tarikoch Etiopia* [Amharic]. [Addis Ababa]: Mesi Matemiya Bet, 2011 E.C.

Abdur Rahman Alfa Shaban. "Shock as Engineer of Ethiopia's GERD Project is Found Dead." *Africanews.en*, July 26, 2018. https://www.africanews.com/2018/07/26/shock-as-engineer-of- ethiopia-s-gerd-project-is-found-dead//.

Abiy Ahmed Ali. Twitter Post. October 2, 2020. https://twitter.com/abiyahmedali/status/1311938748251336704?lang=en.

Addis Ababa University. Department of History. *Kayhut Kemastawisaw: Leul Ras Imru Haile Selassie* [Amharic]. Addis Ababa: Addis Ababa University Press, 2002 E.C.

Addis Regassa. "Mote Enkwan Cheken – Tilahun Gessesse [Amharic]." February 17, 2013. YouTube video, 3.44. https://www.youtube.com/watch?v=OO6HEiy1_ic.

Alemayehu. "World's Last People by Alemayehu". *Ethiopian Culture & Innovations* (blog). *Yerada Lij, Australia,* October 29, 2020. https://wp.me/pbT2rP-17f.

Alfa Tube. "Uneducated Genius: Paulos Gnogno [Amharic]." November 21, 2019. YouTube video, 9.21. https://www.youtube.com/watch?v=bmFe7syU5c4.

Arefaynie Fantahun. "Ethnically Motivated Attacks in Shashemene and Elsewhere." *Ethiopia Observer*, July 06, 2020. https://www.ethiopiaobserver.com/2020/07/06/ethnically-motivated-attacks-in-shashemene-and-elsewhere/.

Asante, S.K.B. "The Italo-Ethiopian Conflict: A Case Study in British West African Response to Crisis Diplomacy in the 1930s." *The Journal of African History*, 15, no. 2 (1974): 291-302. https://www.jstor.org/stable/181074?read-now=1&seq=4#page_ scan_tab_contents.

Asebe Regassa Debelo. "Development by Dispossession? A Reappraisal of the Adola Gold Mine in Southern Ethiopia." *In The Political Economy of Extractives in the Borderlands. Horn of Africa Bulletin*, 28, no. 4 (July-August 2016): 27-31. Life and Peace Institute. https://reliefweb.int/report/kenya/horn-africa-bulletin-volume-28- no-4-july-august-2016-political-economy-extractives.

Asebe Regassa Debelo, Yetebarek Hizekiel, and Benedikt Korf. " 'Civilizing' the Pastoral Frontier: Land Grabbing, Dispossession and Coercive Agrarian Development in Ethiopia." *The Journal of Peasant Studies*, 46, no. 5 (2019):

Bibliography

935-55. Taylor & Francis Online. https://doi.org/10.1080/03066150.2017.1420060.

Bahru Zewde. *A History of Modern Ethiopia 1855–1991*. 2nd ed. Addis Ababa: Addis Ababa University Press, 2002.

Baye Speedy. "Filfilu. Biharu Kegne # 1 [Amharic]". Oct 28, 2008. YouTube video, 6.27 https://www.youtube.com/ watch?v=PmTopvMt3wI.

Campbell, Ian. *The Plot to Kill Graziani: The Attempted Assassination of Mussolini's Viceroy*. Addis Ababa: Addis Ababa University Press, 2012.

CGTN Africa. "Senior Government Officials Netted in Ethiopia Corruption Crackdown." November 13 & 15, 2018. YouTube video, 5.08. https://www.youtube.com/watch?v=fDMTwhGjXLw.

Change.org. "Stop State-sponsored Genocide of Amhara People in Ethiopia." Petition to International Criminal Court, 2016. https://www.change.org/p/stop-state-sponsored-genocide-of- amhara-people-in-ethiopia.

"Children of Gojjam." In *Songs We Learn from Trees: An Anthology of Ethiopian Amharic Poetry*, edited and translated by Beckett, Chris and Alemu Tebeje, 518. Manchester: Carcanet Press, 2020. Kindle.

Clark, Alexis. "When Jim Crow Reigned Amid the Rubble of Nazi Germany." *The New York Times Magazine*. February 19, 2020. https://www.nytimes.com/2020/02/19/magazine/blacks-wwii- racism-germany.html.

Cohen, John M. "Foreign Involvement in the Formulation of Ethiopia's Land Tenure Policies: Part II." *Northeast African Studies*, 7, no. 3 (1985): 1-20. https://www.jstor.org/stable/43660182.

cybraddis. "People to People Tour. Part 1 of 9. National Theatre Troupe of Ethiopia 1987/1988 [Amharic]." September 01, 2008. YouTube video, 10.02. https://www.youtube.com/watch?v=p3vWc7sqz8c.

Ejigayehu Sibabaw. "All Her Music in One [Amharic]." January 21, 2019. YouTube video, 1.46.55. https://youtu.be/fjown8DwG14.

ESAT News. "Meles Zenawi Humiliated in G8 Meeting." May 18, 2012. YouTube video, 9.51. https://www.youtube.com/watch?v=hUVsq-FDFRE.

Ethio Pentatonic. "Asnakech Worku. Tizita, Tisita, a Love Song from Ethiopia Played on the Krar, Lyra [Amharic]." Mar 23, 2015. YouTube video, 7.50. https://www.youtube.com/watch?v=RK9SXtIPw0Y.

Evangadi Production. "Tilahun Gessesse: Ethiopia [Amharic]." Aug 01, 2017. YouTube video, 7.04 https://www.youtube.com/watch?v=p7j2Zzfyt04.

Firew Kebede Tiba. "The Trial of Mengistu and Other Derg Members for Genocide, Torture and Summary Executions in Ethiopia". In *Prosecuting International Crimes in Africa*, edited by Chacha Murungu, and Japhet Biegon, 163-184. Pretoria: Pretoria University Law Press, 2011. http://ssrn.com/abstract=2635348.

Gashaw Ayferam Endaylalu. "Mustard Gas Massacres and Atrocities Committed by Italy in 1939 Against the Inhabitants of Menz, Merhabete, and Jamma in

Bibliography

Amesegna Washa/Zeret Cave." *Journal of Cultural and Religious Studies*, 6, no. 9 (September 2018): 501-13. https://doi.org/10.17265/2328-2177/2018.09.001.

Haddis Alemayehu. *Fikir Eske Mekabir* [Amharic]. Addis Ababa: Birhanna Selam Press, 1965.

Haddis Alemayehu. *Wenjl Danya* [Amharic]. Addis Ababa: nigd Printing Press, 1981.

Haile Selassie, Emperor of Ethiopia, and Edward Ullendorff. *My Life and Ethiopia's Progress. Volume One: 1892-1937: The Autobiography of Emperor Haile Selassie I*. Chicago: Research Associates School Times Publications; Frontline Distribution International, 1999.

Hama Tuma. "Just a Nobody". In *Songs We Learn from Trees: An Anthology of Ethiopian Amharic Poetry*, edited and translated by Beckett, Chris and Alemu Tebeje, 355. Manchester: Carcanet Press, 2020. Kindle.

Hamlin, Catherine, and John Little. *The Hospital by the River: A Story of Hope*. 2nd ed. Oxford; Grand Rapids, Mich.: Monarch Books, 2016. Kindle.

Hussein Ahmed. *Rete and Honey* [Amharic]. n.p.: n.p., 2009 E.C.

International Agency for Research on Cancer Working Group on the Evaluation of Carcinogenic Risks to Humans. "Sulfur Mustard." In *A Review of Human Carcinogens. Volume F: Chemical Agents and Related Occupations*. Lyon, France: World Health Organization, 2012. https://www.ncbi.nlm.nih.gov/books/NBK304425/.

Kasaye Chemeda. *Yeto Meda Welowotch Seka* [Amharic]. 5th ed. n.p.: Inspire Printing Press, 2011 E.C.

Kebede Michael. *Tarik ena Mesale: An Ethiopian Tale* [Amharic and English]. Addis Ababa: Shekla Studio, 2013. Kindle, 2020.

Kebede Mikael. *Japan Indemin Seletenech* [Amharic]. Addis Ababa: Mega Printers, 1974.

Kebelay Geday. *Lalibela* [Amharic]. Addis Ababa: Birhanna Selam Press, 1995 E.C.

Kebra Negast: The Queen of Sheba and Her Only Son Menyelik [Amharic], edited by Wallis Budge. 3rd ed. n.p.: Tsigay Shinbur, 2009 E.C.

Kiunguyu, Kylie. "Plundered Ethiopian Maqdala Treasure in UK Museum Could be Returned on Loan." *This is Africa*, April 10, 2018. https://thisisafrica.me/politics-and-society/ethiopian-maqdala- museum-returned/.

Levine, Donald N. *Greater Ethiopia: The Evolution of a Multiethnic Society*. 2nd ed. Chicago; London: University of Chicago, 2000.

Library of Congress. "The History of Education in Ethiopia with Special Emphasis on Higher Education." October 26, 2010. video, 59.21. https://www.loc.gov/item/webcast-5071.

Melaku Tefera. *The Diary of a Person Sentenced to Death* [Amharic]. Addis Ababa: Abrihot Ethiopia, 2012 E.C.

Bibliography

Moresh Wegenie Amara Organization (MWAO). *A Study Summary on the Crime of Ethnic Cleansing Perpetrated on the Amhara of Ethiopia, 1991-2016.* Washington, DC: MWAO, April 5 2016. https:// docplayer.net/42626849-Moresh-wegenie-amhara-organization- mwao-8221-georgia-avenue-silver-spring-maryland-md-usa.html.

Mr Mirkuzz. "Alemayehu Eshete – Tikur Gissila 1964 E.C. [Amharic]." September 20, 2015. YouTube video, 3.13. https://www.youtube.com/watch?v=FOeQdRR-hmI.

Mueni ma Wuiu. "Colonial and Postcolonial State and Development in Africa." *Social Research*, 77, no. 4 (Winter 2010): 1311-38. https://www.jstor.org/stable/23347128?read-now=1&seq=1#page_ scan_tab_contents.

Nigatu Kifelaw. *Somali Lands* [Amharic]. n.p.: n.p., 2007 E.C. Ostego, Terje, Haustein, Jorg, Fasika Gedif, Kedir Jemal Kadir,

Muhammed Jemal, and Yihenew Alemu Tesfaye. *Religion, Ethnicity, and Charges of Extremism: Dynamics of Inter-Communal Violence in Ethiopia.* European Institute of Peace, 2021. https://www.eip.org/

Pankhurst, Sylvia. *Ethiopia: A Cultural History.* Woodford Green, Essex: Lalibela House, 1955.

Peters, Kathryn. "New Zealand's Attitudes to the Reform of the League of Nations: The Background of the Memorandum to the Secretary-General, 16th July 1936." *New Zealand Journal of History*, 6, no. 1 (1972): 81-98. http://www.nzjh.auckland.ac.nz/docs/1972/NZJH_06_1_06.pdf.

Priselac, Adolphe. *Habesha's Adventure* [Amharic]. Addis Ababa: Addis Ababa University Press, 2003 E.C.

Scriptsource. "Ethiopic (Ge'ez)." *SIL International*, 2020. https://www.scriptsource.org/cms/scripts/page.php?hitem_ id=script_detail&key=Ethi.

Schneidmiller, Chris. "Ethiopia Still Seeking Help with Chemical Weapons." *Nuclear Threat Initiative.* May 03, 2004. http://nti.org/1997GSN.

Solomon Nigus. "Ethiopian Biran Mitshift [Amharic]." November 20, 2017. YouTube video, 25.39. https://www.youtube.com/watch?v=8dFzgvnb49g.

Songs We Learn from Trees: An Anthology of Ethiopian Amharic Poetry, translated and edited by Beckett, Chris, and Alemu Tebeje. Manchester: Carcanet Press, 2020. Kindle.

Sophia Tesfamariam. "Ethiopia: A Classic Case of the Accuser Being the Culprit." *Tesfanews*, August 05, 2011. https://www.tesfanews. net/ethiopia-a-classic-case-of-the-accuser-being-the-culprit/.

tangodaa. "Drastic and Gross Human Right Violation in Ethiopia and Neighbor Countries." *Odaakoo*, February 22, 2012. https://odaakoo.wordpress.com/2012/02/22/drastic-and-gross- human-right-violation-in-ethiopia/.

"Tilahun Gessess." *Addis Herald.* October 13, 2017. https://www.addisherald.com/tilahun-gessess/.

Bibliography

Timkehet Teffera. "Chapter III: Part II." *In Homage to Alemayehu Eshete's Artistic Legacy*, 76-99. San Francisco, Cal.: Academia.edu, 2019.

WikiArt. Visual Art Encyclopaedia. "Gebre Kristos Desta Center." Last modified June 21, 2020. https://www.wikiart.org/en/gebre-kristos-desta.

Young Lives. "Round 5 Longitudinal Education and Learning Fact Sheet," October 17 2017. Oxford: University of Oxford, 2017. https://www.younglives.org.uk/content/education-and-learning-preliminary-findings-round-5-survey-ethiopia.

Young Lives, Oxford Department of International Development (ODID), and Young Lives Ethiopia PDRC. "Lessons from Longitudinal Research with the Children of the Millenium." Young Lives Ethiopia Country Report, Summary, June 2018. Oxford: University of Oxford, 2018. www.younglives.org.uk.

www.ingramcontent.com/pod-product-compliance
Lightning Source LLC
Chambersburg PA
CBHW030252010526
44107CB00053B/1672